VISUAL QUICKSTART GUIDE

Painter 3.1

FOR MACINTOSH

Elaine Weinmann
Peter Lourekas

Peachpit Press

This book is dedicated to our siblings, Harriet and Nia.

Visual QuickStart Guide
Painter 3.1 for Macintosh
Elaine Weinmann and Peter Lourekas

Peachpit Press
2414 Sixth Street
Berkeley, CA 94710
510/548-4393
510/548-5991 (fax)

Find us on the World Wide Web at: http://www.peachpit.com

Peachpit Press is a division of Addison-Wesley Publishing Company

Cover design: The Visual Group
Book design, production, and illustrations, except as noted:
Elaine Weinmann and Peter Lourekas

ISBN 0-201-88371-6

9 8 7 6 5 4 3 2 1

Printed and bound in the United States of America

Welcome to the Painter Visual QuickStart Guide

In Painter, you can do things that can't be done with traditional media, like use art supplies that never run out, paint without washing your hands or brushes and without inhaling turpentine, change paper textures midway through a drawing, build up wet brush strokes with no drying time, erase a watercolor, apply oil paint over pastel on paper, or instant-replay a picture, stroke by stroke. Yet Painter's brushes work uncannily like traditional media: watercolor strokes bleed into the paper like real watercolor, oil strokes smear like real oil paint, and you can even make paint drip.

If Painter's brushes don't interest you, take a look at Painter's special effects commands: an arsenal of intriguing ways to enhance, develop, and rearrange images that simply can't be replicated in traditional media. Many of the artists featured in this book still use traditional media — palette table, drafting table, or silkscreening table right next to their Macintosh. The computer is merely a new tool in their lifelong creative process.

We think the best way to inspire you to learn and explore Painter's features is to show them in the context of drawings and paintings, and we've tried to include a wide range of art styles in this book (we happen to love diversity). Abstract or representational, Painter-ly or illusionistic, messy or neat — you're the artist. We're pretty square when we describe Painter's basic techniques, though, because we know you want to paint, not read. Our aim is to give you enough technical information about Painter to get you started without stifling your creative juices.

We took notes as we created the illustrations for this book so we could write intelligible captions. If you're not a note-taker and you would like to record your methods (the brush you used, at what opacity, etc.), you can use Painter's sessions commands to record and then replay a brush stroke or even a whole work session. Who knows, the next brush stroke you draw might be a "stroke of genius," and you'll be glad you made a record of it.

On the other hand, most of the artists showcased in this book don't remember an iota about how they produce their work because they're so absorbed in art-making and each piece they create is one-of-a-kind. They enjoy surprises and exploring the mysterious workings of new software, and they like the fact that the computer challenges them to try new methods. Trying to find out what commands or brushes they use is like trying to transcribe a recipe from someone's grandmother. We're grateful when they remember they've used Painter!

Phil Allen

Speaking of methods, feel free to be disrespectful to this book. Read it in the bathtub, read it on the bus, fold down the corners, scribble notes on the pages, bend back the spine. We're thrilled when we see beat up copies of our books, because we know they're being used as learning tools. *Painter 3.1 for Macintosh: Visual QuickStart Guide* is not a coffee table book — it's a computer art class-in-a-book. ■

Table of Contents

1 Bare Essentials

Rodney Alan Greenblat (created for the Lands' End Kids' Catalog; detail).

Hardware

CPU

We hesitate to recommend specific models because the Macintosh hardware world changes so fast. By the time this book reaches the bookstores, no doubt there'll be newer models on the market. The faster the machine, the better, because many of Painter's commands are processor intensive. Painter will run fastest, of course, on a Power Mac. Running Painter on a slow machine requires enormous patience. If you're not using a Power Mac, you won't be able to access all Painter's features unless your machine has an FPU (Floating Point Unit). Make sure you have enough empty hard disk space for Painter to use as a scratch disk when it needs more RAM for processing. Painter requires System 7.0 or later.

Color Monitor

Color monitors display 8-bit, 16-bit, or 24-bit color, depending on the type of video card. With an 8-bit card, the screen displays up to 256 colors; with a 24-bit card, 16.7 million colors are available. With an 24-bit card, every possible color can be represented on screen. All Painter 3.1 pictures are saved as 24-bit.

Mouse or Stylus?

You don't have to use a pressure-sensitive tablet and stylus combo with Painter, but we highly recommend that you do so. With a stylus and tablet you'll be able to create more idiosyncratic and personal brush strokes in a wider range of thick-to-thin and dark-to-light variations. And since a stylus is held more like a pen or brush, you'll probably find it to be more comfortable than using a mouse. Tablets by Wacom, CalComp, Hitachi, Kurta, and Summagraphics work with Painter. If you use a pressure-sensitive tablet, you should set Brush Tracking Preferences at the beginning of each work session (see page 179).

Third-party plug-ins

Painter supports third-party plug-ins, including those created for use with Photoshop. In order to access your plug-in files you must install them all together in one folder. You can tell Painter where this folder is when you install the application, or you can use the Edit > Preferences > Plug-ins dialog box. Plug-ins are accessed from Painter's Effects menu.

Memory allocation

To learn how much RAM you have available to allocate to Painter, launch Painter and any other applications that you want to have running at the same time, then choose About This Macintosh from the Apple menu. Total Memory is the amount of hardware RAM installed, and Largest Unused Block is the amount of RAM still available. The applications you launched and their RAM allotments are also displayed.

If possible, you should allocate least 10 to 12 megabytes (MB) of RAM to Painter. To do this, quit Painter, click the Painter application icon in the Finder, choose Get Info from the File menu, then enter the desired amount in the Preferred size field. To enter 10MB, for example, type in "10000". Be sure to reserve enough RAM to run the System.

Can you guess how many megabytes this book weighs? Look for the answer later in the book!

About resolution

- Resolution is a measurement of a file's pixels. At 100% view, one pixel in a file displays as one pixel on screen. When a file is printed, pixels are converted into dots, whose size will vary depending on the resolution of the output device. The higher a file's resolution, the the larger its storage size and the longer image edits will take to process.
- For video, choose a resolution of 72 ppi unless you'll be zooming in on part of the image. For printing, your resolution should be double the line screen your print shop is going to use for color output, or one and a half times the line screen for grayscale output. A lower resolution than that might be adequate for a very painterly image; a picture with sharp line work would require a very high resolution.
- When all the values in the New dialog box are in pixels, choosing a resolution above 75 ppi (pixels per inch) will reduce the file's dimensions without changing the file's storage size (RAM). If the Height and/or Width is specified in a unit other than pixels, the higher the resolution, the more pixels in the file and thus the larger the file's storage size.
- Using Painter's Sessions feature, you can record the creation of a picture at one resolution and then replay it later in a new document at a different resolution (see page 160).

To launch Painter:

Double-click the Painter application icon inside the Painter application folder.

Painter 3.1

Follow these instructions to create a new, blank document. To paint on scanned imagery, see the scanning info on pages 17-18 and the instructions for opening a file on page 5.

To create a new file:

1. Choose File > New (⌘-N).
2. Choose a unit of measure for the Width and Height **2**.
3. Enter Width and Height values **3**.
4. Enter a Resolution value **4**.
5. *Optional:* To choose a different background color, click the Paper Color rectangle, click a color on the color wheel, adjust the Hue, Saturation, or Brightness, if necessary, then click OK. (To reset the Paper Color to pure white, enter Hue, Saturation, and Brightness values of 0, 0, and 65535, respectively.)
6. Click OK or press Return **5**.

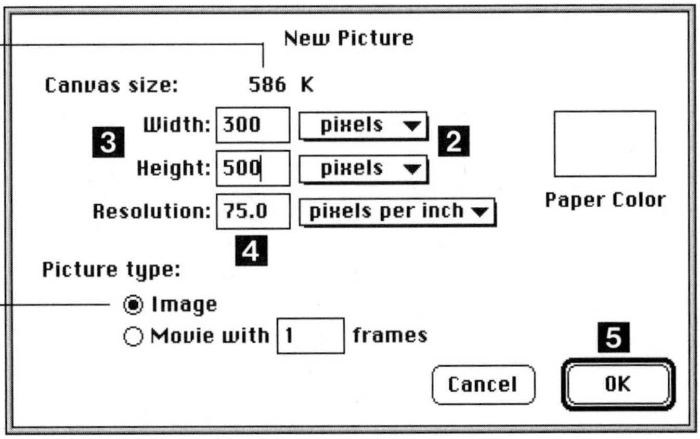

The file's storage size (unless you save the file in the RIFF format with the Uncompressed box unchecked, which reduces the file storage size).

Leave the ***Picture type*** *on* ***Image****, unless you're creating a movie (see Chapter 12).*

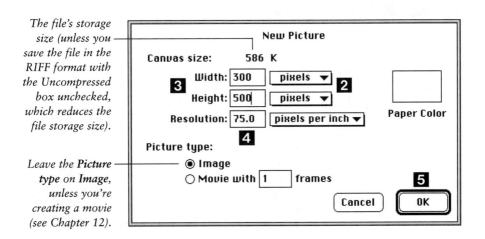

After you save your document for the first time, just choose Save from the File menu (⌘-S) the next time you want to save it.

To save a new file:

1. Choose File > Save As. If you've already starting painting, you can choose Save (⌘-S).
2. Enter a name for the file in the Save Image As field **2**.
3. Choose a file format from the Type pop-up menu **3**.
4. Choose a location in which to save the file **4**.
5. Click Save or press Return **5**.

Use the Save As command to save a file in a different format after it's already been saved.

What file format Type should I choose?

RIFF is Painter's default native format. You must use this format if you want to save your document with floaters, color annotations, or Wet Layer brush strokes. Leave the Uncompressed box unchecked to save file storage space. Floaters are also preserved in the Photoshop 3.0 format, but color annotations are not.

Information about other file formats for opening Painter files in other applications is on page 188.

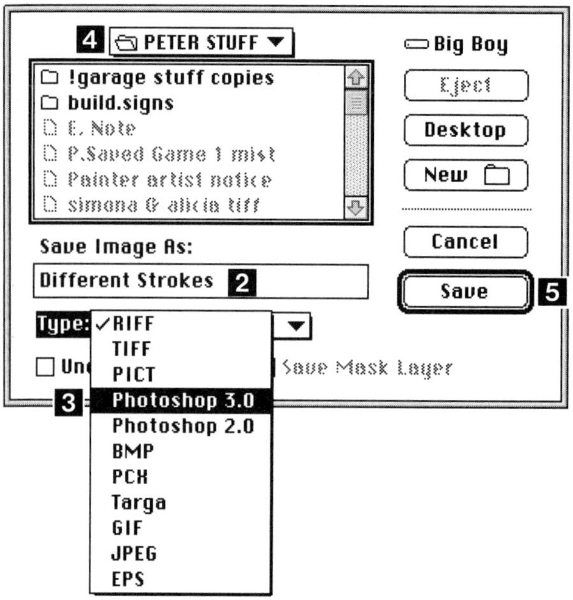

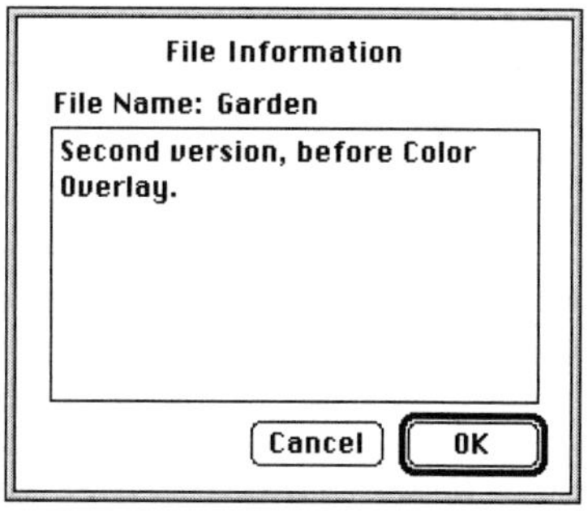

Every file has its own notepad for saving messages or instructions. With the file open, choose Get Info from the File menu, then type anything you want in the information field.

What happens to a Photoshop file if it's opened in Painter 3.1?

- Layers will be converted into floaters in Painter and paths in the Photoshop file will be converted into paths in Painter.
- If the Photoshop file contains a layer mask, it will be converted into a floater mask in Painter. If you reopen the document in Photoshop, however, the layer mask effect will become permanent and the mask itself will be deleted.
- The fourth channel in a Photoshop file will be viewable in Painter as a mask if there were no paths in the original Photoshop 3.0 file. To display the mask in Painter and force its name to appear on the Objects: P. List palette, choose the Path Adjuster tool and click in the document window or click the third Visibility button on the P. List palette. The channel will be deleted if you reopen the file in Photoshop.
- If you import a Photoshop file that has a transparent background, a white background will be created for it in Painter. If you reopen the file in Photoshop, the file will have a new, white background layer, which will contain any brush strokes that were applied to the background in Painter.

These file formats can be opened in Painter: RIFF, TIFF, PICT, BMP, PCX, Targa, Photoshop 2.0, and Photoshop 3.0. **Painter images are bitmapped, and in RGB color mode. Files in CMYK color mode can't be opened in Painter.**

To open a file in Painter:

1. Choose File > Open (⌘-O).
2. Highlight the file you want to open, then click Open.
   or
   Click Browse to view thumbnails of pictures in the currently open folder, then double-click a thumbnail to open that picture (or click a thumbnail, then click Open).

You can also open a Painter file by clicking its icon in the Finder.

To open a numbered file movie, see page 168.

To open a Photoshop file in Painter, first save the document in RGB Color or Grayscale mode in Photoshop 2.5 or 3.0 format.

To open an Illustrator or FreeHand file as a selection, see page 82. You can't open an EPS directly into Painter.

To open a PhotoCD file directly into Painter, use Kodak's PhotoCD Acquire plug-in module. Or open your PhotoCD file in Photoshop, save it in RGB Color mode and Photoshop 3.0 format, then open it in Painter.

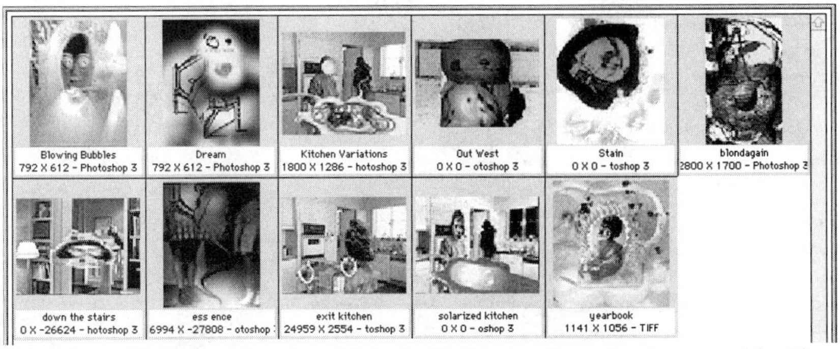

Painter's terrific ***Browse*** *feature, with its large thumbnails, makes it easy to identify and open pictures. Double-click a thumbnail to open that file. (Artwork by David Humphrey.)*

Palettes

You'll be using one or more of the eight main palettes for most of your work in Painter. To open a palette, choose the palette name from the Window menu or use the keyboard shortcut listed at right.

The Art Materials, Brush Controls, Objects, and Advanced Controls palettes contain secondary palettes. To open a secondary palette, click its icon at the top of the main palette. To display a secondary palette by itself, make sure it isn't currently displayed (click a different icon), then drag its icon away from the main palette. To restore a palette to its main palette, just click its close box.

If you want your screen to look neat and tidy, you can manually snap your palettes together edge-to-edge (you'll need a large monitor to do this). To restore the palettes to their default locations — snapped together — choose Window > Clean Up Palettes.

The Painter palettes

Show/hide palette shortcut	
⌘ 1	**Tools**
⌘ 2	**Brushes**
⌘ 3	**Art Materials** *Subpalettes:* **Colors, Papers, Grads, Sets, Weaves**
⌘ 4	**Brush Controls** *Subpalettes:* **Size, Spacing, Bristle, Looks, Nozzle**
⌘ 5	**Objects** *Subpalettes:* **Paths, P. List, Floaters, F. List, Sessions**
⌘ 6	**Controls**
⌘ 7	**Advanced Controls** *Subpalettes:* **Rake, Well, Random, Sliders, Water**
⌘ 8	**Color Set**
⌘H	Hide all open palettes (or display all previously open palettes)

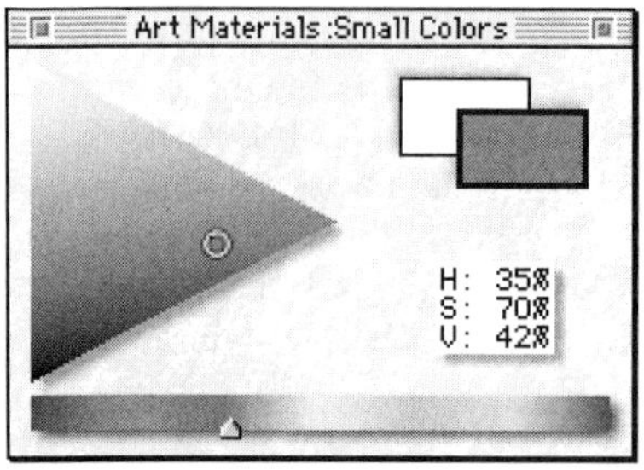

The Colors palette displayed separately from the Art Materials palette.

To close a palette, click its close box or use the shortcut.

To expand a palette, click its zoom box.

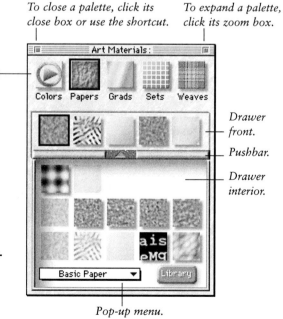

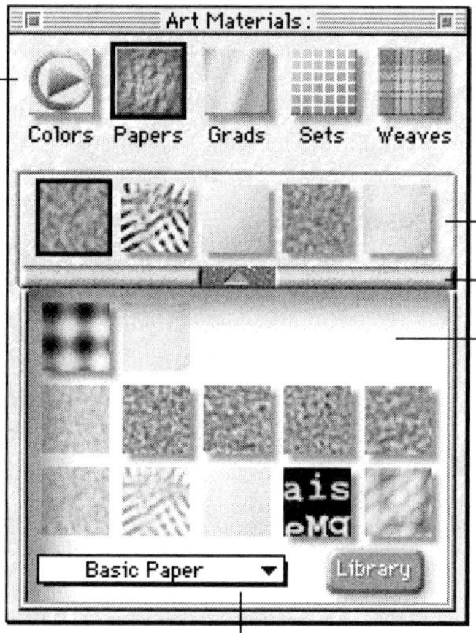

Drawer front.

Pushbar.

Drawer interior.

Pop-up menu.

Colors palette display styles

You can choose from three display types for the Art Materials: Colors palette. We use the Hue Slider+Triangle type (illustrated above) because it takes up less screen space. To change the display style, choose Edit > Preferences > General Preferences, then click a Color Palette Type.

Palette backgrounds

You may have noticed that our palettes have a different background texture than yours. We thought the background texture on the default interface was too distracting for our illustrations. If you'd like to change yours, **turn to page 180.**

Palette drawers

To make a selection from any of the palettes that have drawers, click an icon on the drawer front or in the drawer. When you click an icon in a drawer, the icon is placed on the drawer front and the same icon in the drawer becomes grayed out. The drawer front contains the last five most recently used icons.

To lock an item on the drawer front, press on the icon for a couple of seconds until a green dot appears under the icon. Press on the icon again to unlock it. Only four items can be locked at a time.

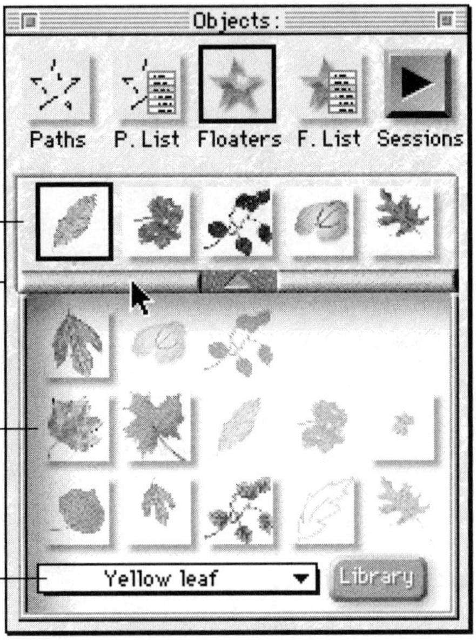

*Click an icon on the **drawer front**.*

*To open a drawer, click anywhere on the **pushbar**.*

*Click an icon in the **drawer**.*

*Or choose from the **pop-up menu**.*

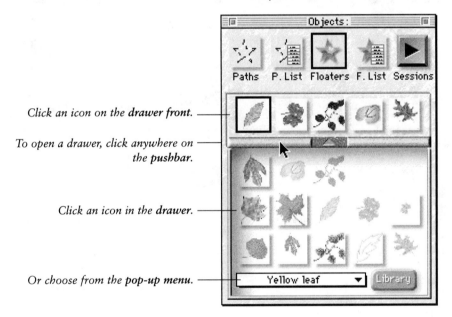

Sliders

Many of Painter's palettes and dialog boxes have sliders.

*Click anywhere in the **bar**.*

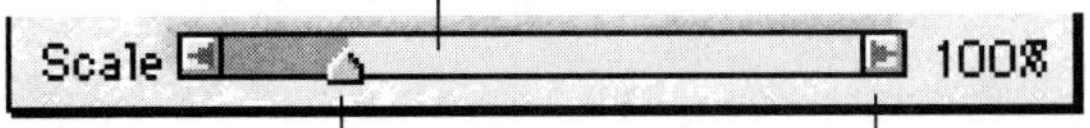

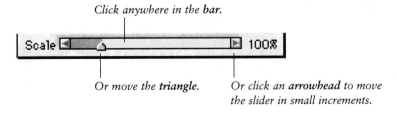

*Or move the **triangle**.*

*Or click an **arrowhead** to move the slider in small increments.*

Tools

There are 12 tools. To open the Tools palette, choose Windows > Tools (⌘-1). To choose a tool, click once on its icon or press the tool's assigned letter on the keyboard (in boldface, below). Once the tool is selected, you can choose special attributes for it from the Controls palette.

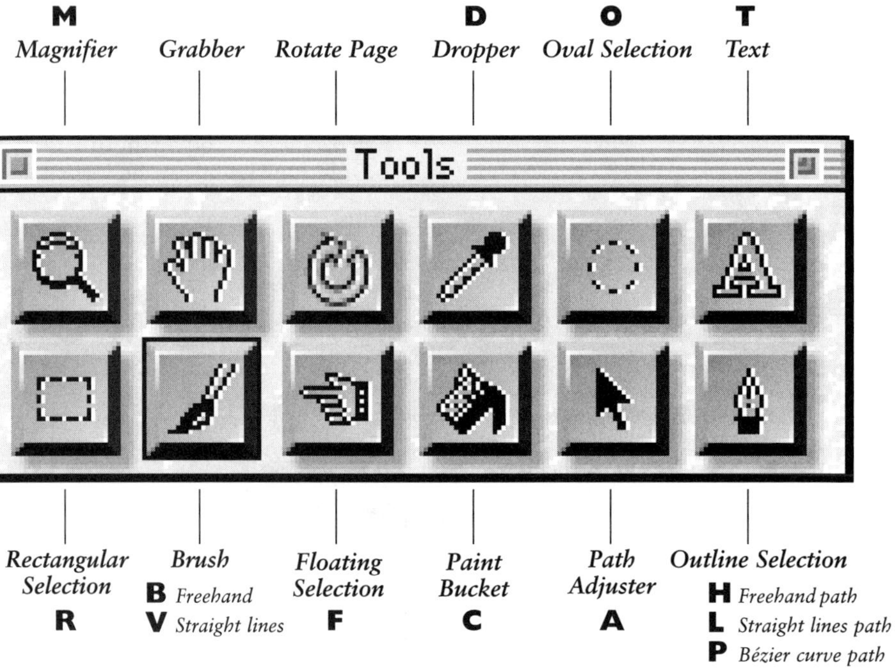

Magnifier: Changes the picture's screen display size.

Grabber: Moves the picture in the image window. (Press Space bar to access the Grabber when another tool is selected.)

Rotate Page: Rotates the canvas for drawing comfort. (Press Option-Space bar to rotate the page when another tool is selected.)

Dropper: Selects a Primary color (front color rectangle on the Art Materials: Colors palette) or a Secondary color (back color rectangle on the Colors palette) from a picture. (Press Command to access the Dropper when another tool is selected.)

Oval Selection: Creates oval or round selections.

Type: Creates text selections.

Rectangular Selection: Creates rectangular or square selections.

Brush: Painter's basic brush tool. Choose individual brushes (Pen, Chalk, etc.), brush variants, method categories, and method subcategories from the Brushes palette.

Floating Selection: Turns an ordinary selection into a floater; selects an existing floater.

Paint Bucket: Fills with color where you press the stylus or click the mouse.

Path Adjuster: Moves, resizes, or reshapes selection paths.

Outline Selection: Creates or reshapes selection paths.

Magnifier tool

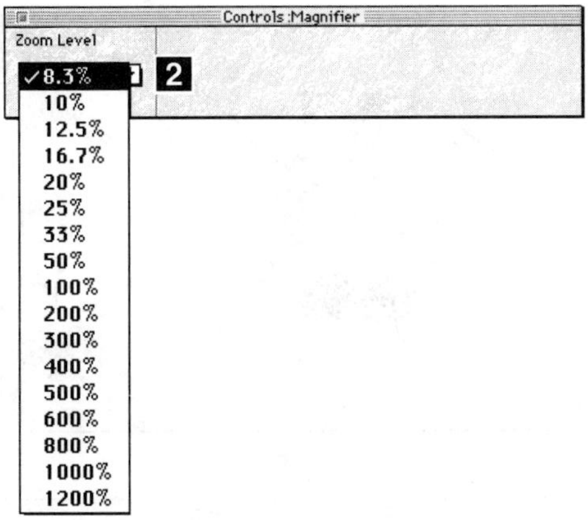

To change the view size without using the Magnifier tool

TO ENLARGE THE VIEW SIZE:

⌘-+ *or* **⌘-Space bar-click in the image window**

TO REDUCE THE VIEW SIZE:

⌘-– *or* **⌘-Option-Space bar-click in the image window**

To change a picture's display size:

1. Choose the Magnifier tool (M).
2. To enlarge the view size, click in the image window.
   or
   To reduce the view size, hold down Option and click in the image window.
   or
   Choose a Zoom Level from the Controls: Magnifier palette pop-up menu **2**.
   or
   Press and drag in the image window. The area you marquee will be magnified.

- The current level of magnification will be indicated on the document title bar.
- To center the image, hold down Space bar and click in the image window.
- To display your entire picture at the largest possible size for your screen, choose Window > Zoom to Fit Screen or double-click the Grabber tool.

Grabber tool

To move the image in the image window:

1. Choose the Grabber tool.
2. Press and drag in the image window.

- Hold down Space bar to use the Grabber tool while another tool is selected.
- When the Grabber tool is selected, you can choose a Zoom Level from the Controls palette.

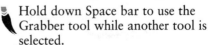

Like an artist working in traditional media, you can rotate the paper/canvas to reach an area of a picture from a more comfortable position, or simply to study the composition from a different angle. **The picture will print from its original orientation.**

To work on a picture from a different angle:

1. Choose the Rotate Page tool **1**.
2. Press and drag in a circular direction in the image window. The arrow will point to the top of the original image as you drag **2** **3**.

- To restore the original vertical orientation, Option-Space bar-click in the image window, or choose the Rotate Page tool and click in the image window, or double-click the Rotate Page tool.
- Hold down Option and Space bar to use the Rotate Page tool while another tool is selected.
- Hold down Shift while dragging to rotate to the nearest 90° angle.

1 *Rotate Page tool*

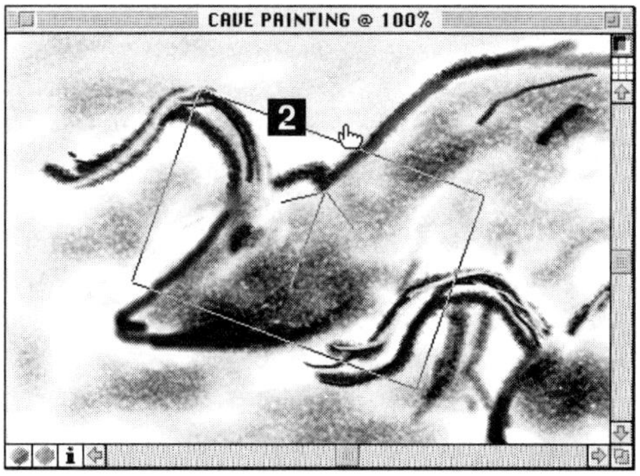

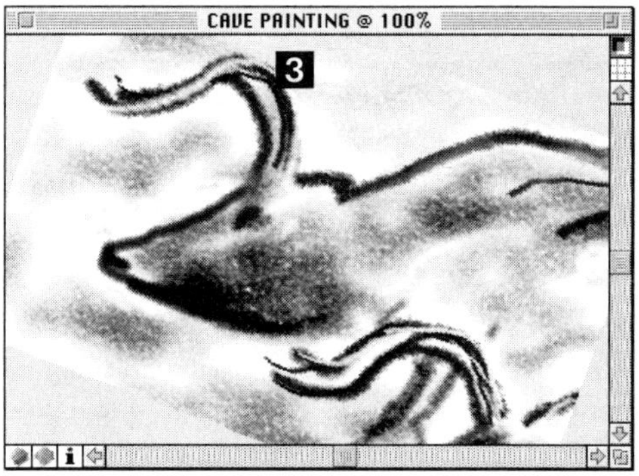

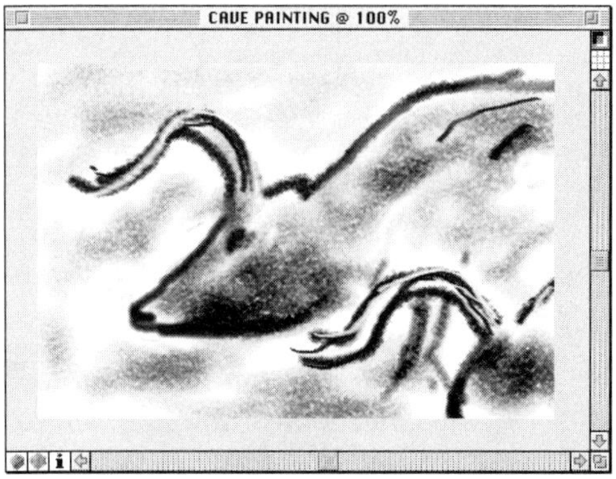

Tip

To prevent clicking in the Finder when you stroke off the edge of your paper, make the image window slightly larger than the picture.

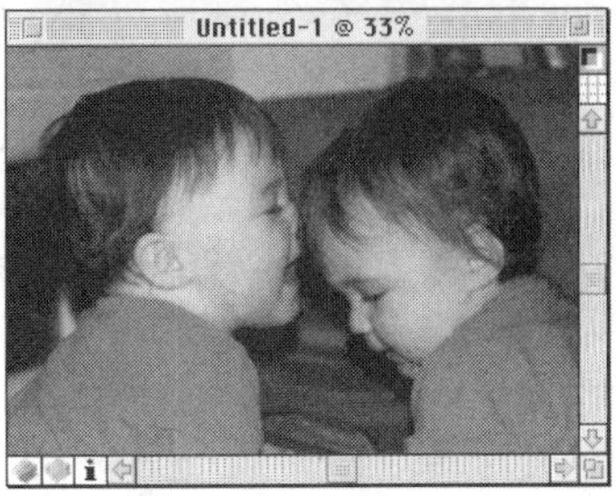

The cropped image appears in a new, untitled image window.

This method is a bit cumbersome, but it works.

To crop a picture:

1. Choose the Rectangular Selection tool.
2. Select the area you want to keep **2**.
3. Choose Edit > Copy (⌘-C).
4. Choose Edit > Paste > Into New Image.

To replace the old document with the new document, choose File > Save As, and don't change the document name. To preserve the original, save the new document under a different name.

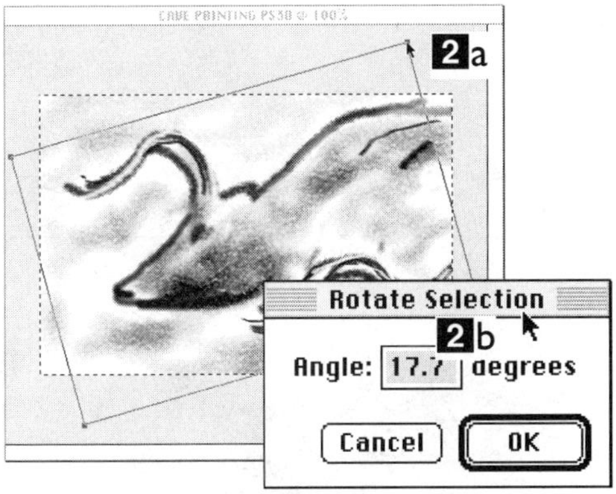

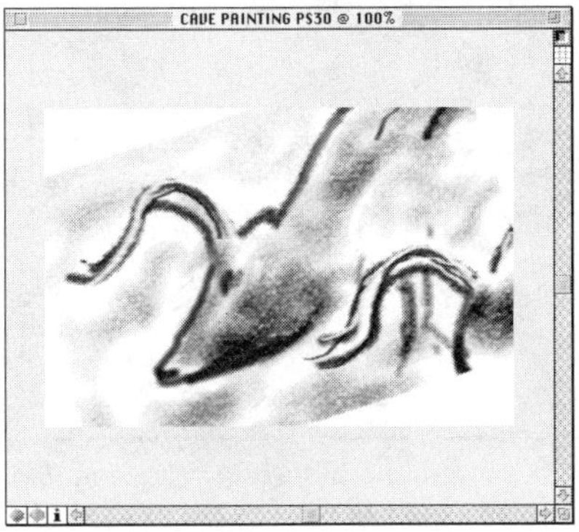

The rotated image.

Use the Rotate command to save and print a picture from a new orientation. **The Rotate command will blur your picture slightly and it will turn it into a floater.**

To rotate the image:

1. Choose Effects > Orientation > Rotate.
2. Press and drag a corner of the image in the image window **2a**.
   or
   Enter a number in the Angle field **2b**.
3. Click OK or press Return.
4. Choose Edit > Deselect (⌘-D).

To create a vertical or horizontal mirror image of your picture, choose Flip Vertical or Flip Horizontal. The image won't become a floater.

Use the Canvas Size command to add new, edtiable pixels to any of a picture's four sides. **You must turn off Wet Paint to access the Canvas Size command.**

To enlarge the canvas size:

1. *Optional:* The new border area will be the Paper Color you chose when you created your document. To change the paper color, choose a Primary color from the Art Materials: Colors palette, then choose Canvas > Set Paper Color.
2. Choose Canvas > Canvas Size.
3. Enter the number of pixels you want to add to the image in any of the Increase Size fields **2**. (To calculate the number of pixels to enter, multiply the number of inches you want to add by your file's pixels per inch resolution.)
4. Click OK or press Return.
5. Click the image window zoom box (upper right corner) to enlarge the window and display the added pixels.

To display your picture in the center of your screen with the image window title bar and scroll bars hidden, choose Window > Screen Mode Toggle (⌘-M). Choose the same command again to restore the normal viewing mode.

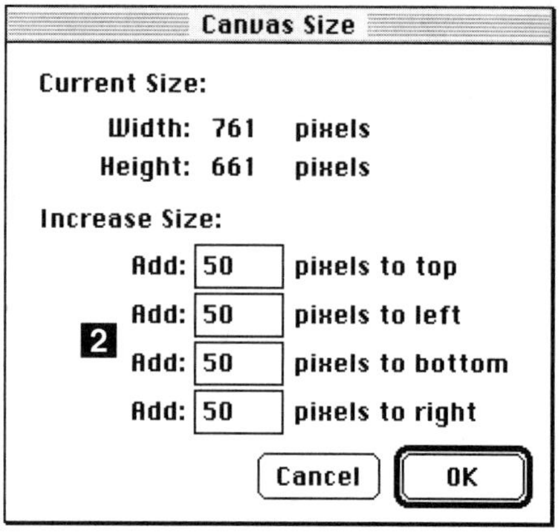

The original picture.

Phil Allen

Pixels added to all four sides of the picture and the image window enlarged.

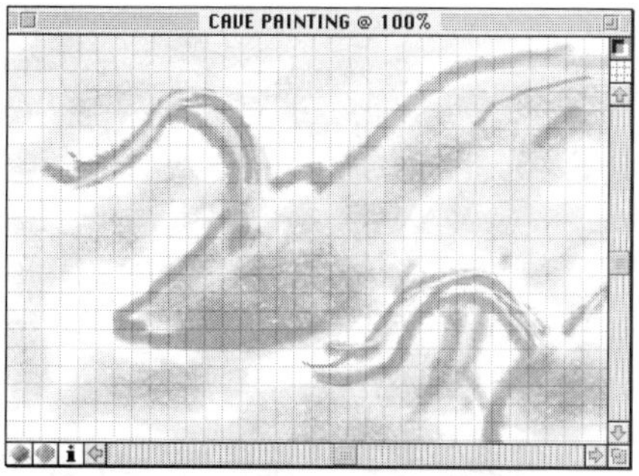

View Grid on and the Transparent Background box unchecked in the Grid Options dialog box.

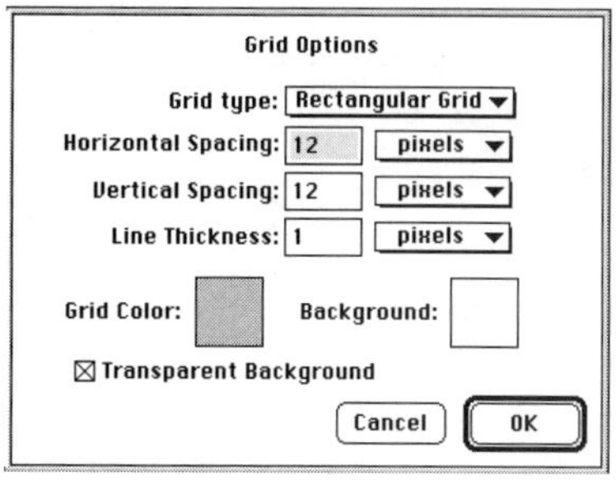

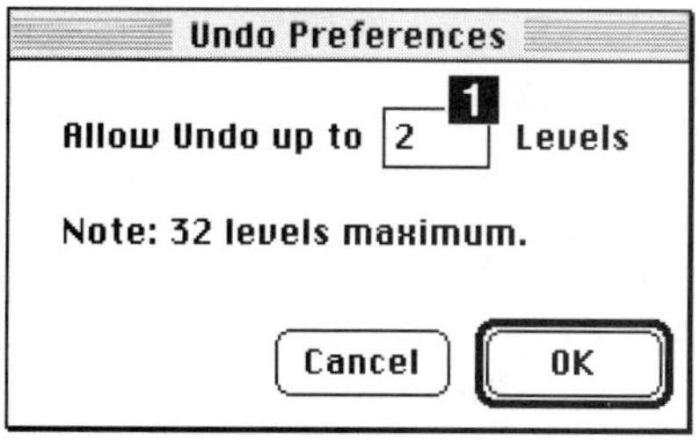

The FADE command

A pat on the back to Fractal Design for the Fade command, which reduces the last modification in increments. Choose Edit > Fade, then watch the preview in the Fade dialog box as you move the Undo Amount slider. If you choose Undo after executing the Fade command, both the Fade and the previous command will be undone.

Techniques for erasing brush strokes are discussed on page 21 and pages 43-44. Cloning techniques for restoring areas from a source document are discussed in Chapter 9.

To display a non-printing grid:

1. Choose Canvas > View Grid (⌘-G) or click the grid icon in the upper right corner of the image window.
2. *Optional:* Choose Canvas > Grid Options, then change the Grid type, Horizontal or Vertical Spacing (space between lines), Line Thickness, or Grid Color (line color). When the Transparent Background box is unchecked, the grid will have a semi-transparent background. When it's checked, you'll see the image at full strength behind the grid. Click OK to display the modified grid.

To turn the grid off, choose Canvas > View Grid or click the grid icon again.

To create a grid that *is* part of the image and does print, choose Effects > Esoterica > Grid Paper **before** you start painting.

Undo options

Choose Edit > **Undo** (⌘-Z) to undo the last operation. Repeat to undo the second-to-last operation, etc. You can undo up to 32 operations (the combined total for all open documents), depending on the Undo Preferences setting (choose Edit > Preferences > Undo and enter a number **1**). The whole picture is saved for each Undo level, so you may want to limit the number of levels to conserve disk space. To take advantage of the Undo command, draw short brush strokes when you're painting. You can Undo after you save your file, as long as it's still open.

Choose File > **Redo** to redo the last undone operation.

Choose File > **Revert**, then click Revert to restore the last saved version of your document.

Choose Edit > **Clear** to fill the current selection with the current paper color. Choose Edit > Select All first if you want to clear your whole picture.

To change a picture's storage size and/or resolution:

1. Choose Canvas > Resize (⌘-Shift-R).
2. To change the file's storage size and not its resolution, choose pixels from the pop-up menus and enter a new number in the Width or Height field **1**. The Constrain File Size box will uncheck automatically. Don't recheck it unless you want to restore the original file size.
   or
   To change the file's resolution and overall dimensions but not its storage size, choose an increment other than pixels from the Width and Height pop-up menus, check the Constrain File Size box, then enter a new number in the Width, Height, or Resolution field. (To change resolution *and* storage size, uncheck the Constrain File Size box first.)
3. Click OK or press Return.

To add pixels to any of the image's four sides, use the Canvas > Canvas Size command (see page 12). If you use the Edit > Orientation > Scale > command to resize a whole picture, it will turn into a floater.

If the Constrain File Size box is checked and you change a picture's width, height, or resolution, the picture's on-screen display size will remain the same, with no loss of pixels. With the Constrain File Size box unchecked, the image is resampled, which means its on-screen size and file storage size change. Resampling down causes pixels to be permanently deleted from the file, and resampling up causes pixels to be added based on existing colors in the picture. Resampling will diminish a picture's crispness, but the degree to which the change will be noticeable depends on how much the resolution is changed and whether the picture contains sharp line work.

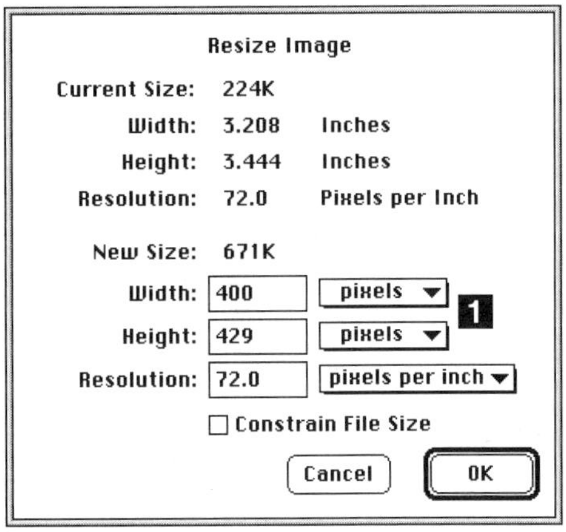

A library icon

How many items should I put in a library?

A maximum of 25 icons can be displayed in the palette drawer at a time, so you might want to limit the number of items you place in one library to that number. If the drawer contains more than 25 items, you'll need to use the scroll bar or arrows to access the ones on the bottom.

You can create a library for papers, paths, brushes, brush looks, sessions, floaters, lighting effects, weaves, and gradations.

To create a library:

1. Choose the type of library you want to create from the Tools > Movers submenu.
2. Click New.
3. Enter a name for the library.
4. *Optional:* Choose a location in which to save the library.
5. Click Save.
6. Highlight the gradation, weave, etc. on the left side of the Mover dialog box that you want to move into the library. (If the item isn't listed, click Close, then click Open to open the correct library.)
7. Click Copy.
8. *Optional:* Click Change Name, enter a new name for the gradation, weave, etc., then click OK.
9. Click Quit or press Return.

To delete a whole library, drag its icon from the Finder to the trash.

To create a new sessions library another way, click Library in the Objects: Sessions palette drawer, then click New. You can do the same on the Art Materials: Weaves palette, Art Materials: Grads palette, or Objects: Paths palette. To create a lighting library, click Library in the Apply Lighting dialog box, then click New.

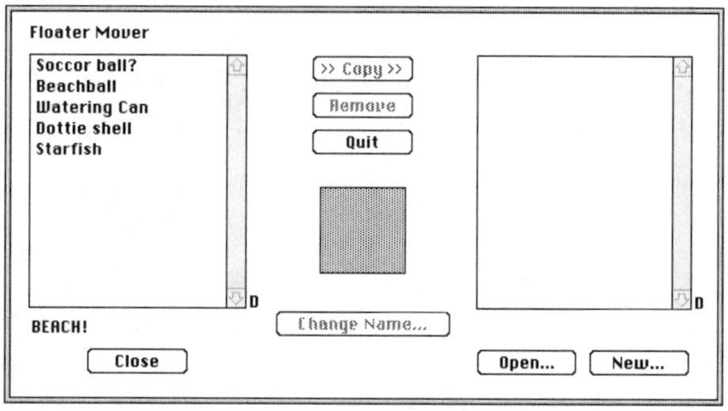

To edit a library:

1. Choose the category of the library you want to edit from the Tools > Movers submenu.
2. *Optional:* To open a different library at any time, click Close, if necessary, click Open, highlight the library you want to open, then click Open.
3. To delete an item from a library, highlight it, then click Remove.

   To rename an item, highlight it, click Change Name, enter a new name, then click OK or press Return.

   To copy an item from one library to another, open the library you want to copy from and highlight the item you want to copy on the left side of the dialog box, open the library you want to move the item to on the right side of the dialog box, then click Copy.
4. Click Quit or press Return.

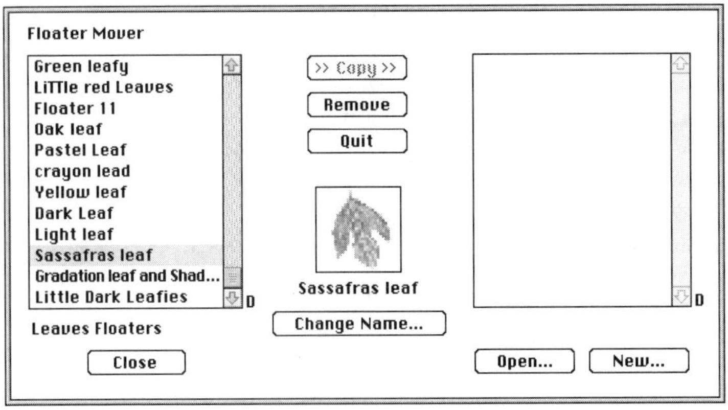

To close a file:
Choose File > Close (⌘-W).

To quit Painter:
Choose File> Quit (⌘-Q).

Scanning

Using a scanning device and scanning software, a slide, flat artwork, or a photograph can be digitized so you can open it and paint on it in Painter. If you install the correct plug-in file, you can scan directly into Painter. (Painter can only access plug-ins from one folder, so install your scanner plug-in with the rest of the plug-ins you want to use in Painter.) If you scan outside Painter, make sure to save the scan in a file format that Painter imports, such as TIFF.

Scanners

The quality of a scan depends on the type of scanner you use. If you are going to apply a lot of brush strokes or Effects menu commands to the image in Painter, you can use an inexpensive flat-bed scanner. If color accuracy is critical, scan a transparency on a slide scanner. Scan a picture that is going to be printed electronically on a high-resolution CCD scanner, such as a Scitex Smart-Scanner, or on a drum scanner. A high-quality scan can be obtained from a service bureau. Unfortunately, high-resolution scans usually have very large file sizes and are sometimes saved in CMYK color mode, which Painter cannot open. You can use another application, like Photoshop, to convert a CMYK color file into an RGB color file, which Painter can open.

Scanner software

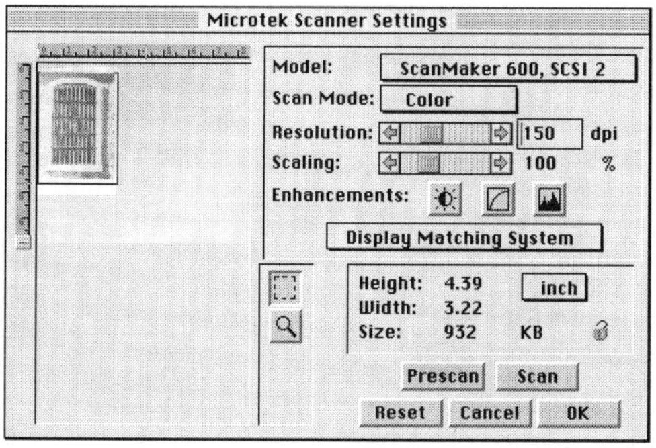

Scanning software usually offers most of the following options, although terminology may vary. The quality and file storage size of a scan are affected by the mode, resolution, and scale you specify, and whether you crop the picture. Set the scanning parameters carefully, weighing such factors as your final output device and storage capacity.

Preview: Place the art in the scanner, then click Preview or PreScan.

(Continued on the next page)

Scan mode: Choose Black-and-White Line Art (no grays), Grayscale or Color. A picture scanned in color will be approximately three times larger in file size than in grayscale.

Resolution: Scan resolution is measured in pixels per inch (ppi). The higher the resolution, the better the scan, and the larger its file size. Choose the minimum resolution necessary to obtain the best possible printout from your final output device. Choosing a higher resolution than is required will just make the picture take up more disk space than is necessary and it will take longer to render on screen and to print, with no improvement in output quality.

For multimedia or video work, choose the monitor's resolution (72 ppi). Before selecting a resolution for printing, ask your print shop what halftone screen frequency they will be using. As a general rule, your image resolution should be one-and-a-half times the printer's halftone screen frequency (lines per inch) for a grayscale picture and twice the halftone screen frequency for a color picture. (If your printer plans to use a 133-line screen for grayscale printing, for example, scan your image at 200 ppi.) We've been told this rule can be broken, though. For smudgy, chalky, or painterly color images, one-and-a-half times screen frequency may be adequate. For crisp line art, use a very high scan resolution (600 ppi or higher), then lower the resolution in Painter to the appropriate output resolution.

Cropping: If you're going to use only part of the picture in Painter, move the handles of the selection box in the preview window to reduce the scan area. Cropping will reduce the scan's storage size.

Scale: To enlarge the image's dimensions, choose a scale percentage larger than 100%. This the time to enlarge your picture, if you need to. Enlarging the picture in Painter may make it blurry because mathematical "guesswork" is used to fill in needed pixel information. A source picture's original information is recorded only at the time of scanning.

Scan: Click Scan and choose a location in which to save the file.

Video capture

To digitize (capture) video frames to edit in Painter, a video board and its accompanying software must be installed in your computer. If your Macintosh is an AV (audio-visual) or a 7500 or 8500 PCI Power Mac model, then you have the necessary hardware and software to capture video built in.

You'll need to use the proper cables to connect the video source (like a VCR) to the Mac. In Painter, choose File > Acquire, and select the appropriate plug-in name for video. In the video capture software dialog box, set such parameters as the video encoding standard used by the input signal (like NTSC for United States video recordings), the source encoding method of the video (like composite or S-video), and the size of the captured video image. A 640 by 480 pixels resolution will produce a full video frame on a 14-inch monitor.

With the video capture dialog box open, start the source video, then click the Grab button (or a similarly-named capture button) to grab a "frame" of the video. If your Mac has built in video capture capability (AV and 7500 or 8500 PCI Macs), use that software to capture a video frame, save the captured image in the PICT or TIFF file format, then open it in Painter.

Keep in mind that the quality of a video captured image will depend on the quality of hardware and software you use to capture and of course the quality of the original videotape.

Painting Basics 2

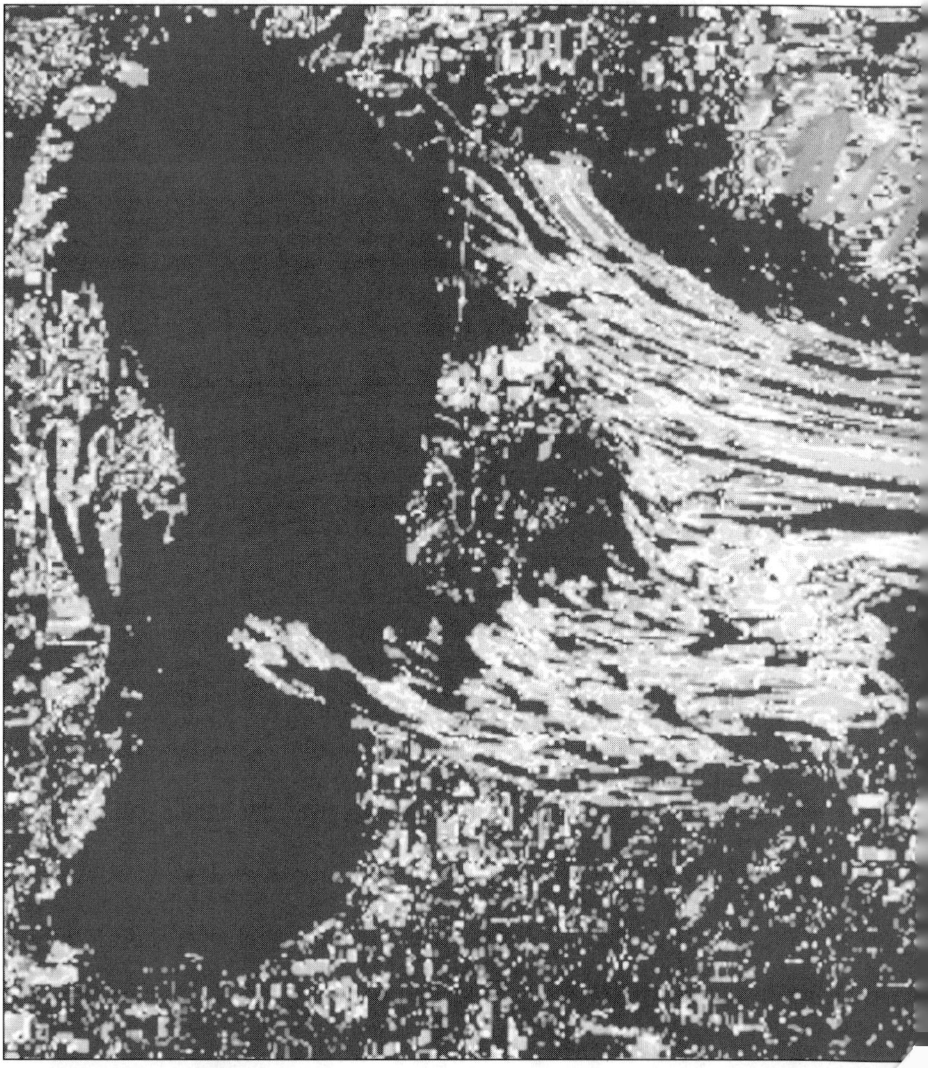

Ron Gorchov, ***Clone of Herophile*** *(detail).*

Follow these instructions if you'd like to get started painting right away using Painter's default brushes. After you learn these basic steps, you'll want to learn more about brushes, paper textures, and color. These topics are covered in this chapter and in the next two chapters.

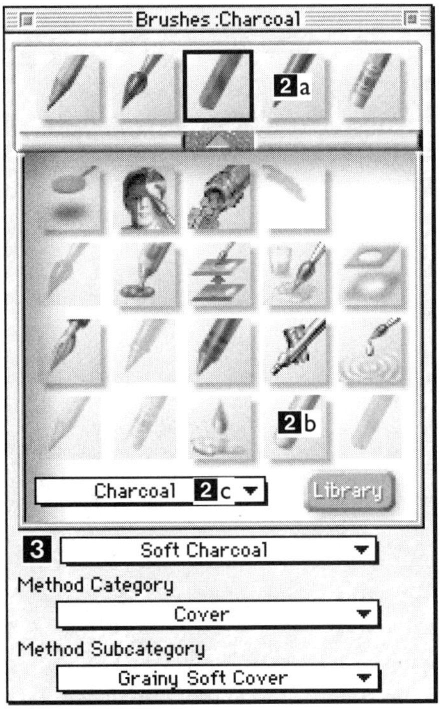

QuickStart Paint:

■ *Choose a brush.*

1. Click the **Brush** tool on the Tools palette.
2. Click a brush icon on the Brushes palette drawer front 2a (⌘-2 to open/close the Brushes palette).
   or
   Click the pushbar to open the drawer, then click a brush icon in the drawer 2b or choose a brush from the pop-up menu 2c. (If an item is already on a palette drawer front, its icon in the drawer will be dimmed.)
3. Choose a variant for the brush from the variant pop-up menu 3.

■ *Choose a paper texture.*

Note: Brush strokes will reveal the paper texture only if your brush has a Grainy method subcategory.

1. Click the **Papers** icon on the Art Materials palette 1 (⌘-3 to open/close the Papers palette).
2. Click a paper texture icon on the Papers palette drawer front 2a.
   or
   Click the pushbar to open the drawer, then click a paper texture icon in the drawer 2b or choose a paper texture from the pop-up menu 2c.

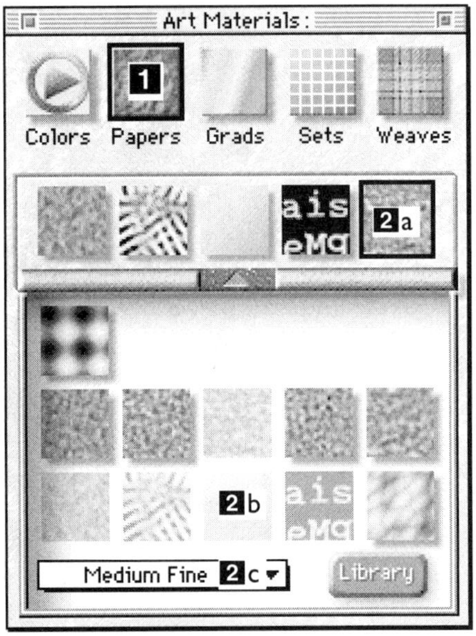

■ *Choose a color.*

1. Click the **Colors** icon on the Art Materials palette **1**.
2. Make sure the Primary (frontmost) rectangle is highlighted **2**. (Click on it to activate it.)
3. To choose a hue, click on the color ring or move the little circle on the color ring **3**. If you switched your Colors palette to the Hue Slider+ Triangle Color Palette Type (General Preferences dialog box), click on the color bar to choose a hue.
4. Click on the triangle or move the circle on the triangle to choose a value and a saturation of that hue **4**.

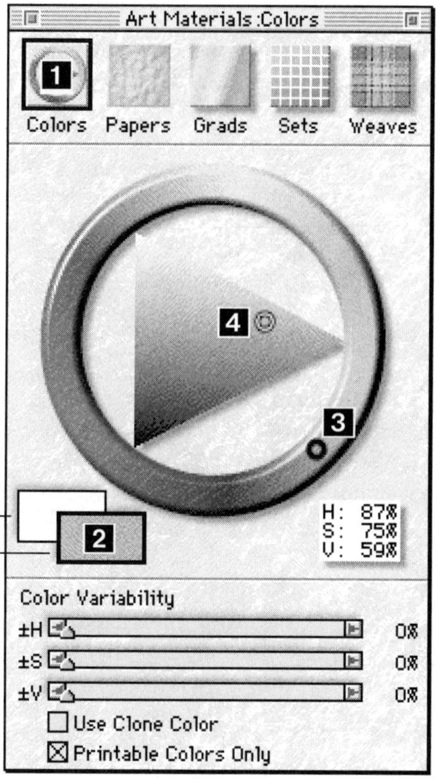

***Secondary** color rectangle*

***Primary** color rectangle*

■ *Paint!*

How to remove brush strokes

Choose Edit > Undo (⌘-Z).

or

Erase using an Eraser brush variant or using the Eraser variant for a non-Eraser brush.

or

Paint with a background color or the current paper color (you can use the Dropper tool to choose a color from the picture).

To delete the whole image, choose Edit > Select All (⌘-A), then press Delete.

The Controls: Brush palette

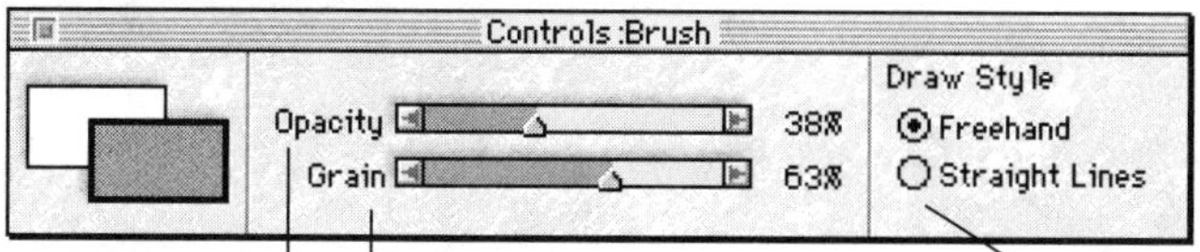

*Move the **Opacity** slider to adjust the transparency of the stroke. Or press a corresponding keypad key (0=100%, 1=10%, 2=20%, etc.)*

*For most brushes for which the chosen submethod category contains the word "Grainy," moving the **Grain** slider to the left will make the paper texture more prominent in your brush strokes. The higher the Grain setting, the more strokes penetrate the paper surface and the less the grain shows.*

*Drag with your mouse or stylus when the **Freehand Draw Style** is selected. Click with your mouse or stylus to create **Straight Lines**. Click the Freehand button or press Return to end a Straight Lines stroke.*

Color

Most of the time you will paint with what Fractal Design calls the **Primary** color. The current Primary color is displayed in the front color rectangle on the Art Materials: Colors palette and on the Controls: Brush or Controls: Dropper palette. You may occasionally choose a **Secondary** color (the back color rectangle) — for the Graduated Brush, to mix color into the Image Hose, or to create a Two-Point gradient.

To choose a Primary color:

1. Click the Colors icon on the Art Materials palette **1**.
2. Make sure the Primary (frontmost) rectangle is highlighted. Click on it if it isn't **2**.
3. Click on the color ring (or the color bar, if you're using the Hue Slider+ Triangle Color Palette Type) on the Colors palette to choose a hue **3**.
   or
   To choose a color from a picture, choose the Dropper tool, then click on a color in any open image window.
   or
   Choose Color Set from the Window menu, then click a swatch. To open a different color set, see the next page.
4. Click on the triangle or move the little circle on the triangle to choose a different value or saturation of that hue **4**.
5. *Optional:* Check the Printable Colors Only box on the expanded Colors palette to restrict subsequently chosen colors to colors that can be printed on a four-color press **5**.

To convert existing colors in a picture into their closest printable equivalents, choose Effects > Tonal Control > Printable Colors, then click OK. To convert existing colors to video legal colors (NTSC for the U.S., PAL for Europe), choose Video Legal Colors from the same submenu.

In Painter, you can choose colors based on their Hue, Saturation, and Value (HSV) components or their Red, Green, and Blue (RGB) components. You can't choose CMYK colors in Painter.

In the HSV color model, hue is the component that gives a color its name, such as red or green; saturation is the intensity of a color; value is the amount of white or black in a color (brightness).

Use the RGB Colors palette to mix RGB colors by number (Choose Edit > Preferences > General, then click the Red-Green-Blue Color Palette Type).

Dropper tool

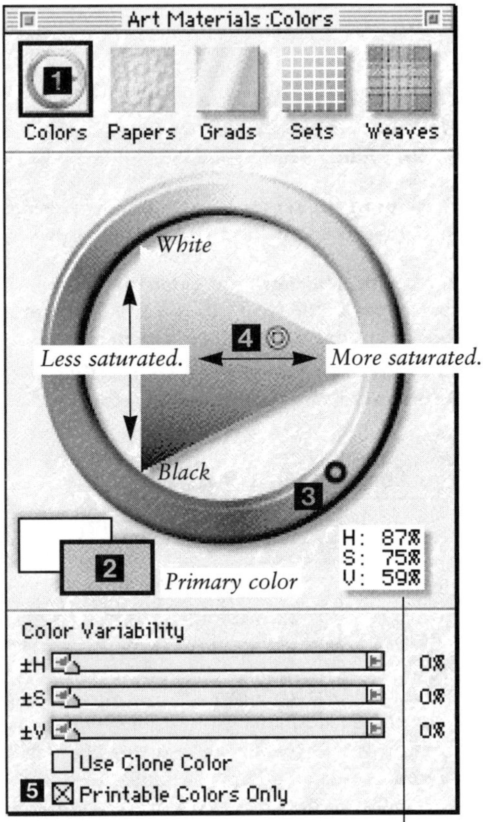

Click this box to switch between HSV and RGB color readouts.

Choose a Color

The **Color Set** palette displays one group of color swatches at a time that you can choose from to paint with. To display the Color Set palette, choose Window > Color Set (⌘-8). Choose Color Set again to close the palette, or click the palette close box. To choose a color in a set, simply click on a swatch.

The color you choose from the Color Set palette will also be displayed in whichever color rectangle is active on the Art Materials: Colors palette and the Controls: Brush palette.

Painter Colors is Painter's default color set. The Pantone Matching System color set as well as many other color sets, including Grayscale, Muted Tones, and Candy, are also supplied with Painter. You can create your own color sets to make it easier to grab colors that you use frequently or to assemble special colors for specific projects.

To display a different color set:

1. Click the Sets icon on the Art Materials palette **1**.
2. Click Library **2**.
3. Locate and highlight the color set you want to open. The Painter Colors color set is on the first level of the application folder. The other Painter color sets are in the Colors, Weaves, Grads folder. Color sets that you create may be stored anywhere you like.
4. Click Open.

Read more about color sets in Chapter 4, More Painting.

Use Painter's Grayscale color set to create a grayscale picture **3**.

3 *The Grayscale color set.*

Paper Textures

There is a rich assortment of methods for applying paper textures in Painter. If you use a brush for which you've chosen a Grainy method subcategory, the paper texture currently selected on the Art Materials: Papers palette will be revealed under your brush strokes. You can choose a different paper texture at any time while you're painting. Many Effects menu commands, including Adjust Colors, Adjust Selected Colors, Apply Screen, Apply Surface Texture, Color Overlay, Dye Concentration, Express Texture, and Glass Distortion apply a texture to a whole painting or to a selected area. If you use an Eraser brush on a texture applied using either method, you'll erase texture along with color.

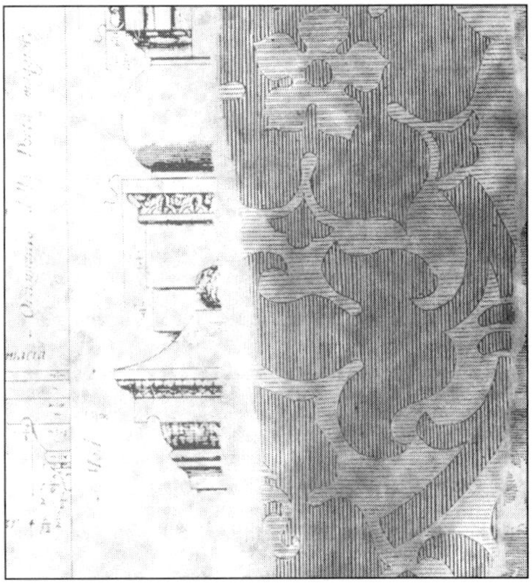

Fabric Effects, Inc. (detail)

Grainy brushes used to add texture.

To reveal a paper texture under brush strokes:

1. *Optional:* To choose a different paper texture, click the Papers icon on the Art Materials palette, then click a paper texture icon on the palette drawer front or in the drawer.
2. Make sure the brush method subcategory you have selected contains the word "Grainy."
3. Paint.
4. *Optional:* To make the paper texture more prominent, move the Controls: Brush palette Grain slider to the left.

HELP!

You chose a brush and color, tried to paint, and nothing happened?

Remember to choose the Brush tool from the Tools palette!

Still nothing?

Check to make sure your paint color doesn't match your background color (i.e., white-on-white).

Still nothing?

Make sure you haven't unintentionally activated a floater or a path selection (check on the Objects: F. List and P. List palettes).

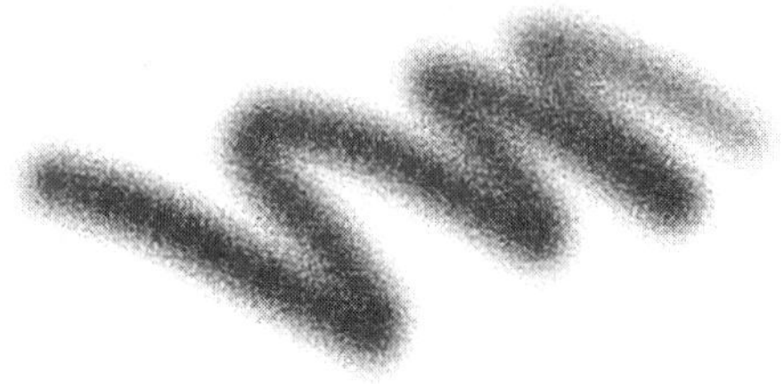

Default Charcoal variant, Grainy Hard Cover method subcategory: Brush stroke reveals paper texture.

Default Charcoal variant, Soft Cover method subcategory: Brush stroke doesn't reveal paper texture.

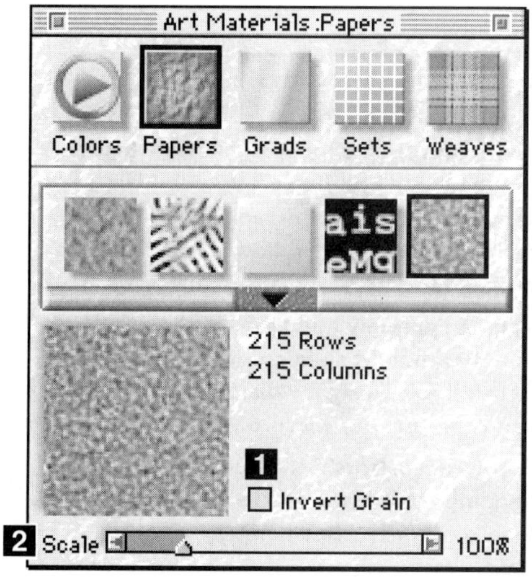

If you're ready to expand beyond the default Paper Textures library...

To choose Art Materials: Papers palette options:

- To switch the raised and depressed areas of the paper, check the Invert Grain box **1**.
- To shrink or enlarge the texture, move the Scale slider **2**.
- To display an alternate set of paper textures, open the drawer, click Library, highlight a library, then click Open. Several paper texture libraries are supplied with Painter, and of course you can create your own paper textures and paper texture libraries.

Painter's default Wicked Wicker paper texture.

The Invert Grain box checked.

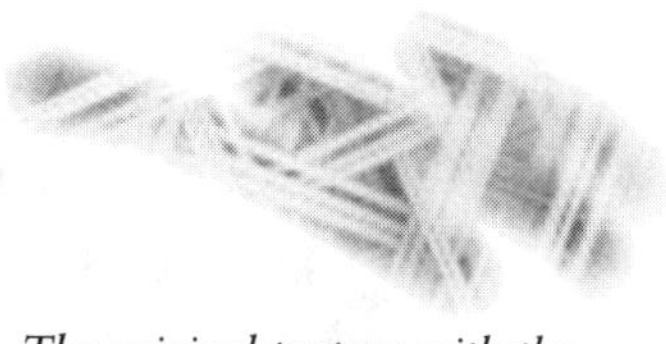

The original texture with the Scale slider moved to 340%.

Texture and then a brush stroke (Grainy Buildup method subcategory) applied with the Invert Grain box unchecked. The brush stroke darkens the positive areas of the texture.

Texture applied with the Invert Grain box unchecked, and then a brush stroke applied with the Invert Grain box checked (Water Color brush, Grainy Wet Abrasive method subcategory). The brush stroke affects the negative areas.

Brushes

When you use a default brush **variant**, a **method category** and **method subcategory** are selected for you automatically. To customize a brush, you can start by choosing a different category or subcategory from the Brushes palette. For the Pencil brush, for example, you can choose a variant like the 2b Pencil, then choose a different method category like Cover, and then choose a different method subcategory like Soft Cover. There are an immense number of possible variant/category/subcategory combinations. Other ways of customizing brushes are discussed in Chapter 4.

Default brush settings

If you choose non-default settings for a brush and then choose a different brush or variant, your non-default settings will be lost. To save a customized variant so you can choose it again, follow the instructions on page 57.

You can preview and test brush variants and brush-and-paper combinations in the Brush Look Designer dialog box before you use them in your picture.

To restore a brush's default settings while keeping the brush selected, Option-click its icon on the Brushes palette.

THE METHOD CATEGORIES

Buildup *strokes combine with existing strokes underneath them, producing darker areas where they crisscross. Choose a light Opacity from the Controls: Brush palette to slow down the buildup.*

Cover *strokes cover existing strokes underneath them. Choose a light Opacity from the Controls: Brush palette to make cover strokes less opaque.*

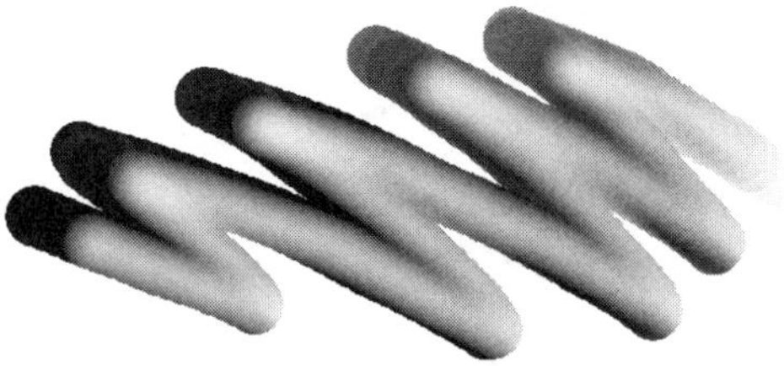

Eraser *strokes erase completely to the current paper color when the Controls: Brush Opacity slider is at 100%. Choose a lower Opacity to partially erase strokes (we chose 40% for the eraser stroke above). And of course you can use of the Eraser brush itself, with its own variants.*

Drip *strokes smear existing colors. The Liquid brushes automatically have the Drip method category.*

Mask *strokes create masked (protected) areas. (See Chapter 7)*

Cloning *brush strokes reproduce pixels in a clone document from the source document. (See Chapter 9)*

Wet *strokes stay wet on the special Wet Paint layer until you choose Canvas > Dry. Water Color brush variants automatically have this method category. (Before drawing the Large Simple Water brush stroke above, the Diffusion slider on the Advanced Controls: Water palette was moved to 13.)*

THE METHOD SUBCATEGORIES

Soft: Smooth, anti-aliased edge.
Flat: Hard, jagged edge.
Edge: Thick, opaque edge.
Hard: Semi-anti-aliased edge.
Grainy: Brush strokes reveal paper texture.

Cover method subcategories hide underlying pixels.

Flat Cover *Hard, jagged edge. Doesn't reveal paper grain.*

Soft Cover *Anti-aliased edge. Doesn't reveal paper grain.*

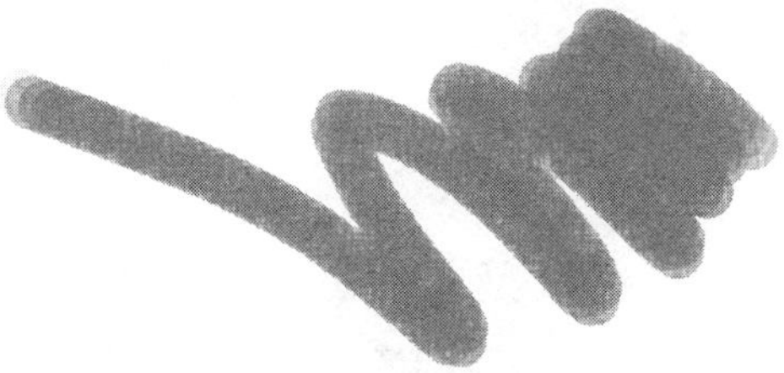

Grainy Flat Cover *Paper grain sensitive, hard-edged.*

Grainy Soft Cover *Paper grain sensitive, anti-aliased.*

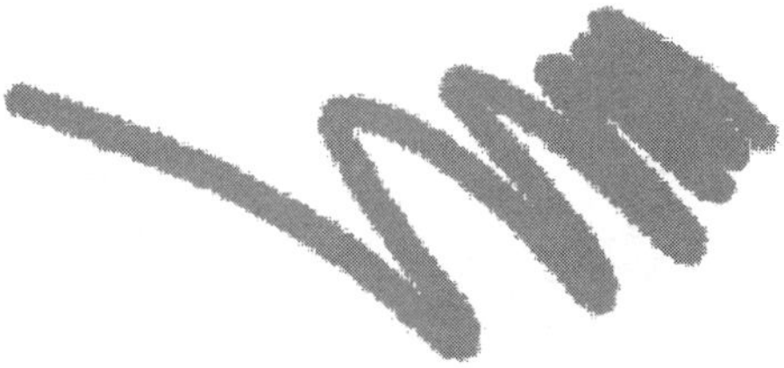

Grainy Edge Flat Cover *Hard-edged, paper grain visible on the brush stroke edge.*

Grainy Hard Cover *Paper grain sensitive, semi-anti-aliased.*

Buildup method subcategories build up to black.

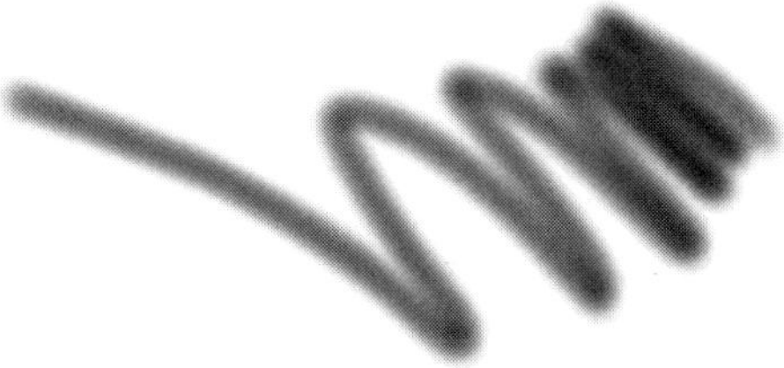

Soft Buildup *Anti-aliased.*

You can see the difference between Cover and Buildup brush strokes where the stroke crisscrosses itself.

Grainy Soft Buildup *Paper grain sensitive, anti-aliased.*

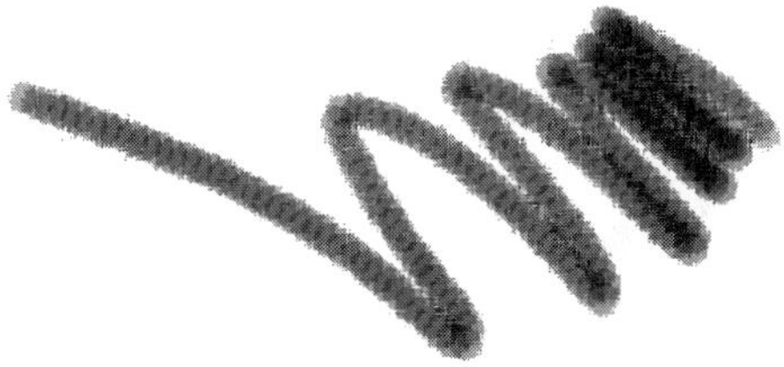

Grainy Edge Flat Buildup *Paper grain sensitive, hard-edged.*

Grainy Hard Buildup *Paper grain sensitive, semi-anti-aliased.*

How can I change my brush size?

To change the brush size interactively, hold down Command (⌘) and Option and drag in the image window. If you make the brush tip large, you may get a prompt to Build the brush when you start to use it.

To change the brush size another way, click the Size icon on the Brush Controls palette, move the Size slider, and click Build, if the button lights up. (More about Brush Controls in Chapter 4.)

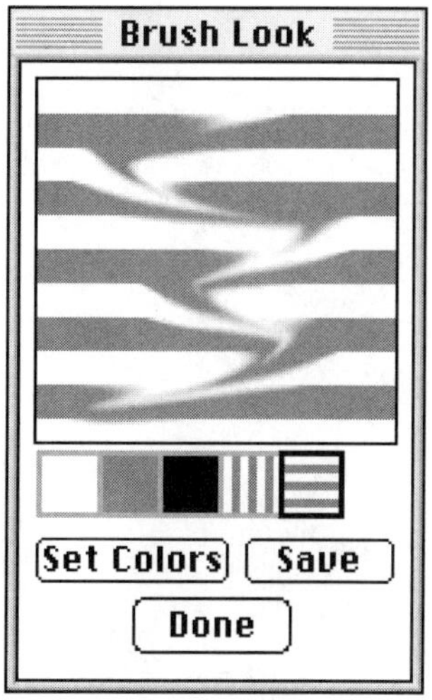

The Brush Look Designer

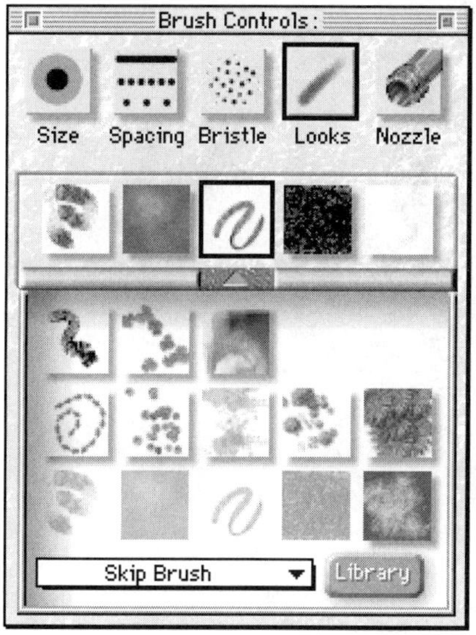

To choose a saved brush look

Click the Looks icon on the Brush Controls palette, then click an icon on the drawer front or in the drawer or choose from the pop-up menu. (To create or edit a brush looks library, see pages 15-16.)

You can use the **Brush Look Designer** simply to preview a brush variant or a customized brush before you use it. Or use the Brush Look Designer to save a brush look, which is a brush-and-paper texture combination. Once a brush look is saved, you can reuse it at any time.

To preview and save brush-and-paper combinations (Brush Look Designer):

1. Open the palettes you want to use (Art Materials, Brushes, Color Set, etc.).
2. Choose Tools > Brushes > Brush Look Designer.
3. Draw a stroke in the preview window.
4. Do any of the following:

   Choose a different brush, variant, method category, method subcategory.

   Change the brush size (see page 28).

   Choose a different paper texture.

   Choose a different Primary color.

   Fine-tune the brush using the Brush Controls or Advanced Controls palette.

   Click a different background color icon for the preview window: White, the last color applied via the Set Colors button, Black, or stripes. Use the stripey background to test a Liquid or Water brush stroke or the Drip or Wet variant.

   To change the Brush Look Designer background color, choose a Primary color from the Art Materials: Colors palette or the Color Set palette, then click Set Colors.
5. Click Done if you don't want to save the current brush look.
   or
   To save the brush look to the currently open Looks library, click Save, enter a name for the brush look, then click OK. (To open a different brush looks library, click Library in the Brush Controls: Looks palette drawer, then locate and double-click a library.) An icon for the brush look will appear on the Brush Controls: Looks palette.

Diane Margolin

Margolin is a computer graphics instructor, so of course she's fluent in many software programs, but she likes to explore novel ways of using program features. She builds rich textures by applying different kinds of brush strokes at a low opacity, often with custom brushes that she creates using Painter's Capture Brush command, and by applying a series of commands or filters. For her figurative work, Margolin draws her initial image directly on the computer, though she sometimes refers to an actual photograph as she draws. She rarely uses scanned imagery. Sometimes she'll mask an image based on luminosity and then layer another image over it. Margolin uses other applications — Photoshop, Illustrator, ColorStudio, Gallery Effects, Director, and Paint Alchemy — in conjunction with Painter. In addition to her other professional work, Diane Margolin has created a series of over one thousand original textures and patterns designed for print, multimedia, and video. The collection was conceived as an imaginative, functional, and innovative alternative design solution to the standard photographic products.

Default Brushes 3

Nancy Stahl, ***Island Woman*** *(detail).*

Brushes that apply color

The following is a description of Painter's default brushes, which are designed to mimic traditional media. Illustrations of special brushes that erase, dilute, smear, lighten, or darken begin on page 43.

Various methods for customizing brushes — choosing a different brush size, method category or subcategory, etc. — are covered on pages 26-28 and in Chapter 4, More Painting.

Terms you'll see in the brush variant descriptions in this chapter:

ANTI-ALIASED
Smoothed edges. Semi-anti-aliased edges are semi-smoothed.

PRESSURE AFFECTS OPACITY/REVEAL PAPER TEXTURE/PRESSURE AFFECTS STROKE WIDTH
The harder you press with your stylus, the more opaque and the less apparent the paper grain, and/or the wider the stroke.

DIRECTION AFFECTS STROKE WIDTH
Vertical strokes are wider than horizontal strokes, provided the ± Size slider on the Brush Controls: Size palette is above 1.4.

SPEED AFFECTS STROKE WIDTH
The faster you drag the mouse/stylus, the thinner the stroke.

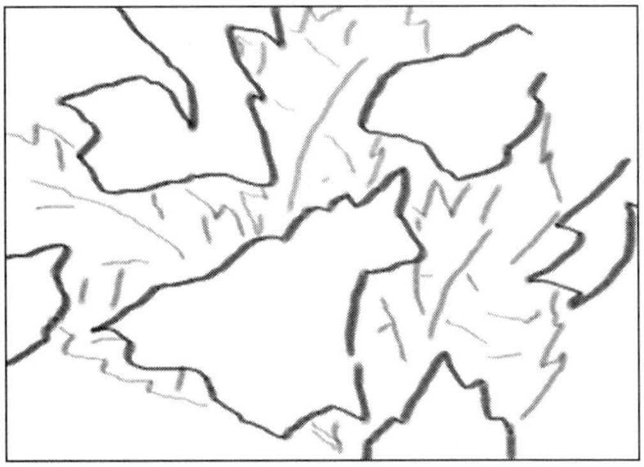

PENCILS 

Main characteristics
Reveal paper texture.

Pressure affects opacity.

Buildup method category.

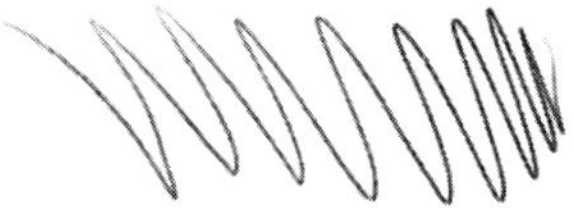

2B Pencil
Thin, soft, anti-aliased.

500 lb. Pencil
Fat, semi-anti-aliased.

Colored Pencils
Semi-anti-aliased.

Sharp Pencil
Thin, hard, semi-anti-aliased.

Single Pixel Scribbler
One pixel wide.

Thick & Thin Pencils
Semi-anti-aliased. Stylus/mouse direction and stylus pressure produce widely variable stroke widths.

CHALK

Main Characteristics

Like pastels.

Pressure affects opacity.

Reveal paper texture.

Cover method category.

Artist Pastel Chalk
Medium width, semi-anti-aliased.

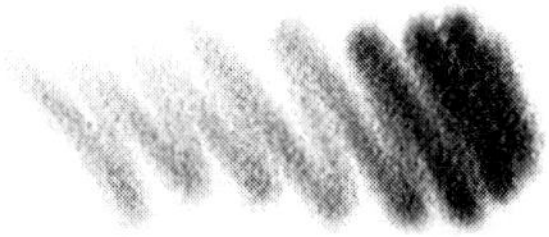

Large Chalk
Wide version of Artist Pastel Chalk.

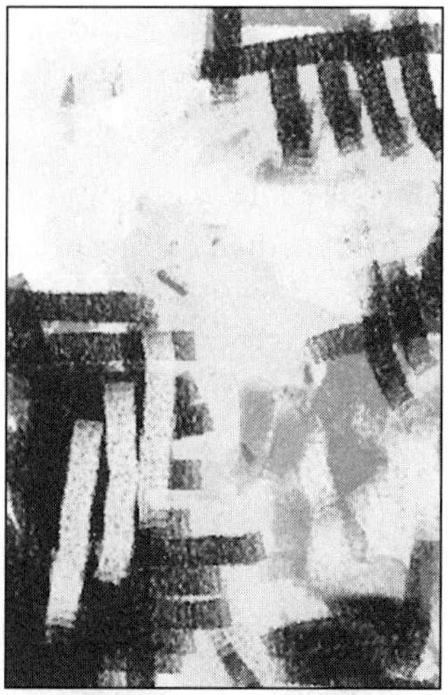

Square chalk

Oil Pastel
Captured rectangular tip. Smears underlying colors and applies color.

Sharp Chalk
Thin, anti-aliased version of Artist Pastel Chalk.

Square Chalk
Like Artist Pastel Chalk with a square, captured rectangular tip.

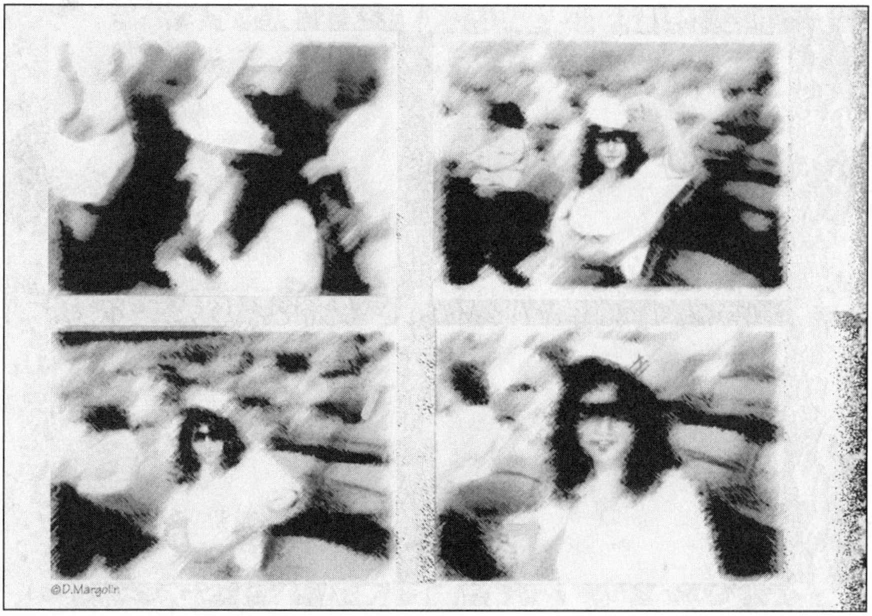

Diane Margolin

Chalk

CHARCOAL

Main Characteristics
Reveal paper texture.

Pressure affects opacity.

Cover method category.

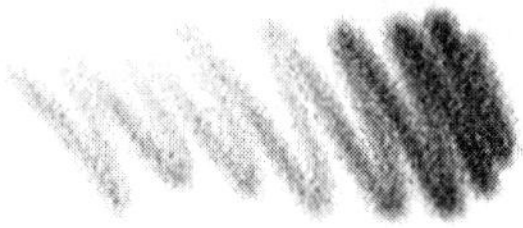

Default Charcoal
Grainy, semi-anti-aliased.

Gritty Charcoal
Semi-anti-aliased. Stylus/mouse direction affects stroke width.

Soft Charcoal
Soft, anti-aliased.

PENS

Main Characteristics
Like ballpoint or fountain pens.

Pressure doesn't affect opacity.

All Cover method category, except Fine Point and Smooth Ink Pen.

Calligraphy
Opaque. Stylus/mouse direction and stylus pressure affect stroke width. Like India ink.

Fine Point
Like a ballpoint pen. Reveals paper grain.

Flat Color
Very wide, consistent width.

Leaky Pen
Ink drops. The farther you drag the stylus/mouse, the larger the blobs become.

Pen and Ink
Opaque, smooth. Stylus/mouse speed affects stroke width.

Pixel Dust
Fine, random spray of pixels.

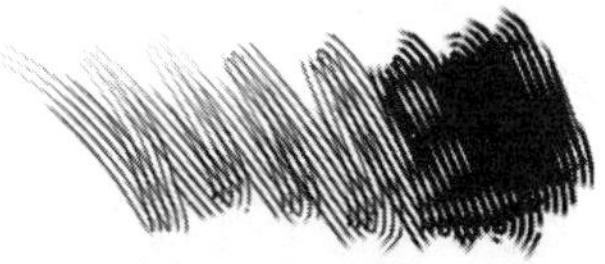

Scratchboard Rake
Multi-bristle stroke. Use for crosshatching. Pressure affects width and opacity. Adjust via Advanced Controls: Rake palette.

Scratchboard Tool
Like a traditional scratchboard tool. Try it on a Black background (choose Black as the paper color when you start your new document). Pressure affects stroke width.

Single Pixel
Not pressure sensitive.

Smooth Ink Pen
Like pen-and-ink. Stylus pressure affects stroke width. Reveals grain.

Tip: To create a leaky pen effect with the Scratchboard Tool, move the Brush Controls: Size palette Size Step slider above 50% and move the Advanced Controls: Sliders palette Size slider to Velocity.

Two images created with the Scratchboard Tool

Steve Gorney

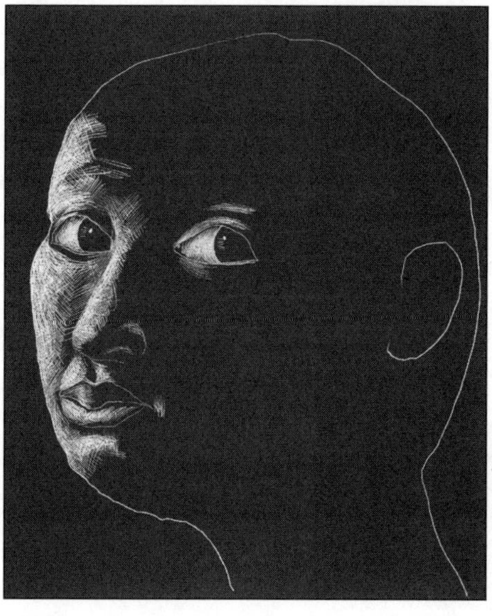

Caty Bartholomew

Calligraphy pen "tips"

Use the Rotate Page tool to tilt your page to a comfortable angle for writing.

To display non-printing horizontal lines to help you align the letters, choose Canvas > Grid Options, and choose Horizontal Lines from the Grid type pop-up menu. Then choose Canvas > View Grid.

Are you left-handed? You can change the brush angle via the Brush Controls: Size palette Angle slider.

FELT PENS

Main Characteristics
Smooth, anti-aliased.

Buildup method category.

Pressure affects opacity.

Dirty Marker
Direction affects stroke width. Fast buildup.

Felt Marker
Lighter than Felt Pens. Direction affects stroke width.

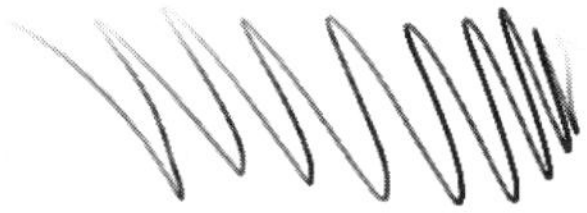

Fine Tip Felt Pens
Thin.

Medium Tip Felt Pens
Medium width. Stylus/mouse speed affects stroke width.

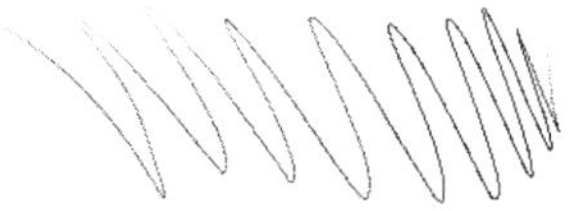

Single Pixel Marker
Ultra thin version of Fine Tip.

CRAYONS

Main Characteristics
Semi-anti-aliased.

Reveal paper texture.

Pressure affects opacity.

Buildup method category.

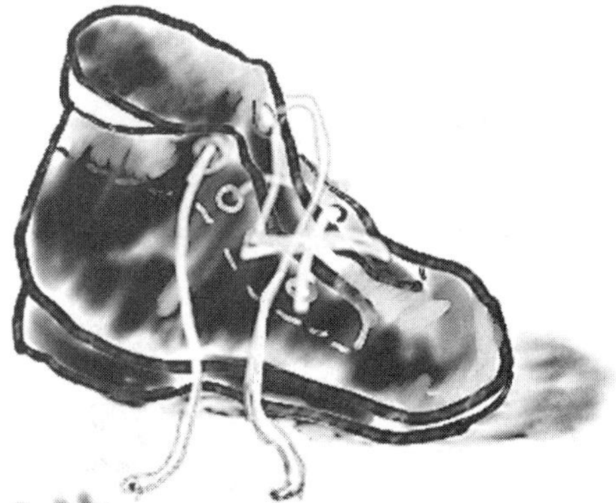

Default
Crayon–crayon.

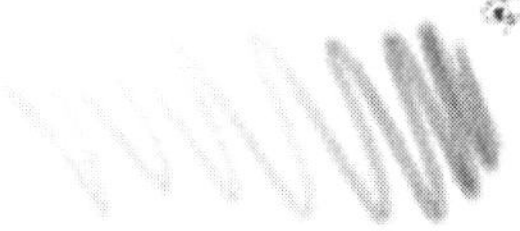

Waxy Crayons
Smears underlying color with paint color.

AIRBRUSH

Main Characteristics

Sprays color.

Cover method category.

Anti-aliased (except Spatter Airbrush).

Pressure affects opacity.

Doesn't reveal paper grain (except Spatter Airbrush).

Fat Stroke
Wide, soft, medium opacity.

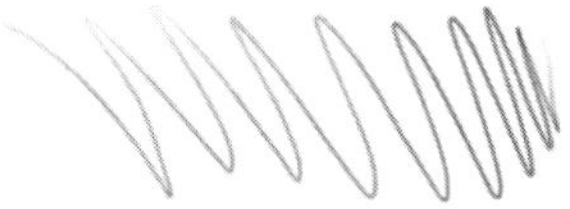

Feather Tip
Narrow, more opaque.

Single Pixel Air
Narrow spray.

Spatter Airbrush
Semi-anti-aliased. Reveals paper grain.

Thin Stroke
Thinner version of Fat Stroke.

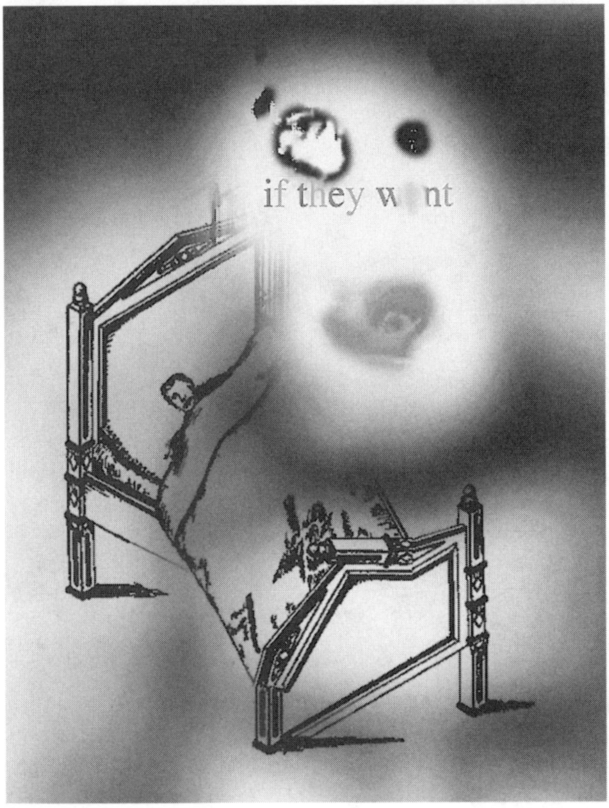

David Humphrey, ***Dream***

BRUSH

Main Characteristics
Like acrylics and oils.
Full coverage.
Pressure affects opacity.
Reveal paper grain.

Illustrator Nancy Stahl likes to use the Camel Hair Brush variant and the Smeary Mover variant of the Liquid brush. She also creates her own paper textures, which she applies using grainy brushes or the Apply Surface Texture command. Take a look at her work in the color section.

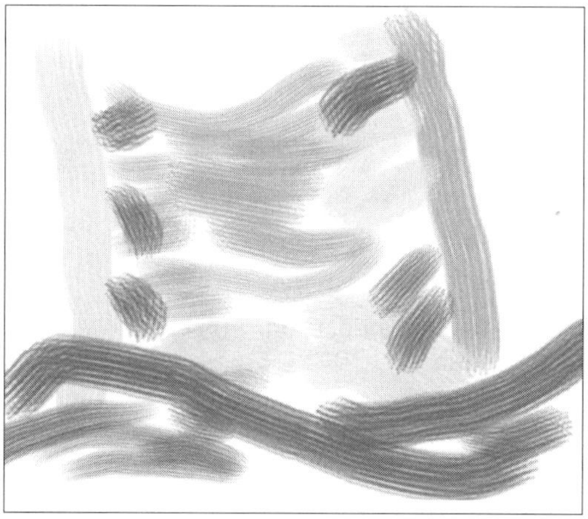

Lourekas

Fine Brush

Big Loaded Oils
Wide, raked, multicolored bristle stroke. Stylus pressure affects width and opacity.

Big Rough Out
Stylus/mouse speed affects stroke width. Reveals paper grain.

Big Wet Oils
Wide, raked, multicolored bristle stroke. Similar to Big Loaded Oils, but less opaque.

Brushy
Runs out of paint as the stroke finishes. Multi-bristle. Smears existing paint. Stylus pressure affects stroke width.

Camel Hair Brush
Anti-aliased, opaque, raked stroke. Stylus/mouse speed affects bristle width.

Coarse Hairs
Noticeable bristles. Stylus pressure easily affects width and opacity.

Cover Brush
Anti-aliased, raked. Doesn't reveal paper grain. Stylus pressure affects width.

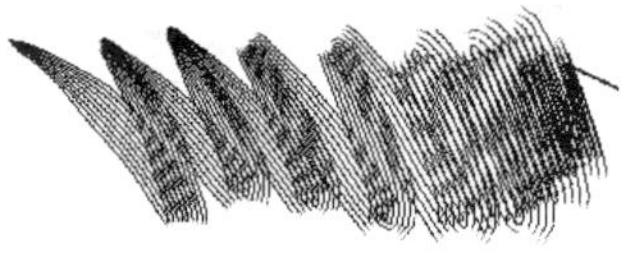

Digital Sumi
Uniform, raked, noticeable bristles. Stylus pressure affects stroke width.

Fine Brush
Smooth, but noticeable bristles. Stylus pressure easily affects width and opacity.

Graduated Brush
Semi-anti-aliased. Reveals paper grain. Stylus pressure affects stroke width. Uses Primary and Secondary colors with strong or light stylus pressure, respectively.

Hairy Brush
Semi-anti-aliased, bristle stroke. Takes time to render. Reveals paper grain. Stylus pressure affects width and opacity. Experiment by changing the Spacing palette and Bristle palette settings.

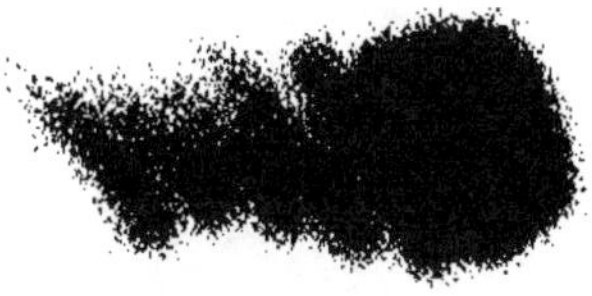

Huge Rough Out
Very wide. Reveals paper grain.

Loaded Oils
Medium size version of Big Loaded Oils.

Oil Paint
Hard, aliased. Reveals paper texture. Stylus pressure affects opacity and stroke width.

Penetration Brush
Hard, aliased rake stroke. Stylus pressure affects opacity and width.

Rough Out
Reveals paper grain, opaque.

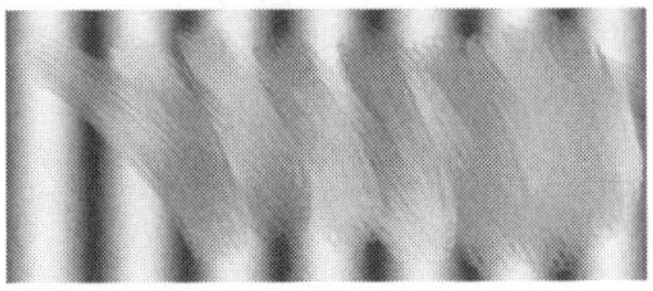

Sable Chisel Tip Water
Smears existing color; doesn't apply color. Soft bristle stroke. Pressure affects width. This is a beauty.

Small Loaded Oils
Small version of Big Loaded Oils.

Smaller Wash Brush
Thin, closely spaced bristles. Soft, translucent stroke.

Ultrafine Water Brush
Wider version of Smaller Wash Brush, with thinner bristles.

To make brush strokes look more three dimensional, clone an image, apply brush strokes to the clone, then use the Apply Surface Texture command (Using: 3D Brush Strokes).

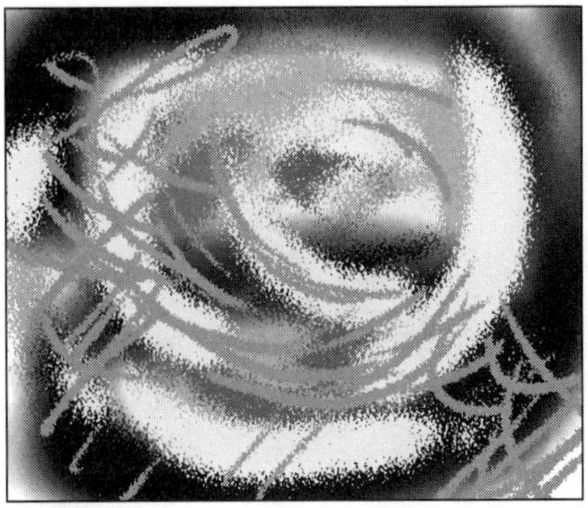

Huge Rough Out

ARTISTS 

Auto Van Gogh
Use this variant to create a "Van Gogh" clone (instructions on page 129).

Flemish Rub
A 16th Century massage? No, it's a brush that smears underlying pixels (Flemish Smear?). Doesn't apply color.

Impressionist
Multicolored, orzo-shaped dabs.

Piano Keys
We admit we slept through some of our art history classes, but as far as we know, Piano Keys wasn't an artist. This brush falls into the miscellaneous category. Creates wide, multicolored ribbons, as if applied with a palette knife. Try using at a low opacity.

Seurat
Multicolored, anti-aliased dot clusters. Use the Brush Controls: Size palette to adjust dot size.

Van Gogh
Oh that it were so easy to be Van Gogh! We differ with Fractal Painter's description of Van Gogh's paint strokes as "multicolored brush strokes." Van Gogh actually applied clean strokes, but when he worked wet-on-wet, his brush strokes dragged color from underneath. Painter's Van Gogh brush is multicolored, anti-aliased, full coverage, similar to Small Loaded Oils. Pause between short strokes.

Textile designer Bernice Mast uses the Seurat variant to create flower centers.

WATER COLOR

Main Characteristics

Water Color brush strokes automatically appear on the Wet Paint layer. Choose Canvas > Wet Paint to turn it on or off. To save a picture with its Wet Paint layer still wet, choose the RIFF file format. Choose Canvas > Dry to dry Wet Paint layer strokes and merge them into the background. To layer translucent brush strokes, apply them at a low opacity (or use the Fade command), and then dry them periodically as you work. Selection tools, masking tools, and Effects menu commands don't affect the Wet Paint layer.

Stylus pressure affects stroke width and opacity for all Water Color variants. The Grain slider on the Brush Controls palette works the reverse of normal — move it to the right to accentuate the paper grain. All Water Color variants have the Circular Dab Type (Brush Controls: Size palette).

To adjust the pooling (concentration of color at the edges) or diffusion (pigment bleed into paper) of Water Color strokes, use the Advanced Controls: Water palette (see page 66). To diffuse all the Wet Paint brush strokes into the current paper texture after they're created, use the Shift-D shortcut as many times as you like.

To remove Wet Paint layer strokes, choose the Wet Remove Density method subcategory for any Water Color variant, or choose the Wet Eraser Water Color variant.

Broad Water Brush
Wide, bristle stroke.

Diffuse Water
Stroke edges bleed after stroke is drawn.

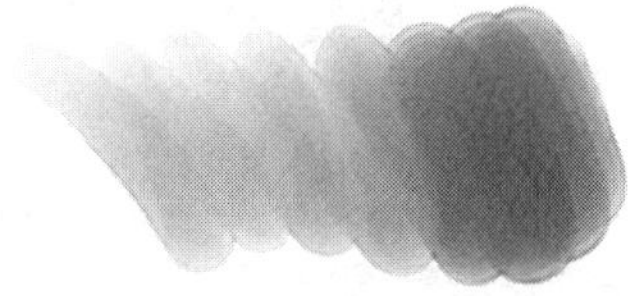

Large Simple Water
Very large version of Simple Water. Stylus pressure affects opacity and width.

Large Water
Wider version of Simple Water.

Simple Water
Smooth, non-bristle stroke. Pressure affects opacity and stroke width.

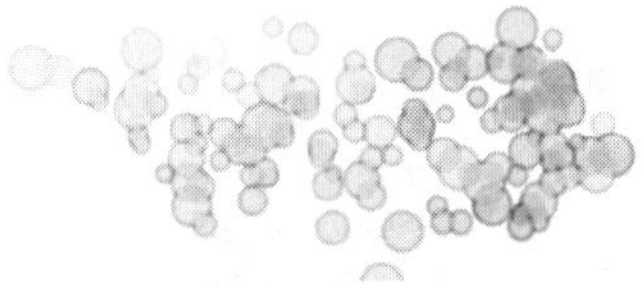

Spatter Water
Sprays random droplets. High Wet Fringe setting (Water palette).

Water Brush Stroke
Bristle. Pause between strokes.

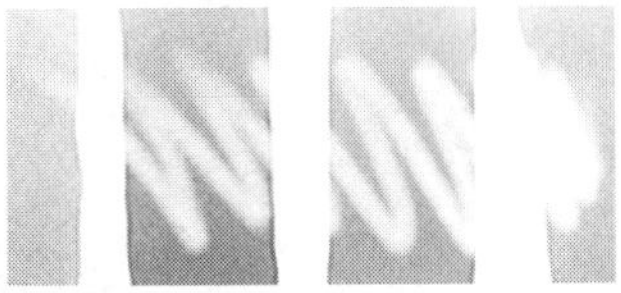

Wet Eraser
Erases on the Wet Paint layer only. Amount of erasure is affected by stylus pressure.

Lourekas

Fabric Effects, Inc.

Fabric Effects, Inc. is a textile firm whose services cover the gamut of innovative computer assisted design and manufacture on the one hand, and traditional fabric design, hand painting, dyeing, and silkscreening techniques on the other. Many tasks formerly done by hand are now accomplished using a variety of proprietary and off-the-shelf software. To reduce electronic images to screen printable colors, create repeats, and execute other important tasks, for example, Fabric Effects uses proprietary software developed by Monarch Computex. Richard Lerner, president of Fabric Effects and of RSL Digital Consultants, specializes in system design and hardware and software integration for digital imaging, graphics, and textile design.

To create the textile designs by Fabric Effects that are reproduced in this book, scanned imagery was composited and then color and texture were applied in Painter using grainy brushes. White lines were drawn using Bleach variants of the Eraser brush.

Fabric Effects, Inc.

Special brushes

The following brush variants don't apply color — they erase, dilute, smear, lighten, or darken color (except for the Liquid brushes, which apply color when used at an Opacity above 0).

ERASER

Main Characteristics
Stylus pressure affects opacity.

Eraser "tips"

You don't have to use the Eraser brush to erase — you can choose the Eraser variant for any brush.

To change the color that the Eraser erases to, choose a Primary color, then choose Canvas > Set Paper Color. This won't change the paper color you chose when you created your document. Adjust Eraser strength via the Controls: Brush palette Opacity slider.

The Eraser variants erase to the paper color.

Flat Eraser

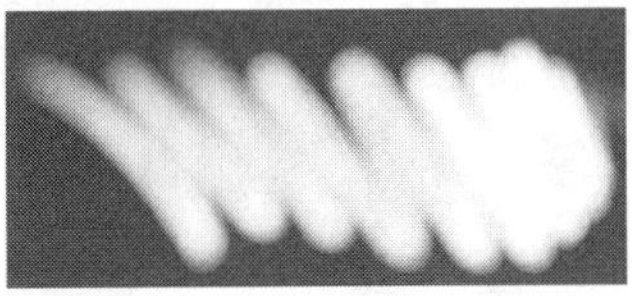

Fat Eraser

Medium Eraser

Small Eraser

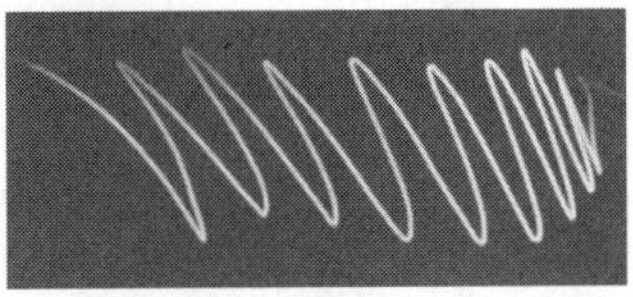

Ultrafine Eraser

The Eraser method subcategories

These categories are available when you choose the Eraser method category for any brush.

Soft Paper Color: Erases to the current paper color.

Soft Paint Remover: Erases to white.

Soft Paint Thickener: Darkens color. Similar to the Buildup method. Try using a low opacity.

Soft Grain Colorize: Applies the current paper texture using the current Primary and Secondary colors.

Soft Mask Colorize: Applies the current Primary color to opaque areas of a mask and the current Secondary color to partially masked areas when the third Drawing button is selected. To produce grayscale strokes using this subcategory, apply the Auto Mask command (Using: Image Luminance), then draw with Black as the Primary color and White as the Secondary color.

The Bleach variants erase to White, regardless of the paper color.

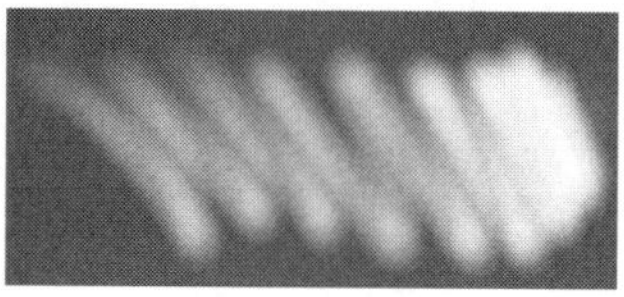

Fat Bleach

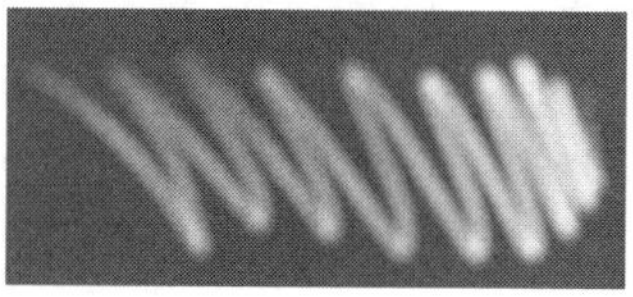

Medium Bleach

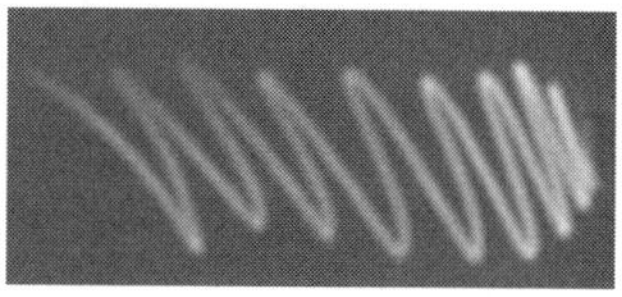

Small Bleach

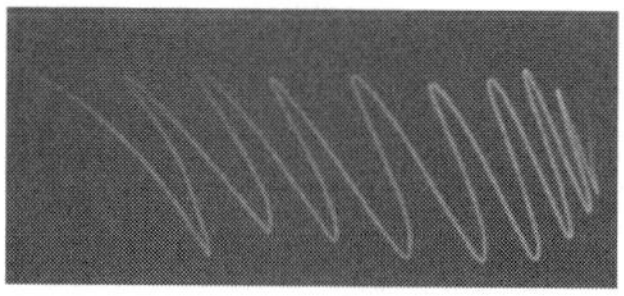

Ultrafine Bleach

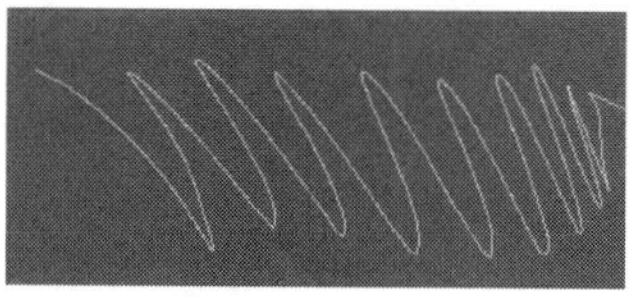

Single Pixel Bleach

Textile artists Mandy Leonard and Bernice Mast both use the Bleach variants of the Eraser brush like traditional bleach — to produce white lines. Look at Leonard's work in the color section (Fabric Effects, Inc.). Look at Mast's work on pages 40 and 113.

The Darkeners build up and saturate color — the opposite of erasers.

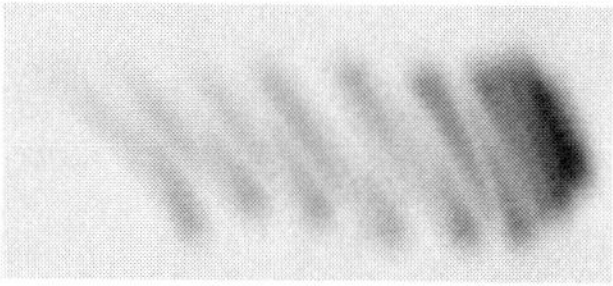

Fat Darkener

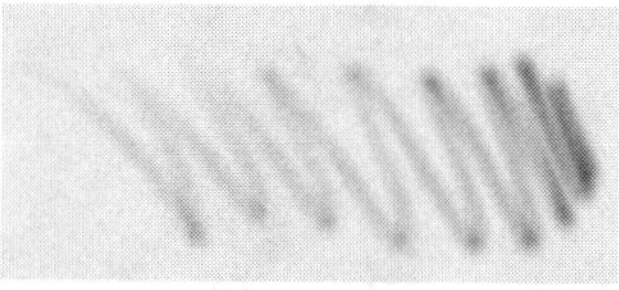

Medium Darkener

Small Darkener

Ultrafine Darkener

The Burn tool works like the Darkeners, except it has a lower opacity setting, so it darkens color more slowly.

WATER

Main Characteristics
Watery smudge. The Water variants don't apply color. Stylus pressure affects opacity. Most reveal paper grain.

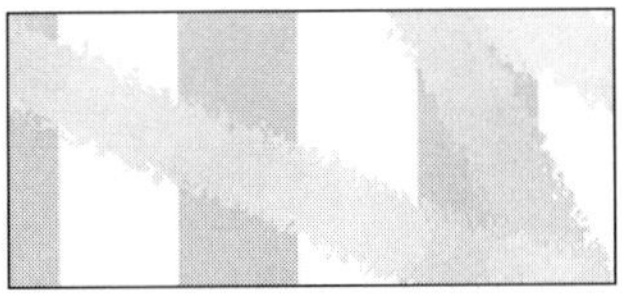

Big Frosty Water
Aliased stroke. Reveals paper grain.

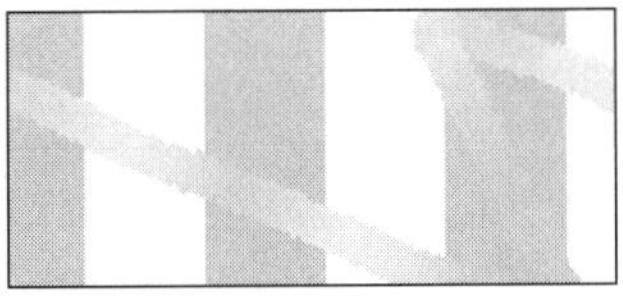

Frosty Water
Smaller version of Big Frosty Water.

Grainy Water
Reveals paper grain.

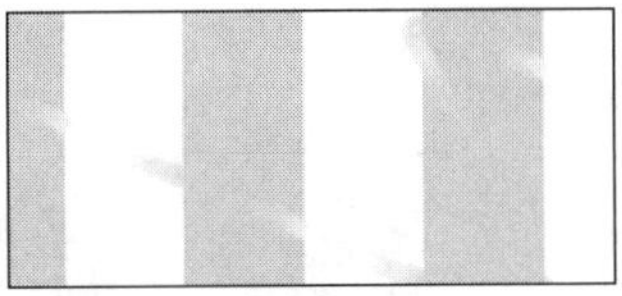

Just Add Water
Smooth, anti-aliased stroke. Doesn't reveal paper grain.

Single Pixel Water
Very thin.

Tiny Frosty Water
Smaller version of Frosty Water. Reveals paper grain.

Water Rake
Wide, bristle stroke. Reveals paper grain.

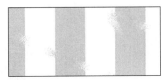

Water Spray
Water mist.

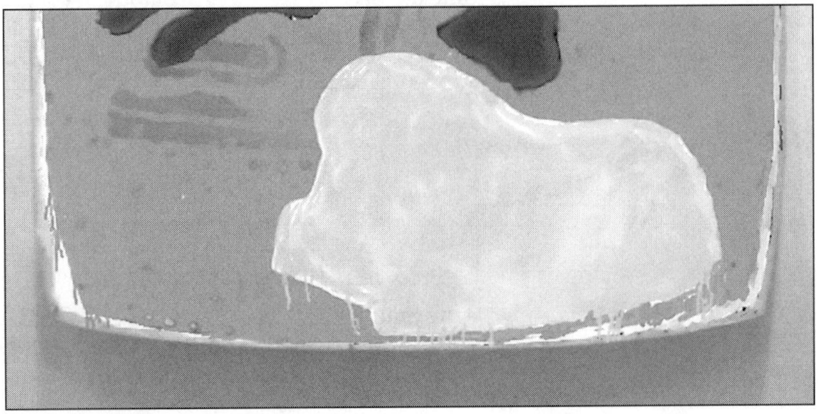

Ron Gorchov, ***Knossos*** *(detail). Gorchov uses Water brush variants to create drips.*

LIQUID

Main Characteristics

At zero opacity (Controls: Brush palette), the Liquid variants smear existing color without applying color, like a palette knife. At an opacity greater than zero, they smear existing color and apply the current Primary color.

With the exception of the Tiny Smudge variant, stylus pressure affects stroke width, the degree of smearing, and the amount paper grain is revealed. The heavier the pressure, the more paper grain is revealed.

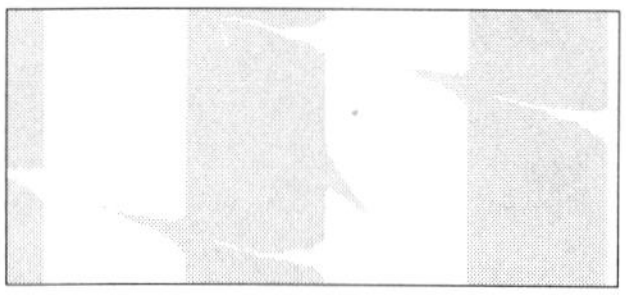

Coarse Distorto
Semi-anti-aliased. Smears existing paint only. Doesn't apply color.

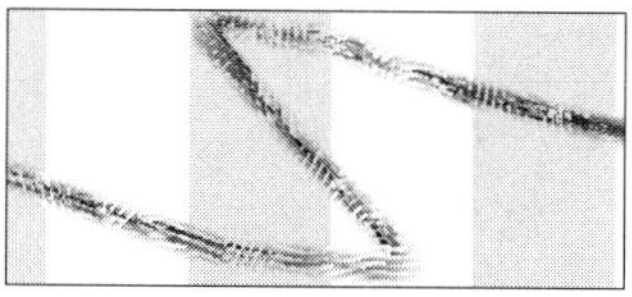

Coarse Smeary Bristles
Semi-anti-aliased version of Smeary Bristles. Applies and smears color.

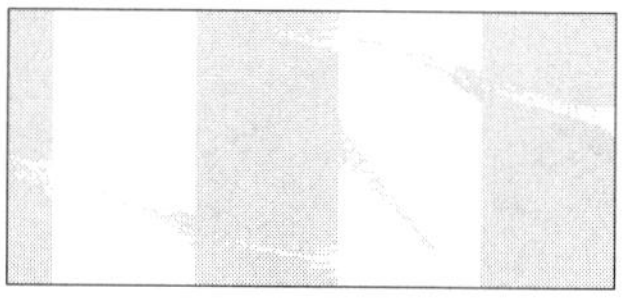

Coarse Smeary Mover
Smears existing paint only. Semi-anti-aliased.

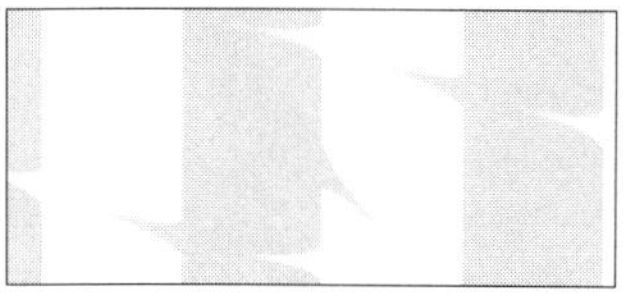

Distorto
Wet, smooth mover. Doesn't reveal paper texture. Smears existing paint.

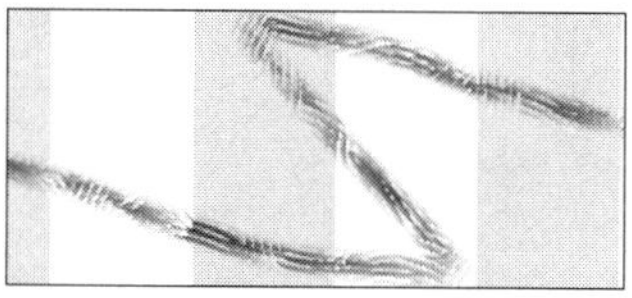

Smeary Bristles
Pressure affects grain/opacity. Applies color.

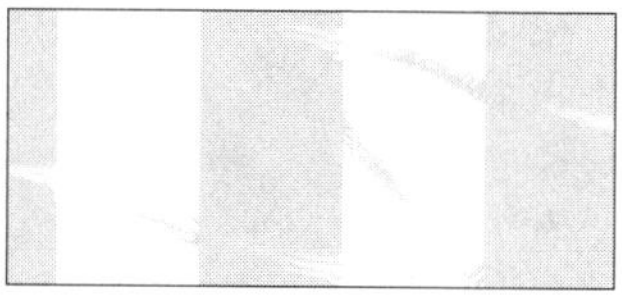

Smeary Mover
Zero opacity version of Smeary Bristles. Doesn't apply color.

Thick Oil
Thick, oily, wet, cover brush. Applies color.

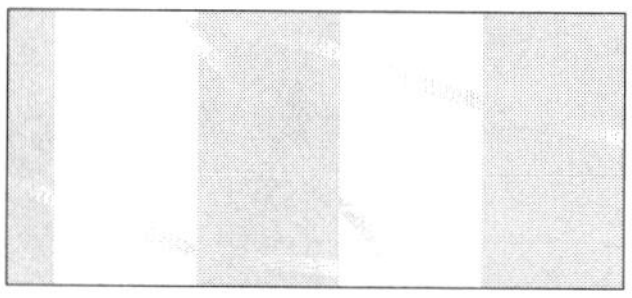

Tiny Smudge
Zero opacity, thin, multibristled smudger.

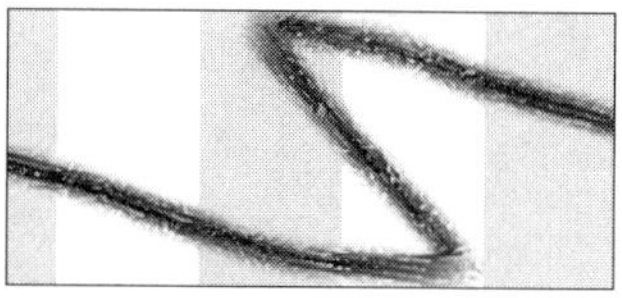

Total Oil Brush
Thinner version of Smeary Bristles.

David Humphrey, **Yearbook**

Two examples of Distorto

David Humphrey, *Essence*

BURN

Main Characteristics
Darkens existing color.

DODGE

Main Characteristics
Lightens existing color.

MASKING

The Masking brush variants are discussed on page 103.

IMAGE HOSE

The Image Hose is discussed on pages 97-100.

CLONERS

The Cloners brush variants are discussed on pages 126-127.

David Humphrey

David Humphrey is a painter who has had numerous one-man shows in New York City and his first retrospective, this year, at the Contemporary Arts Center in Cincinnati, Ohio. Humphrey has been making computer images for a few years in conjunction with his traditional media paintings and drawings, and he frequently combines traditional media and computer techniques. He uses various methods to digitize imagery: he uses a digital camera, scans his own traditional media drawings, scans photographs, scans photocopies of photographs, scans his own sculpture, and captures video images with his AV Macintosh.

Humphrey has been working with images from his own family albums for several years, in an exploration of the process of remembering. Ironically, Humphrey discovered that a horror movie was filmed in the house he lived in as a child, which his family had sold long ago. For his piece Solarized Kitchen (see the color insert), he video-captured a shot of his family kitchen from the movie, digitally removed the film actors, and then added brush strokes in Painter.

Humprey likes to use the computer because it challenges him to work in new, less comfortable ways, and like many artists, he particularly likes to use the Water Color, Liquid, and Water brushes. Humphrey feels his work on the computer has influenced his continuing work in traditional media. "The computer," he says, "has altered how I think about organizing pictures. I think that the computer helped me develop different voices within a picture. I'm also interested in how the computer can give photography some of the powers that painting has; that increased power to retouch. What I've been trying to do in some of these paintings is to act out the notion of retouching as a living component of remembering. We seem to remember according to conditions of the present. The computer can rehearse this process in anticipation of the paintings. Some computer imaging software was designed to imitate effects of painting. In some of my newer works I'm trying to make representations of the effects the computer uses to imitate paintings. There's a feedback loop."

From an interview with Elaine A. King, curator of Humphrey's Contemporary Arts Center exhibition.

More Painting 4

Ray Rue, ***Minotaur*** *(detail).*

Color

To create a new color set:

1. Click the Sets icon on the Art Materials palette.
2. Click New Set **2**. A tiny Color Set palette will appear on your screen.
3. Click on a color in any open image window using the Dropper tool or choose a color from the Art Materials: Colors palette.
4. Click Add Color.
5. Repeat steps 3 and 4 for any other colors you want to add to the set.
6. To save the new color set, click Library, click Save, enter a name for the set, choose a location in which to save it, click Save, then click Cancel. (We wish there was a Save button on the Art Materials: Sets palette.)

The currently open color set.

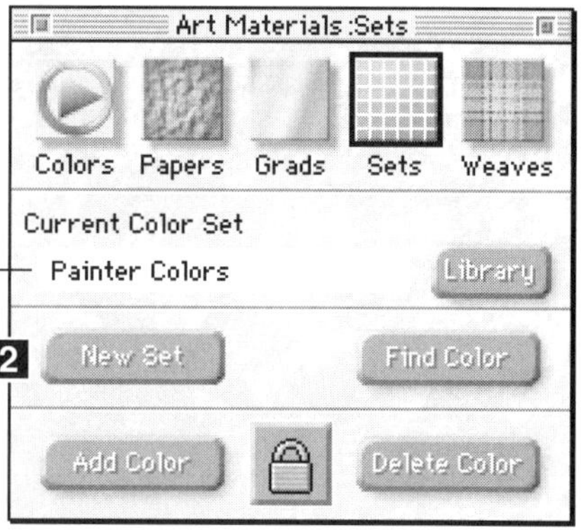

A new color set....

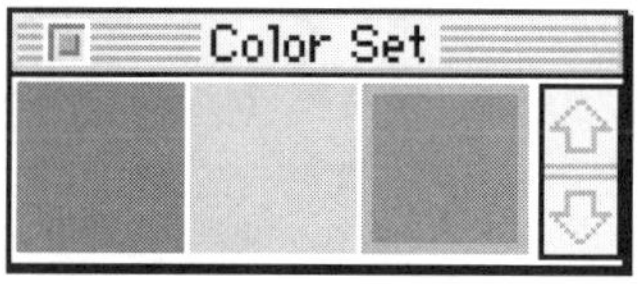

Three colors added to it.

To edit a color set:

1. Open the color set you want to edit, and display the Color Set palette.
2. If the color set is locked (closed padlock icon), click the padlock icon.
3. To **add** a color, choose a color from the Colors palette or click on a color in any open image window with the Dropper tool, then click Add Color (⌘-Shift-K).

   To **delete** a color, click the color swatch, click Delete Color on the Sets palette, then click Yes.

   To **replace** a color, choose a color from the Colors palette or from a picture using the Dropper tool, then hold down Option and click on the color swatch you want to replace.

   To **name** or **rename** a color, double-click the swatch, type a name, then click OK.
4. To save the edited color set, click Library, click Save, open the set's folder, click Save, click Replace, then click Cancel.

Dropper tool

Dropper tip

Hold down Command (⌘) to use the Dropper while the Oval Selection, Rectangular Selection, Brush, Floating Selection, or Paint Bucket tool is selected.

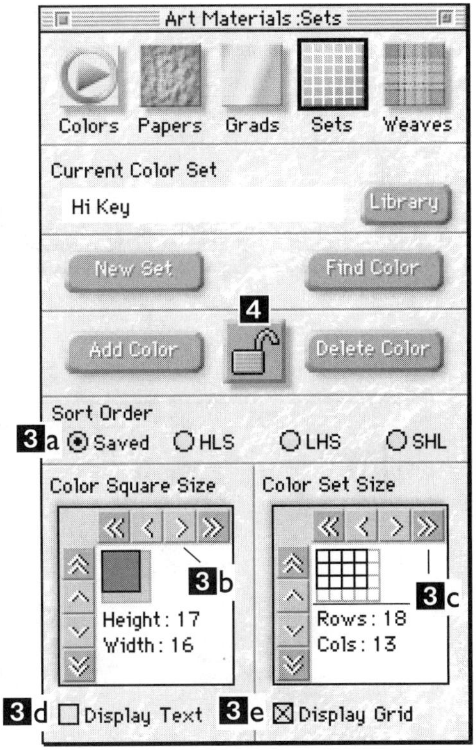

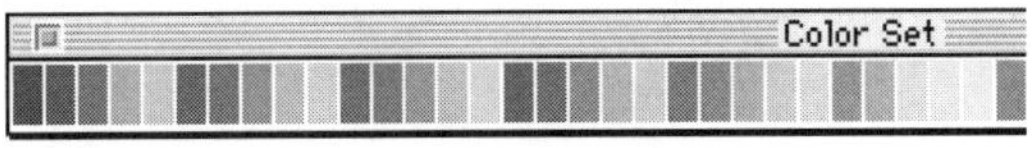

The default Hi Key color set.

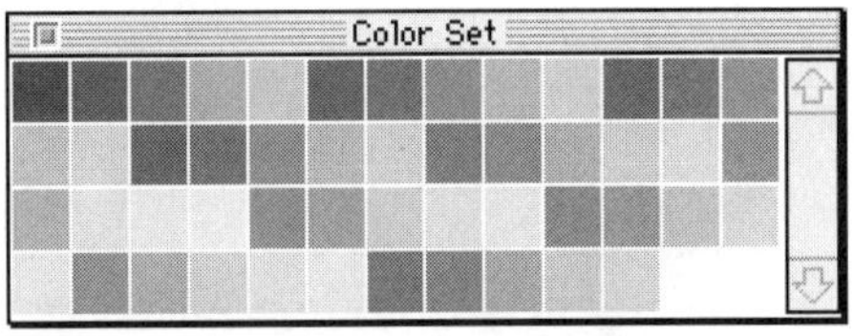

The Hi Key color set with modified display settings, as shown in the Art Materials: Sets palette screenshot above. The swatches were widened and the palette was made taller.

To change a color set's display style:

1. Click the Sets icon on the Art Materials palette to display the Sets palette.
2. If the color set is locked (closed padlock icon), click the padlock icon.
3. On the expanded Sets palette, do any of the following:

   Click a different **Sort Order** button to rearrange the swatches **3a**. "Saved" is the default arrangement. Click HLS to arrange colors by hue, luminance, and saturation, click LHS to arrange colors by luminance, hue, and saturation, or click SHL to arrange colors by saturation, hue, and luminance.

   Click a single **Color Square Size** arrow **3b** to enlarge or shrink the swatches by one pixel, or click a double arrow to enlarge or shrink the swatches by half their current size.

   Click the single or double down **Color Set Size** arrow **3c** to make the palette taller or shorter, and/or click the left or right arrow to make the palette wider or narrower.

   Check the **Display Text** box **3d** to display color names, if there are any, below the swatches. Make sure the swatches are wide enough for the text to appear. The Pantone colors are automatically named.

   Uncheck the **Display Grid** box **3e** and the Display Text box to eliminate the white grid lines between swatches. Colors are harder to distinguish without grid lines.
4. Click the padlock **4** to lock the palette.
5. *Optional:* To save the edited color set, click Library, click Save, open the set's folder, click Save, click Replace, then click Cancel.

You can search for a color by name or search for the closest color to the current Primary color. The color set you search through must be the Current Color Set, but the Color Set palette doesn't have to be open.

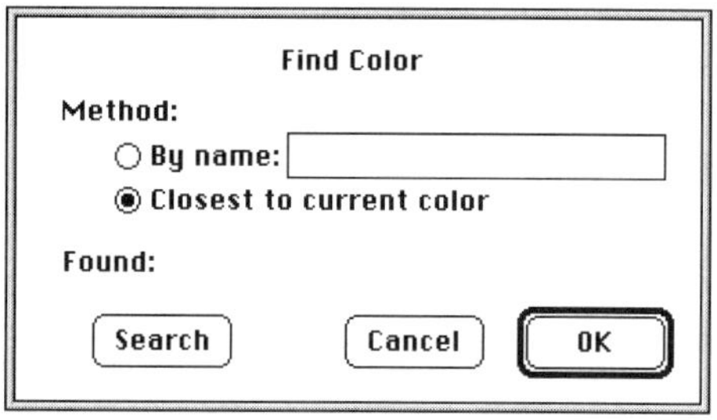

To find a color in a color set:

1. Click Find Color on the Art Materials: Sets palette.
2. Click "By name" and enter a color name. Be sure to enter the correct word spacing. For example, enter a space between Pantone numbers and letters (100 CV, etc.).
   or
   Click "Closest to current color."
3. Click Search.
4. Click OK. If the OK button is unavailable, the color name you entered was not found.

   If the Color Set palette is open, the found swatch will be highlighted.

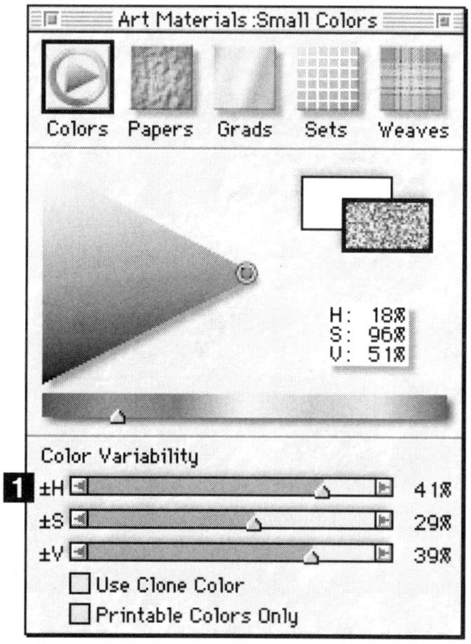

To produce multicolored brush strokes:

On the expanded Art Materials: Colors palette, move the **H**(hue) Color Variability slider **1** to add more hues to the stroke.

and/or

Move the **S**(saturation) slider to increase the saturation range in the stroke.

and/or

Move the **V**(value) slider to increase the range of brightness values in the stroke.

Note how the color changes in the Primary color rectangle.

For a nice effect, try raising the H and V settings. The default Loaded Oils and Hairy Brush variants of the Brush brush and the Van Gogh and Seurat variants of the Artists brush produce multicolored strokes.

The Hairy brush variant of the Brush brush, normal Color Variability.

The same brush, with the V Color Variability slider at 48%.

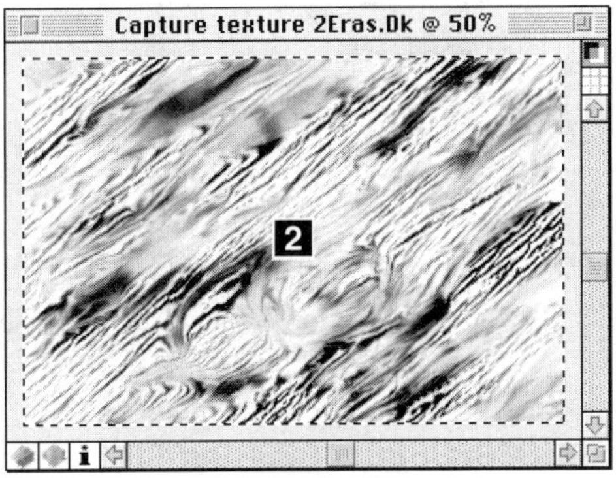

Paper textures

In addition to the paper textures that Painter supplies, you can create your own textures using the Capture Texture or Make Paper Texture command. Apply a texture that you create as you would any other texture: use an Effects menu > Surface Control submenu command or use a brush with a Grainy submethod category.

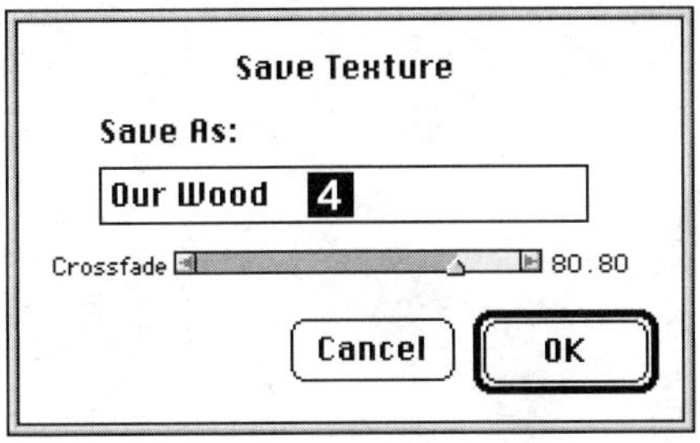

To capture a paper texture from a picture:

1. Choose the Rectangular Selection tool.
2. Select an area of a painting [2]. (Hold down Control while dragging to create a square selection.)
3. Choose Tools > Textures > Capture Texture.
4. Enter a name for the texture [4].
5. Choose a Crossfade setting. The higher the Crossfade, the more the borders between paper texture tiles will be blended.
6. Click OK or press Return. The new texture will appear on the Art Materials: Papers palette and it will be added to the currently open paper library. (To create a papers library, see page 15.)

The texture applied in a brush stroke.

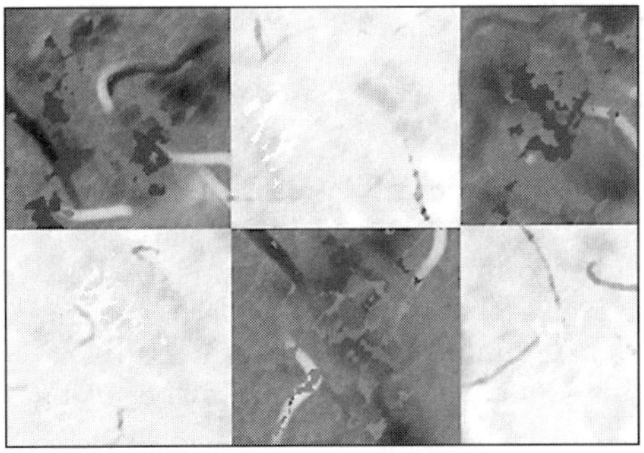

Our Marble texture.

To create a paper texture from an existing texture:

1. Choose Tools > Textures > Make Paper Texture.
2. Choose from the Pattern pop-up menu.
3. Move the Spacing slider to change the size of the pattern. Pause to preview.
   and/or
   Move the Angle slider to rotate the pattern. Pause to preview.
4. Enter a name for the paper texture in the Save As field.
5. Click OK or press Return. The texture will appear on the Art Materials: Papers palette and it will be saved in the currently open paper library.

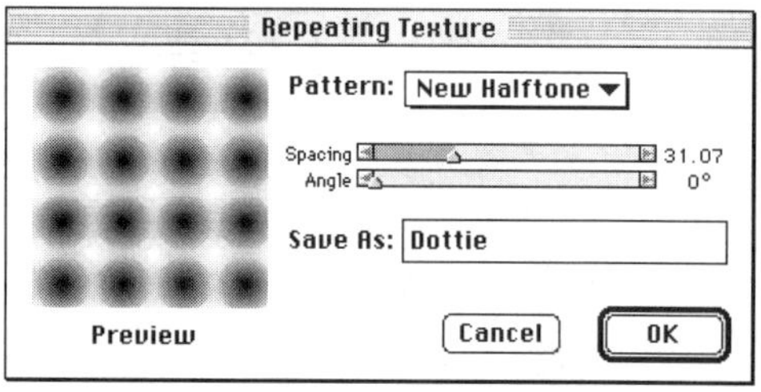

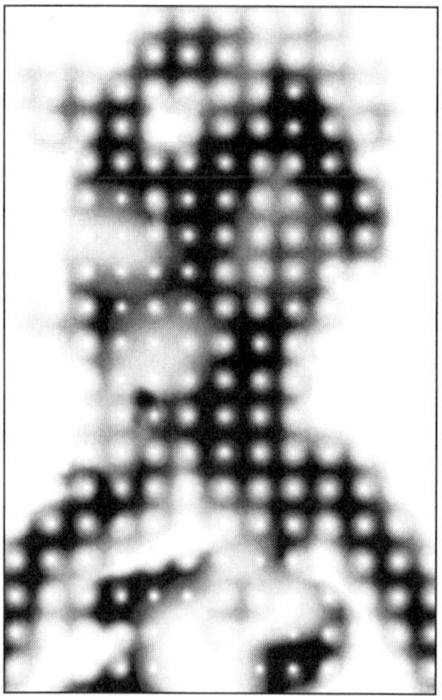

Weinmann

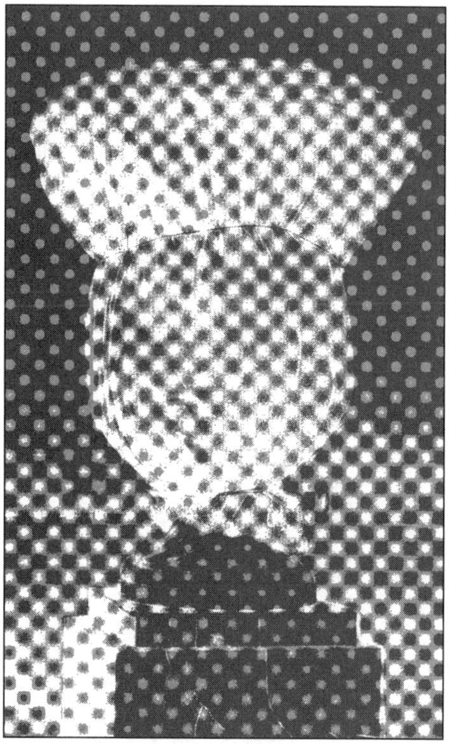

Lourekas

The **Make Fractal Pattern** command produces irregular grayscale patterns in a new document whose size you select. Alone, Painter's fractal patterns make good cloud, stone, or fabric textures, but you can develop them further using any Effects menu command, such as Sharpen or Brightness/Contrast.

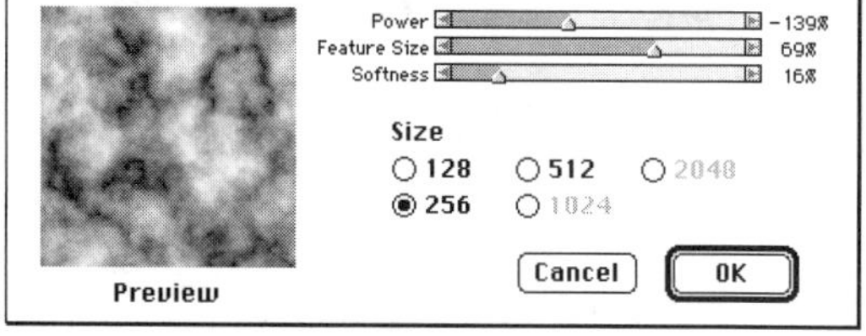

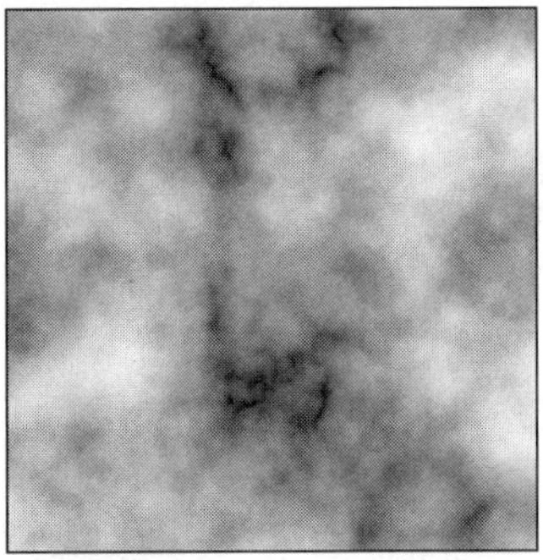

Power -139%, Feature Size 69%, Softness 16%.

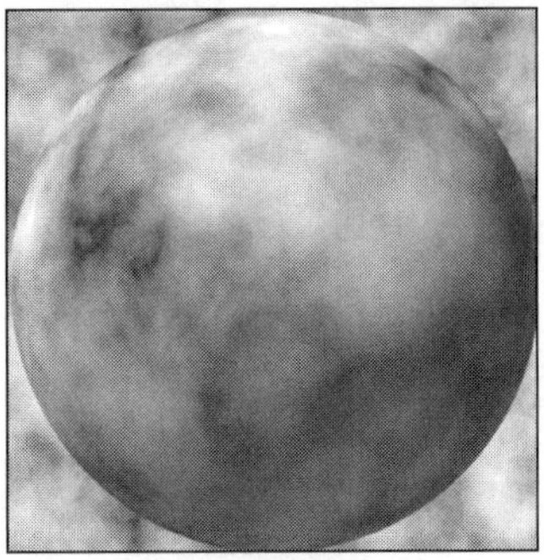

The above pattern after applying Kai's Power Tools Glass Lens Normal filter.

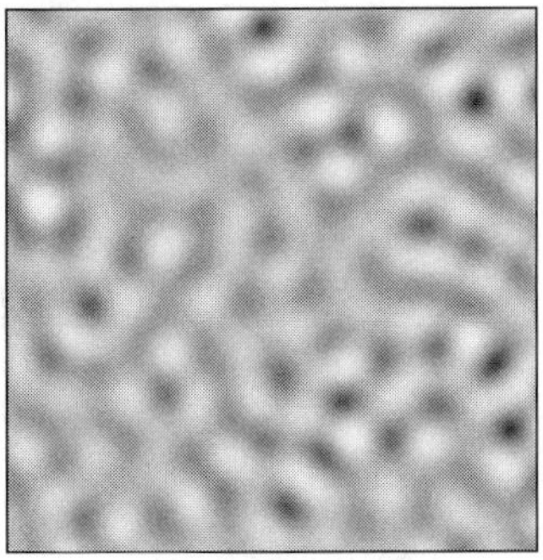

Power -194%, Feature Size 8%, Softness 95%.

You can apply a Fractal Pattern to your image as you would any paper texture or pattern. To add it to the currently open Paper texture library, follow the instructions on page 53. Or use the Patterns > Capture Pattern command and use the pattern as a fill.

To make a fractal pattern:

1. Choose Tools > Patterns > Make Fractal Pattern.
2. Do any of the following:

   Move the **Power** slider to the left to enlarge the shapes in the pattern or to the right to make them smaller.

   Move the **Feature Size** slider to the left to increase the number of repetitions per tile.

   Move the **Softness** slider to increase/decrease blending between pattern elements.

   Click a **Size** button — the pattern's tile size (document size) in pixels. The dpi will be 72. The number of available Size buttons depends on the amount of RAM allocated to Painter.
3. Click OK or press Return.

Use the Effects > Surface Control > Color Overlay command (Using: Paper Grain and Hiding Power option) to colorize the pattern and apply a paper texture.

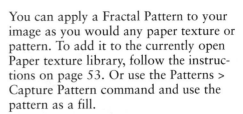

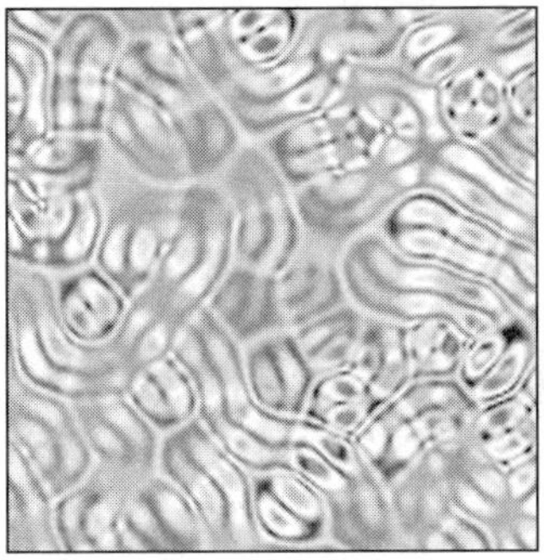

The above pattern after applying Effects > Focus > Glass Distortion, (Image Luminance, Amount 1.63, Variance 1), and Effects > Tonal Control > Brightness/Contrast.

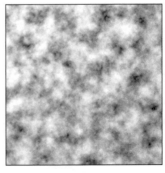

Power -126%, Feature Size 17%, Softness 0%, then Effects > Surface Control > Apply Lighting.

Brushes

As we said earlier in this book, if you choose non-default settings for a brush and then choose another brush or variant, you'll lose your non-default settings. To save a customized brush so you can choose it again, save it as a new variant for an existing brush (such as a Zen variant of the Water Color brush) or save it over an existing variant. You can also create a whole new brush category (like Pencils or Crayons), and then create variants for it. To save a brush using the Brush Look Designer, see page 29.

To create a new brush category:

1. Create an image for the brush's icon that will appear on the Brushes palette drawer (or open an existing picture that you want to use).
2. Choose the Rectangular Selection tool (R).
3. Hold down Control and drag to create a square selection **3**.
4. Choose Tools > Brushes > Save Brush.
5. Enter a name for the brush **5**.
6. Click OK. An icon for your new brush will appear on the Brushes palette drawer front **6**.

   The new brush won't have any variants. To create variants for it, follow the instructions on the next page.

- Use the Brush Look Designer to preview brush variations.
- To change the brush name, choose Tools > Movers > Brush Mover, highlight the name you want to change, click Change Name, enter a new name, click OK, then click Quit.
- To change the brush icon, follow steps 1 through 3 above, choose Tools > Movers > Brush Mover, highlight the name of the brush whose icon you want to change, click Change Picture, click OK, then click Quit.

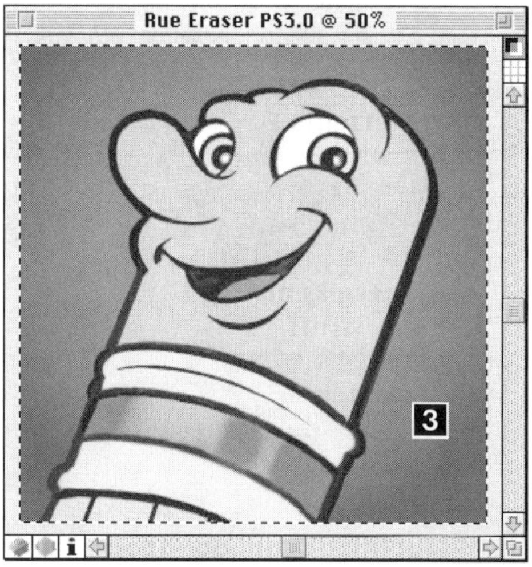

Select an area to become the new brush icon. This is Ray Rue's Eraser brush icon.

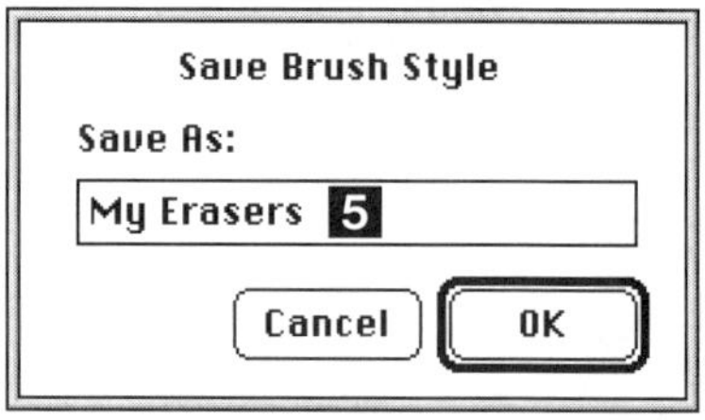

Enter a name for the new brush.

The new brush icon appears on the Brushes palette. (Ray Rue's Brushes palette.)

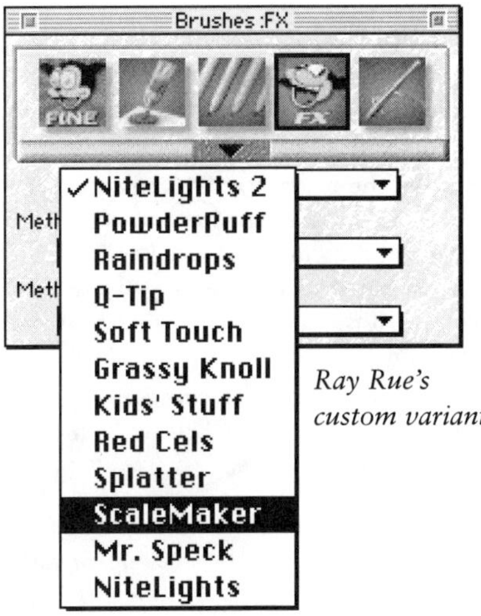

Ray Rue's custom variants.

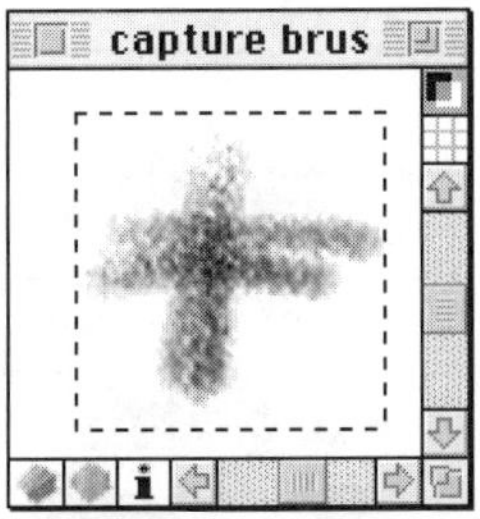

Select an area to become the brush tip.

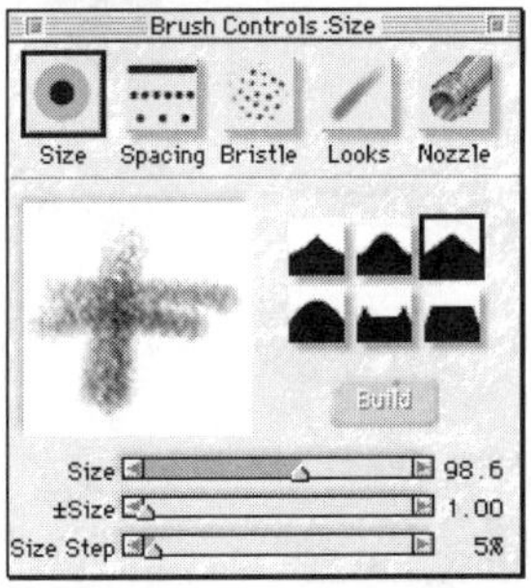

Adjust the captured brush size using the Brush Controls: Size palette.

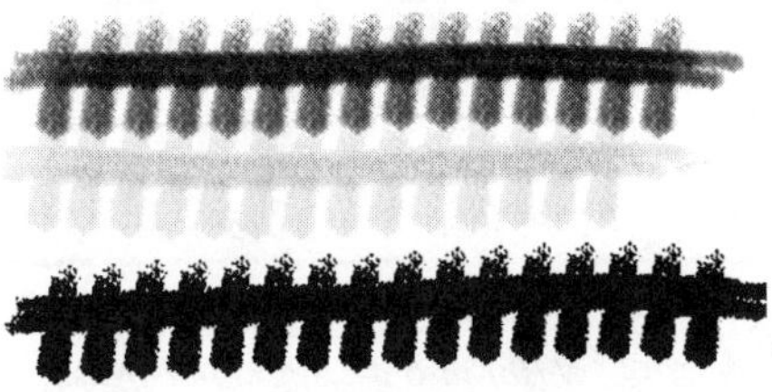

Captured brush strokes drawn with the Soft Buildup, Grainy Soft Cover, and Grainy Edge Flat Cover submethod categories chosen.

A brush can have up to 32 variants.

To save a new or modified brush variant:

1. Customize your brush in whatever way you like (method category or subcategory, Color Variability, Brush Controls, etc.).
2. To add the variant to the variant pop-up menu, choose Tools > Brushes > Save Variant, enter a name for the variant, then click OK.
   or
   To save over the currently selected variant, choose Tools > Brushes > Save Built Variant.

To restore the brush's original default variant, make sure it is selected on the Brushes palette, then choose Tools > Brushes > Restore Default Variant. Choose Tools > Brushes > Delete Variant to delete the variant altogether.

To capture a brush from a painting:

1. Open an existing image. Or draw with 100% black on a white background to define opaque parts of the brush tip; use a lower opacity brush to define semi-transparent areas.
2. Choose the Rectangular Selection tool (R).
3. Hold down Control and drag to create a square selection.
4. Choose Tools > Brushes > Capture Brush. The brush shape will display in the preview window on the Brush Controls: Size palette.
5. *Optional:* Modify the new tip using the Brush Controls: Size palette. Move the Spacing/Size slider on the Brush Controls: Spacing palette to adjust the spacing between dabs. Click the Build button, if necessary.
6. Save the new brush. If you don't save it, it will disappear as soon as you choose a different brush.

To change brush size and/or shape (Brush Controls: Size palette):

SIZE

Move the **Size** slider to the right to make the tip wider. Large tips take longer to preview and render on screen.

Move the **± Size** slider to the right to increase the amount the stroke width can vary with stylus pressure. A large ± Size setting takes more time to build.

The **Size Step** slider controls the smoothness of the transition between the thin and thick parts of the stroke. Move the slider to the right to make the transition more abrupt.

ANGLE CONTROL *(expanded Size palette)*

The **Squeeze** slider controls the shape of the tip. Rounder to the right...

...more elliptical to the left.

The **Angle** slider changes the angle of the tip relative to the horizontal axis. The Angle slider has no effect if the tip is a circle (100% Squeeze). 0° Angle is a horizontal tip. Lefties, this is for you! You can rotate the tip to a more natural angle for your hand.

DAB TYPES

The Dab Type is the dab shape. The **Circular Dab Type** is a single round shape. The spacing between Circular dabs is controlled via the Brush Controls: Spacing palette.

The **Bristle Dab Type** is comprised of multiple dots. Adjust the character of the bristle dabs using the Brush Controls: Bristle palette.

Speed tips

Click Build (⌘-B), if the button lights up, after you've made *all* your Size, Spacing and Bristle palette adjustments.

To change the brush size without using the Size palette, hold down Command (⌘) and Option and drag in the image window. If you make the brush tip large, you may get a prompt to Build the brush when you start to use it.

To restore a whole brush category's default settings, Option-click the brush's icon on the Brushes palette.

Click here to toggle between a preview of the overall brush shape (right) or the individual dabs in the brush tip (left) (shown at the same time here just for illustration purposes).

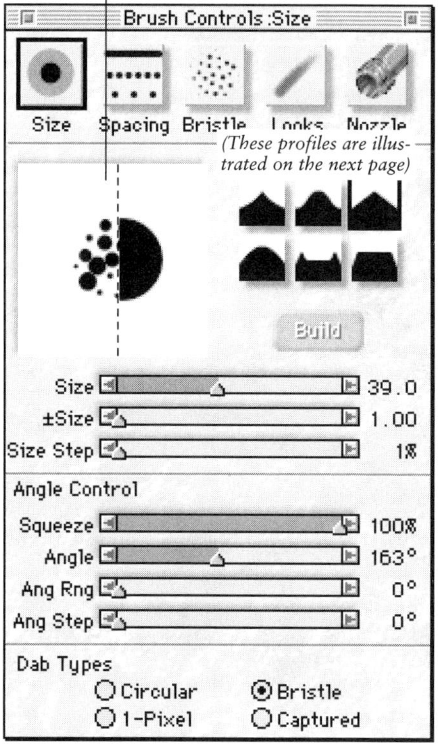

To turn a variant (like Small Wash) into a calligraphic brush, choose the Circular Dab Type, move the Squeeze slider to the left, and adjust the Angle slider.

Brush tip profiles

The brush tip **profiles** on the Brush Controls: Size palette (⌘-4) affect color flow. Brush tip profile changes are noticeable with "hard" media brushes, like the Felt Pens, Pencils, Chalk, Crayons, and Charcoal.

To produce a coiled "Slinky" stroke, choose a hard medium brush, choose the Water Color profile and the Circular Dab Type on the extended Size palette, and choose the Single or Multi Stroke Type from the Spacing palette.

TOP ROW

Pointed *profile. Color is densest at the center of the stroke and falls off quickly toward the edge. The narrowest profile.*

Medium *profile. Like the Linear profile, except with a wider area of density, and thus a wider stroke.*

Linear *profile. Color is concentrated in the center of the stroke and falls off smoothly towards the edge.*

BOTTOM ROW

Dull *profile. Color spreads over a wide area. More density at the edge than the Linear profile.*

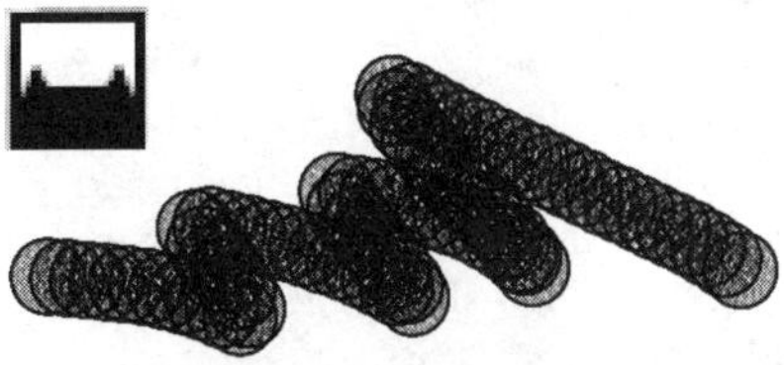

Water Color *profile. Color is concentrated at the edge of the stroke. This is the default Water Color profile.*

One-pixel edge *profile. Very wide density. Color falls off rapidly at the one-pixel, anti-aliased edge.*

To change dab spacing (Brush Controls: Spacing palette):

Pigment is actually applied in dabs, the flow of which you can adjust via the Brush Controls: Spacing palette.

The **Spacing/Size** slider controls the continuousness of the dab flow. Move to the right to produce a less dense stroke.

The **Min Spacing** slider controls the minimum spacing between dabs. For maximum space between dabs, move both the Spacing/Size and Min Spacing sliders to the right.

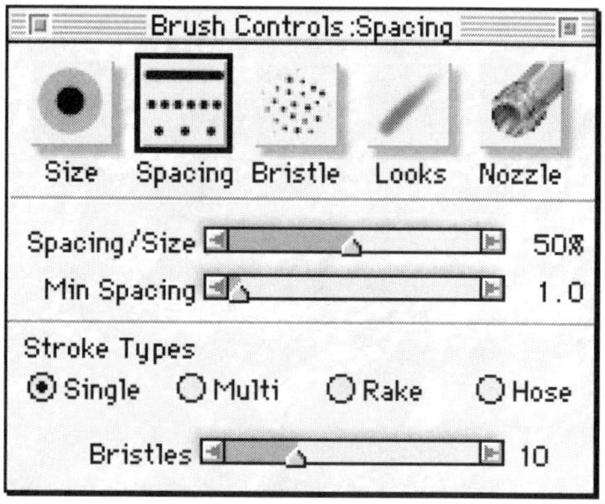

The **Stroke Types** options control the number of bristle paths in the stroke:

Single creates one path of bristle dabs per stroke. Single Stroke Type brushes are affected by both the Spacing/Size and Min Spacing sliders.

Multi strokes are comprised of a group of dab paths that are precomputed, so they take time render. Draw short strokes and pause between them for this Stroke Type. The Min Spacing slider affects this Stroke Type more.

Rake strokes are comprised of grouped dab paths with some spacing between each path. The Digital Sumi, Penetration Brush, Loaded Oils, and Camel Hair Brush variants of the Brush brush and the Scratchboard Rake variant of the Pen brush are Rake brushes. The Min Spacing slider affects this Stroke Type more.

If you change the Stroke Type from Single to Rake and the stroke is too light, raise the Resaturation slider setting on the Advanced Controls: Well palette to add pigment to the paint flow.

Spacing/Size 50%

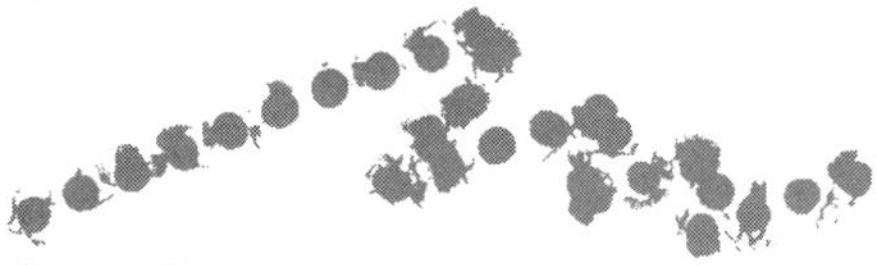

Spacing/Size 100%

Min Spacing 2.

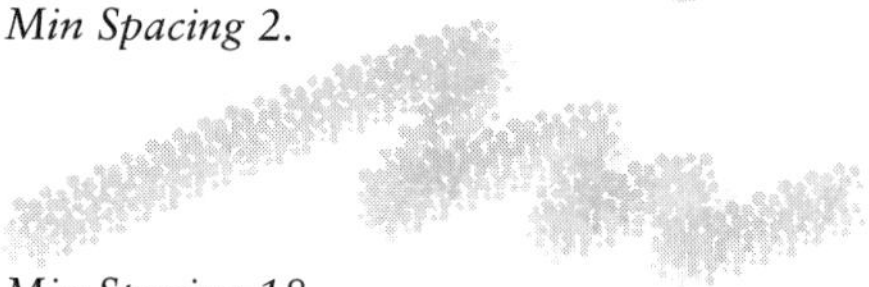

Min Spacing 18

Multi Stroke Type — Hairy Brush. Increasing Color Variability (expanded Colors palette) produces nice effects with this Stroke Type.

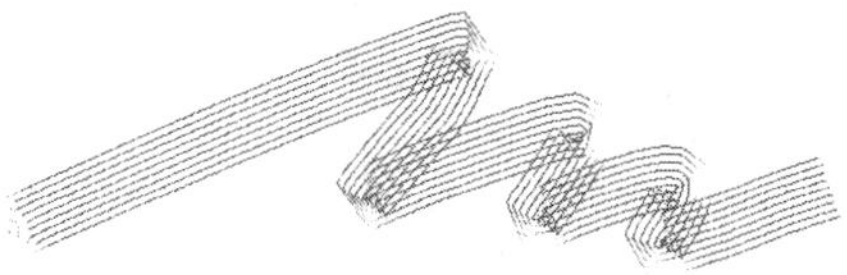

Rake Stroke Type — Digital Sumi

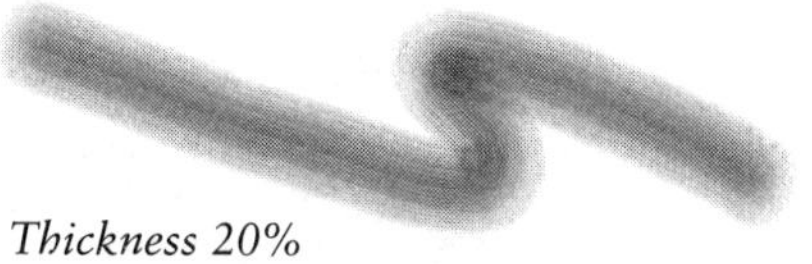
Thickness 20%

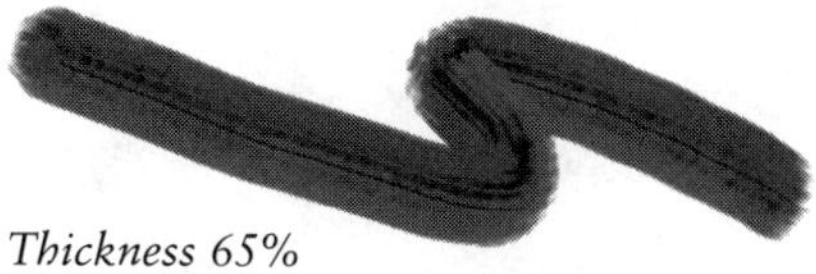
Thickness 65%

Clumpiness 2%

Clumpiness 100%

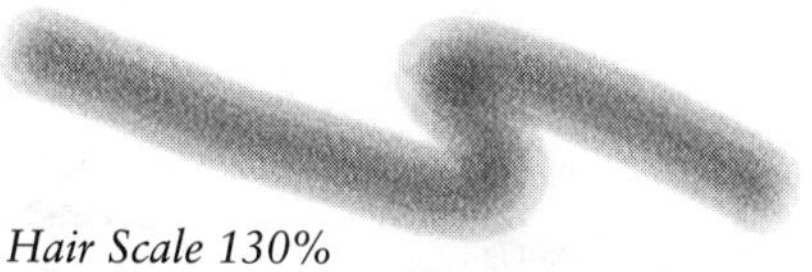
Hair Scale 130%

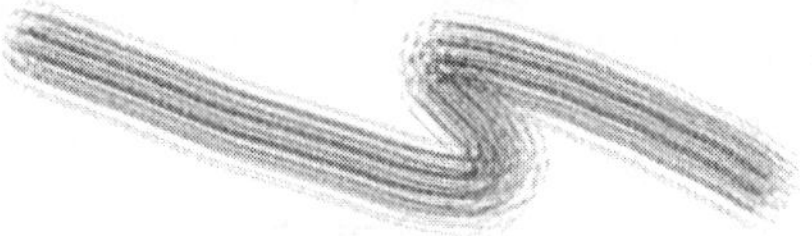
Hair Scale 900%, Thickness 30%

[Loaded Oils, Soft Cover submethod category.]

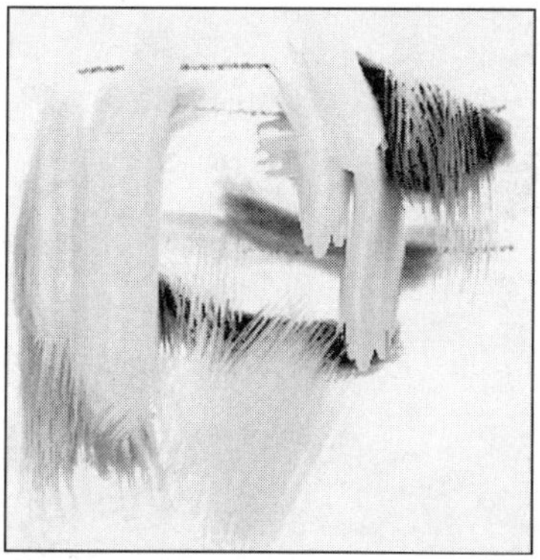
Brush variants: Fine Wet Oils and Smaller Wash Brush; Bristle Thickness and Clumpiness lowered, Hair Scale raised.

To change stroke character (Brush Controls: Bristle palette):

You must choose the Bristle Dab Type on the Brush Controls: Size palette for your brush for Bristle palette settings to have any effect. You can preview the Brush Controls: Bristle palette changes on the Size palette — just drag the Size palette away from the main Brush Controls palette and click the preview to display the bristle dots.

The higher the **Thickness,** the thicker the bristles and the denser the stroke.

The higher the **Clumpiness,** the more bristles clump together.

The higher the **Hair Scale,** the larger and denser the bristle dots and the more separate and noticeable are the bristles.

The **Scale/Size** slider controls jumps in size variations in the bristle dots in the tip. For the Scale/Size slider to have any effect, the Brush Controls: Size palette ±Size setting must be above 1.0. Scale/Size changes will be noticeable with these bristly variants of the Brush brush: Big and Small Loaded Oils, Big Wet Oils, and Smaller and Ultrafine Wash Brush.

Scale/Size 0%

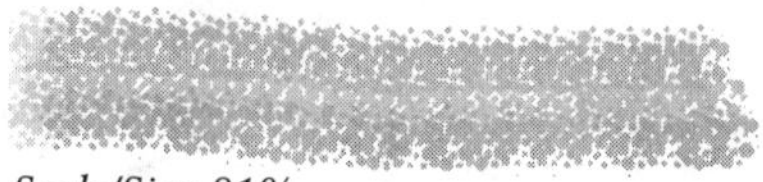
Scale/Size 81%

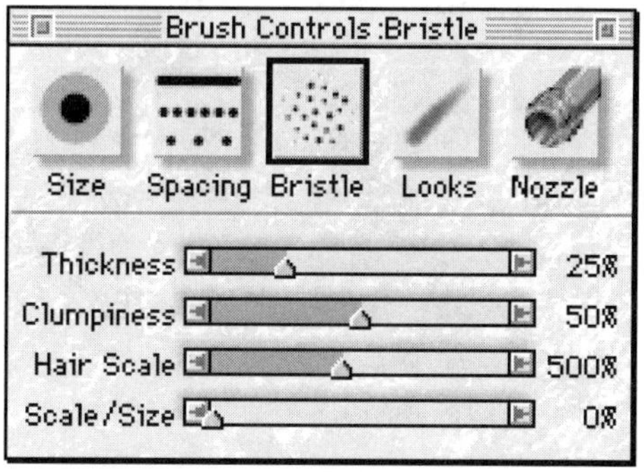

To fine-tune a raked brush (Advanced Controls: Rake palette):

Before using the Rake palette, you must choose the Rake Stroke Type from the Brush Controls: Spacing palette.

The **Contact Angle** slider controls how much of the brush touches the canvas. The higher the Contact Angle, the wider the stroke or the more pigment is applied.

The higher **Brush Scale**, the wider bristles are spread. Adjust in small increments!

The higher the **Turn Amount**, the more bristles will lift up sporadically as you move the stylus in a new direction, mimicing traditional brush behavior.

With the **Spread Bristles** box checked, bristles are spread apart. Stroke width will vary with stylus pressure.

With the **Soften Bristle Edge** box checked, bristles edges are more transparent.

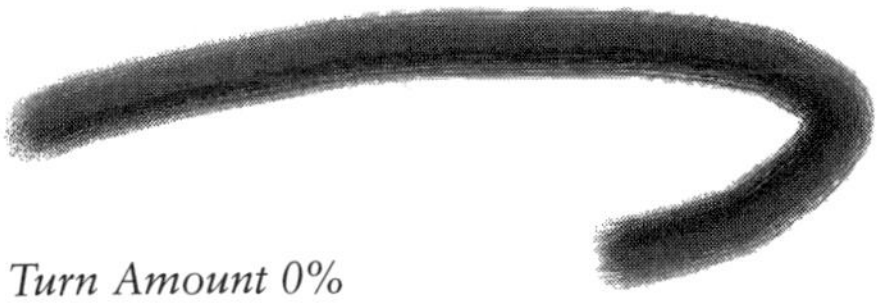

Turn Amount 0%

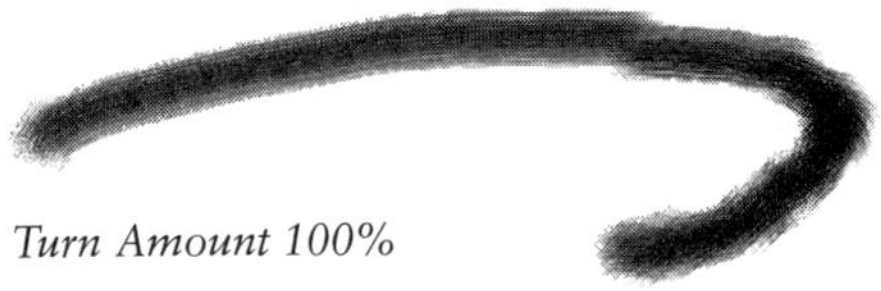

Turn Amount 100%

[Brush brush, Loaded Oils, Soft Cover submethod category.]

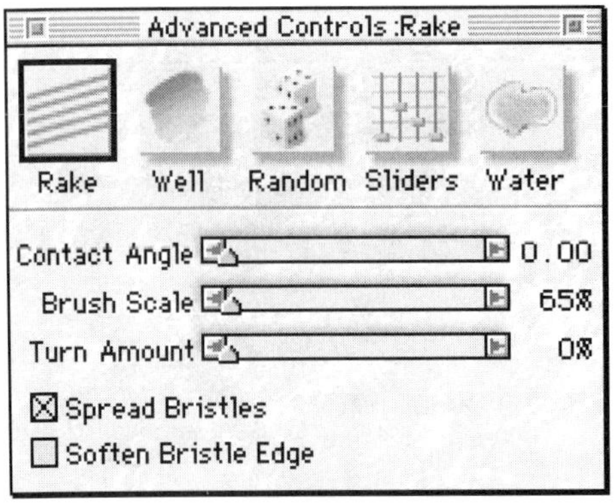

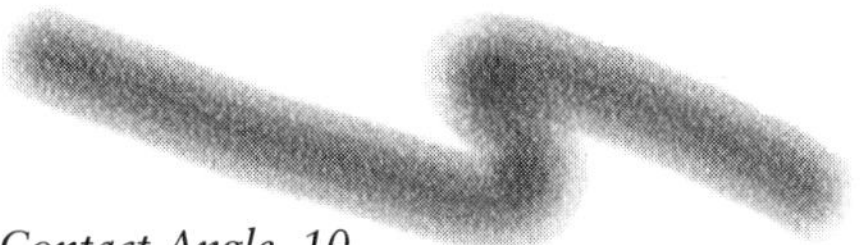

Contact Angle .10

Contact Angle 2.8

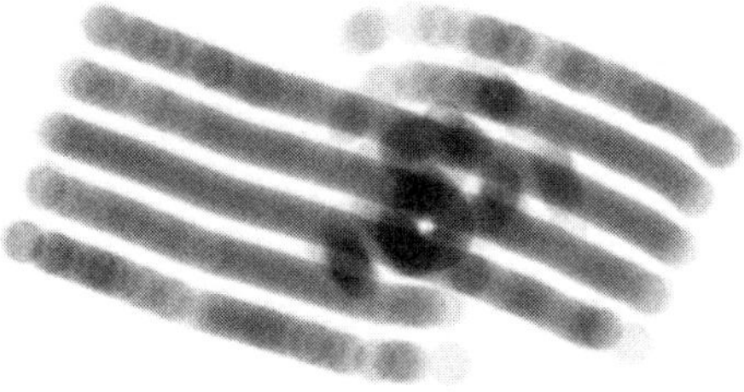

Contact Angle 2, Brush Scale 400%

Spread Bristles on

Spread Bristles off

Soften Bristle Edge on, Contact Angle 1.44

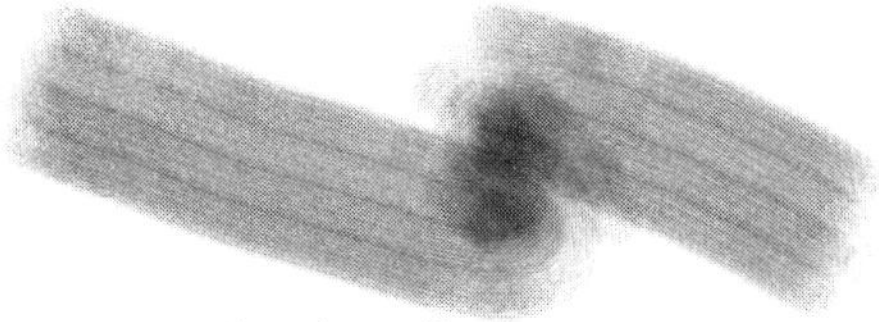

Soften Bristle Edge off

Resaturation 10%

Resaturation 88%

Bleed 15% (low Restauration setting)

Bleed 90% (low Restauration setting)

Dryout 1285

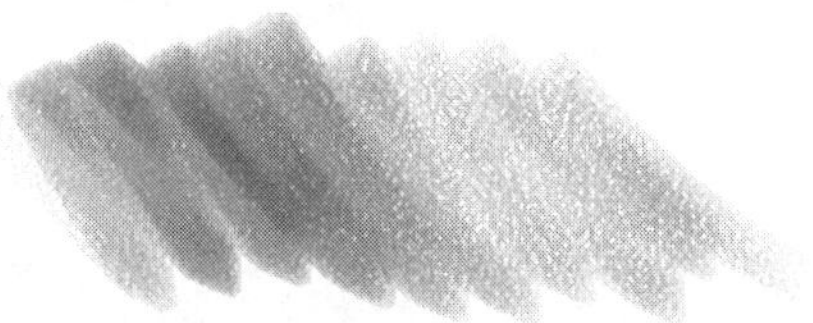

Dryout 22026

[Brush brush, Cover Brush variant, Buildup method category, Soft Buildup submethod category.]

To change the paint flow (Advanced Controls: Well palette):

The higher the **Resaturation** setting, the more concentrated the color in the paint flow.

The higher the **Bleed** setting, the more a brush stroke bleeds into colors beneath it. You may have to lower the Resaturation setting to observe any Bleed effect.

The higher the **Dryout** setting, the slower a brush stroke runs out of paint. There is no dryout with the Dryout slider at its rightmost setting.

Dryout works with brushes that have the Single or Multi Stroke Type (Spacing palette). Brushes of this type include the Water Color brush variants, the Coarse Hairs, Fine Brush, Brushy and Smaller Wash Brush variants of the Brush brush when the Bleed setting is above 0%, the Oil Pastel variant of the Chalk brush, the Dirty Marker and Medium Tip Felt Pens variants of the Felt Pens brush, and the Waxy Crayons variant of the Crayons brush.

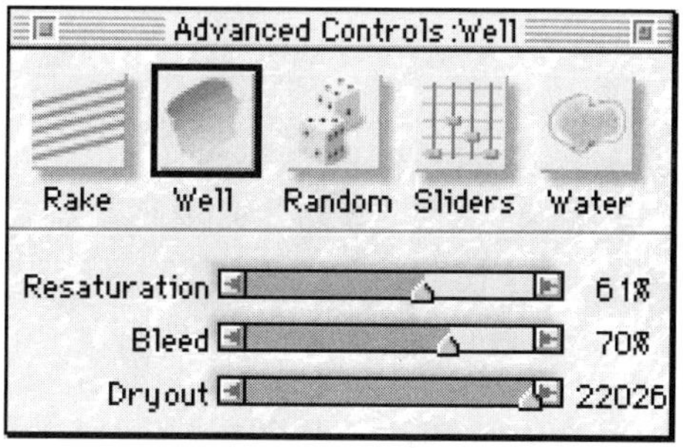

To change a stroke's randomness (Advanced Controls: Random palette):

Use the Random palette to control how variegated your strokes are.

Move the **Dab Location: Placement** slider to the right to scatter the dabs in the stroke and produce a noticeable "jitter." Most noticeable when the Single Stroke Type is selected for the brush (Brush Controls: Spacing palette).

Dab Location Placement .15

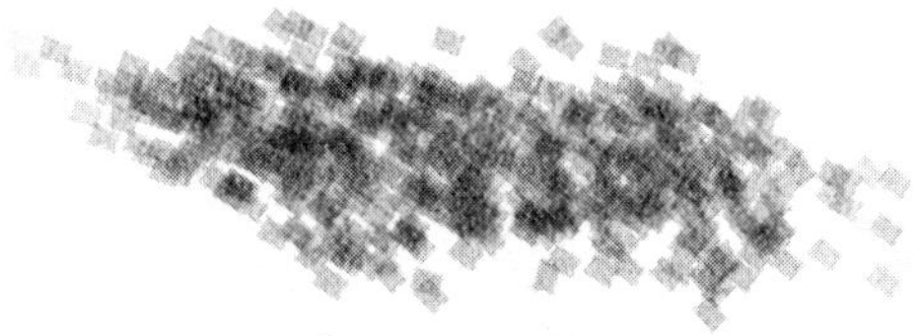

Dab Location Placement 3.41

[Square Chalk variant, Grainy Soft Cover sub-method category.]

Check the **Random Brush Stroke Grain** box to make the current paper texture appear more randomly. Choose a Grainy method subcategory for your brush and a paper texture with a large pattern.

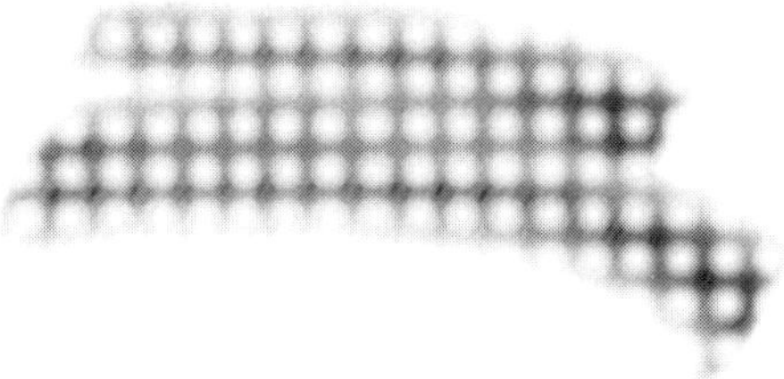

Random Brush Stroke Grain box unchecked

Random Brush Stroke Grain box checked

[Gritty Charcoal brush, Grainy Soft Cover sub-method category, Dottie paper texture.]

The Seurat variant of the Artists brush has a high Dab Location Placement setting (flower center). Artwork by Bernice Mast.

To clone areas of a source image more haphazardly, push the **Clone Location: Variability** slider to the right. Check the **Random Clone Source** box for maximum haphazardness. The further left the **How Often** slider is, the more frequently areas are displaced as you clone, and the rougher the stroke (set Variability above 0).

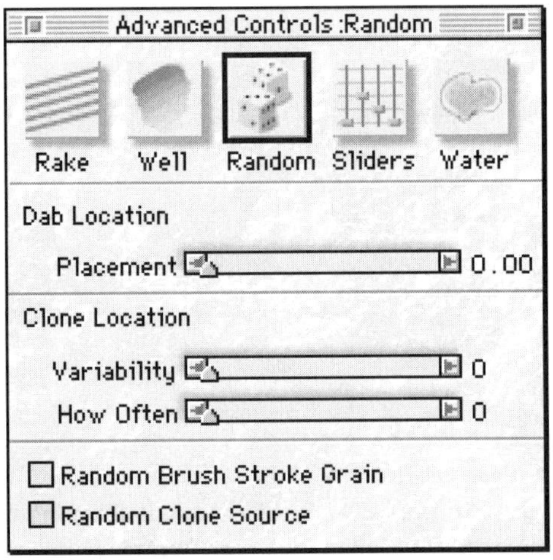

To change the stylus/mouse–stroke connection (Advanced Controls: Sliders palette):

Fractal also calls the Sliders palette the Expression palette because the Sliders control how stylus or mouse actions, like speed, direction, and pressure, express themselves through stroke characteristics, like size, jitter, and opacity.

If you're using a stylus/tablet, you might want to set stroke characteristics to Pressure. If you're using a mouse, experiment with Direction or Velocity.

BRUSH STROKE CHARACTERISTICS:

Size affects brush tip size when the ± Size slider setting on the Brush Controls: Size palette is above 1.2.

Jitter affects the randomness of the placement of brush dabs. Jitter parameters are set on the Advanced Controls: Random palette.

Opacity affects how quickly colors mix to black when a brush Buildup method category is selected or what level of coverage a brush has when the Cover method category is selected.

Grain affects how much the current paper texture shows through a stroke.

Color controls how the Primary and Secondary color mix in a brush stroke, in conjunction with the Color Variability sliders on the Art Materials: Colors palette.

Angle sets the direction (orientation) of the brush dabs.

Resat(uration) controls the level of color concentration that flows from a brush, in conjunction with the Resaturation setting on the Advanced Controls: Well palette.

Bleed controls how much colors mix together.

STYLUS/MOUSE ACTIONS:

Link any of these stylus actions to any of the stroke characteristics described at left.

Random sets the level of the selected stroke characteristic randomly.

Source uses the source document's light and dark distribution to assign different amounts of the selected brush stroke characteristic in the clone document.

Bearing, Tilt and **Pressure** are functions found only on some styluses. Most brushes have their Size and Opacity set to Pressure as a default.

Direction and/or **Velocity** (speed) of stylus or mouse affect the selected stroke characteristic.

None — the stroke characteristic is unaffected by cursor motion.

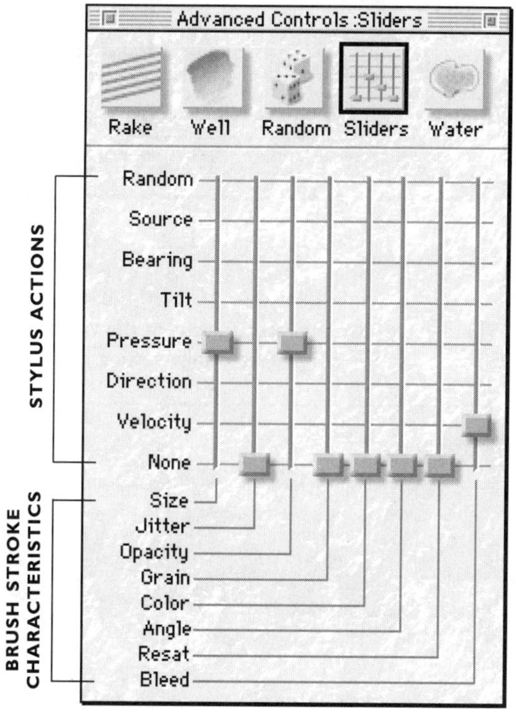

Sliders Palette

To fine-tune a Water Color brush (Advanced Controls: Water palette):

Water palette settings only affect strokes made on the Wet Paint layer. When you choose a default Water Color brush or choose the Wet variant for any other brush, the Wet Paint layer is turned on automatically (Canvas > Wet Paint).

When the **Diffusion** setting is above zero, pigment will feather outward from the edge of brushstrokes into the current paper texture, like traditional watercolor on wet paper. Diffusion may take a few seconds to render.

The higher the **Wet Fringe** setting, the more paint pools at the edges of wet strokes, like traditional watercolor pigment on dry paper. The Wet Fringe slider affects **all** strokes currently on the Wet Paint layer.

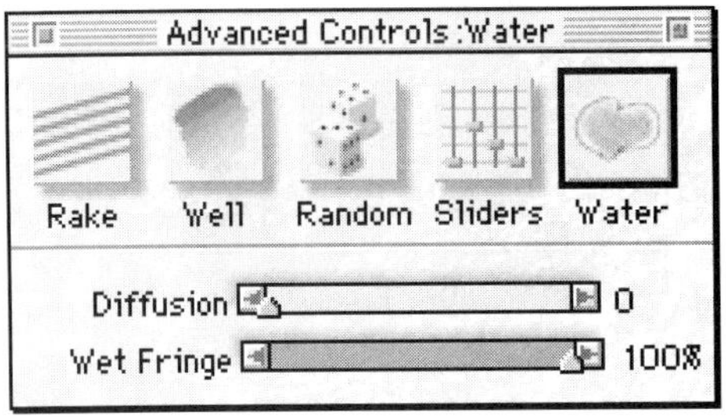

[The default Spatter Water variant of the Water Color brush has a high Wet Fringe setting.]

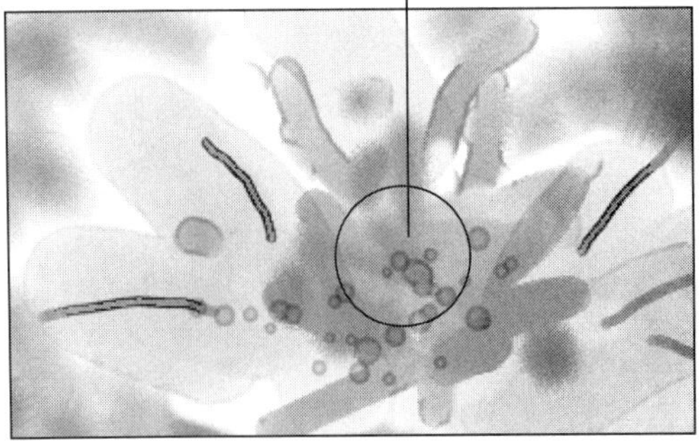

To diffuse strokes after they're made

The Shift-D shortcut diffuses existing strokes on the Wet Paint layer in small increments. Repeat the shortcut to diffuse more.

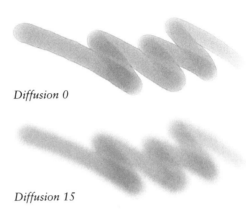

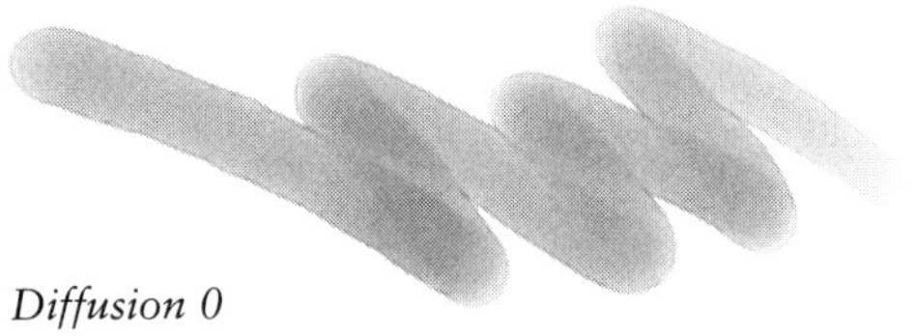

Diffusion 0

Diffusion 15

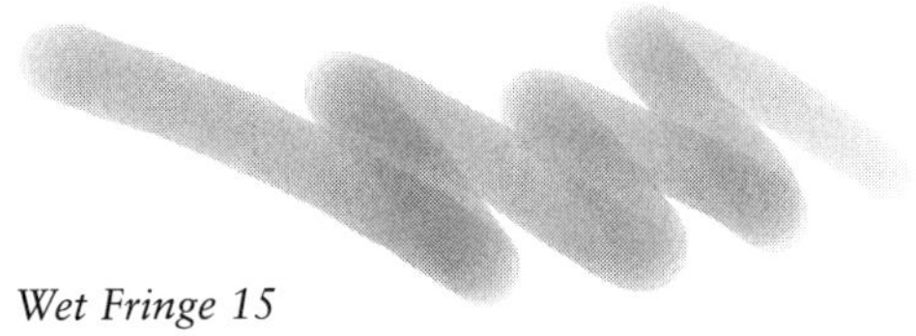

Wet Fringe 15

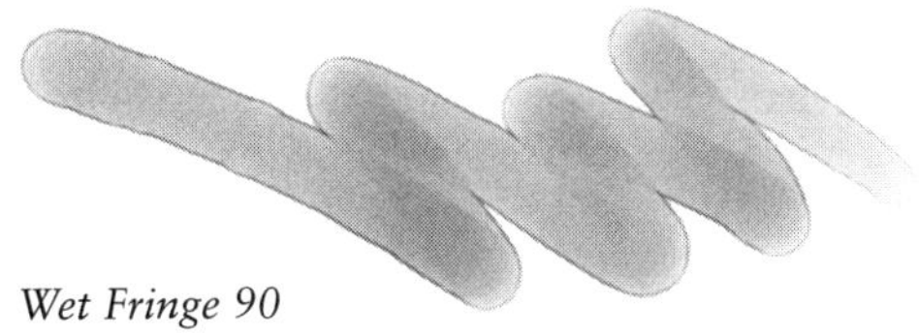

Wet Fringe 90

Selections/Paths 5

Elaine Weinmann (detail).

Selections/Paths

If you create a path (an outline shape) using the Oval Selection tool, the Outline Selection tool, or the Text tool, the area inside the path will automatically be selected. When a path is displayed as a selection it has a black dashed marquee. You can apply any Painter editing feature to it or fill it and you will modify the pixels inside the selection without changing the surrounding, unselected areas.

When a path is highlighted but is not displayed as a selection, it has a solid outline and it stays on its own layer, independent of the background pixels. You can move, reshape, resize, rotate, skew, or feather a non-selection path without affecting the background pixels. To reshape a path very precisely, convert it into a Bézier curve path and then adjust its control points and handles.

Paths are automatically saved with the document in which they are created, but if you save a path in a paths library, you can then place the path onto any picture.

The Objects: P. List palette is used to activate/deactivate paths and masks, to control whether a path is displayed as a marquee or as a mask, and to control whether painting and editing occurs inside or outside an active selection or ignores the selection altogether. The P. List palette is also used to group/ungroup, widen or shrink, smooth, and clear (delete) paths. More than one path can be active at a time.

Note: Selections don't affect the Wet Paint layer.

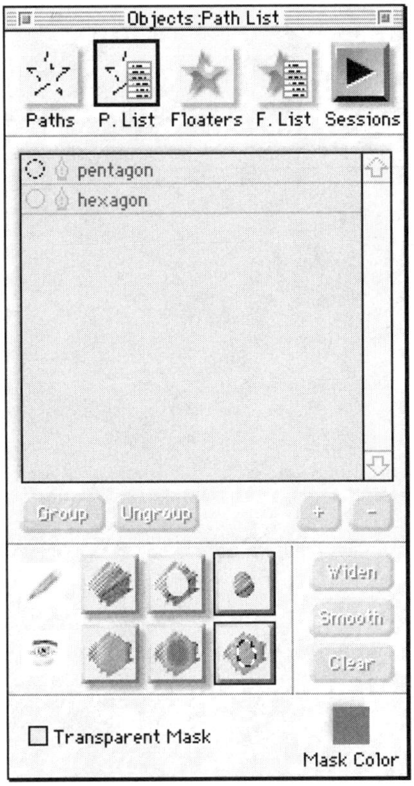

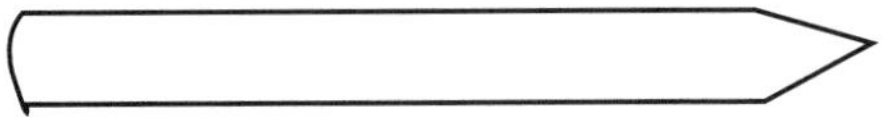

A path that is active, but not a selection.

A path displayed as a selection.

A path displayed as a mask.

Double-click any path name on the Objects: P. List palette to display this list of path types.

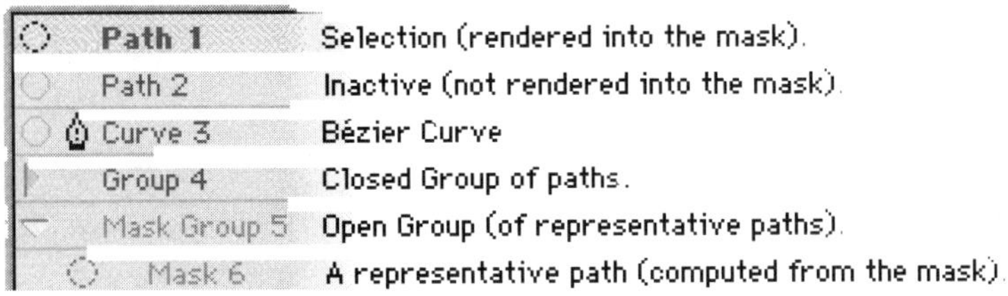

Rectangular Selection tool

To select an entire picture:

Double-click the Rectangular Selection tool. If you already have a selection on your picture, double-click the Rectangular Selection tool twice.

or

Choose Edit > Select All (⌘-A).

Note: If you choose Select All when the Path Adjuster tool is selected and a path is displayed as a selection (its circle icon is dashed), you will select all the file's paths instead of selecting the image.

Press Delete to fill the entire picture with the current paper color.

Oval Selection tool

To create an oval selection:

1. Choose the Oval Selection tool (O).
2. Drag diagonally to create a selection marquee.

Hold down Control before and while dragging to create a circular selection. Release the mouse before you release Control.

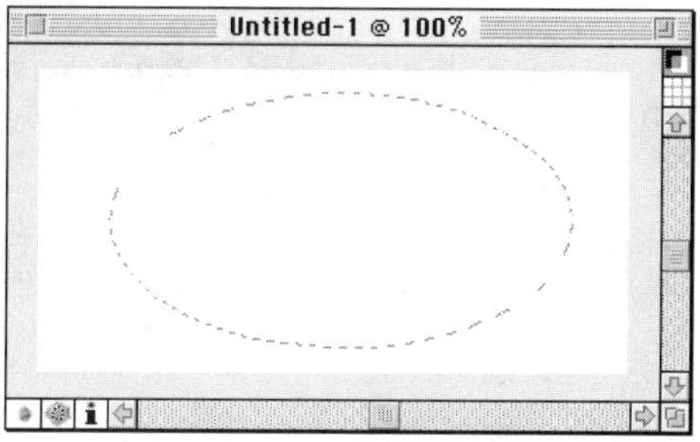

An oval selection.

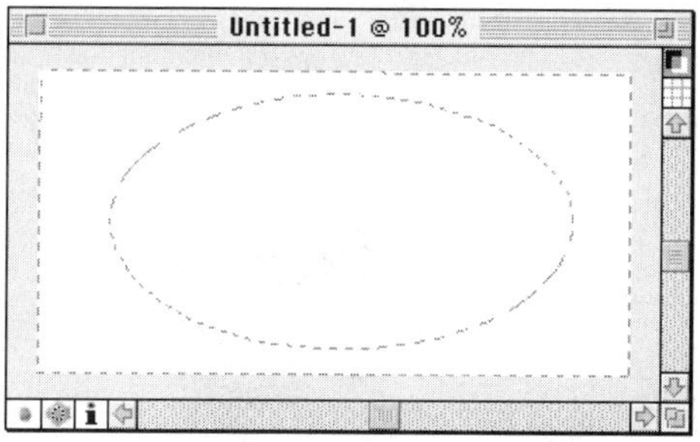

*After choosing the **Invert Mask** command.*

To switch the selected and unselected areas:

Choose Edit > Mask > Invert Mask (⌘-Shift-I).

Use Invert Mask to make unselected parts of an image editable when you apply an Effects menu command.

To deselect a selection:

Choose Edit > Deselect (⌘-D).

or

Double-click the Rectangular Selection tool.

You can't Undo the Deselect command. Choose Edit > Reselect (⌘-R) to reselect a selection. The Reselect command won't work if the selection was created using the Rectangular Selection tool.

The **Rectangular Selection** tool creates a temporary rectangular or square selection area that functions differently from other Painter paths and from rectangular selections in other programs in that it won't limit paint strokes. A rectangular selection *will* limit Effects menu commands, however.

Rectangular Selection tool

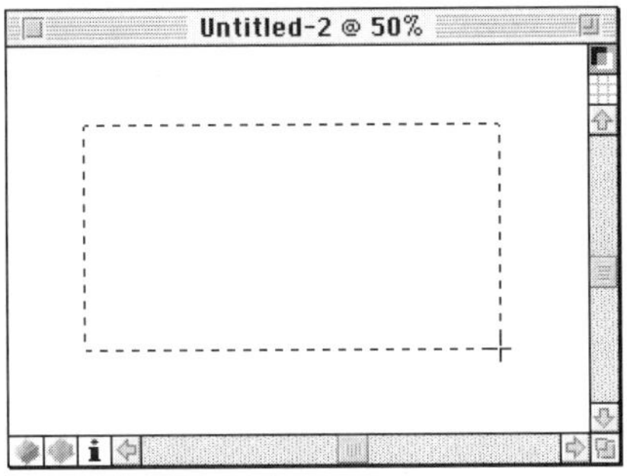

To create a rectangular selection:

1. Choose the Rectangular Selection tool (R).
2. Drag diagonally over the area of the picture you want to select.

Hold down Control while dragging to create a square selection area.

To limit brushstrokes to a rectangular selection

After creating your selection using the Rectangular Selection tool, turn it into a floater (instructions on page 84). Click on it before paint on it, and then drop it into the background when you're finished painting (click Drop on the Objects: F. List palette). Or use the Outline Selection tool, Straight Lines Drawing Style (Controls palette), to create the rectangular selection instead, which will limit brush strokes automatically. This tool creates a path, which will be listed on the P. List palette.

To resize a rectangular selection:

To resize a selection manually, with the Rectangular Selection tool still selected, hold down Shift and drag toward or away from any corner of the rectangle. (You don't have to click right on the corner.)

or

To resize a rectangular selection using a dialog box, choose Tools > Selections > Edit Rectangular Selection (⌘-Shift-E), enter new Height and Width values, then click OK. (Check the Show Bottom and Right box to resize the selection using the bottommost and rightmost position values.)

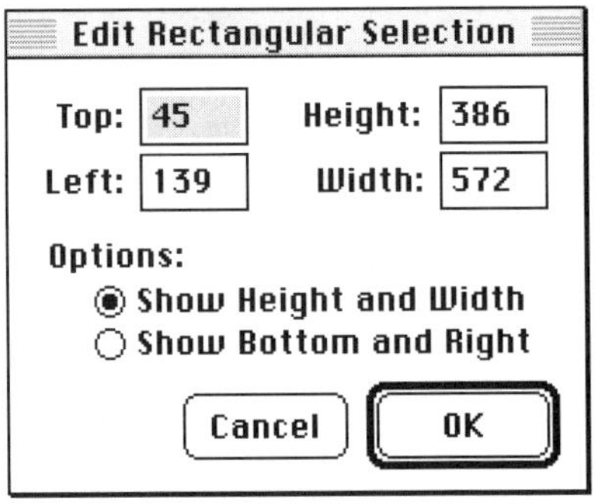

In the Edit Rectanglular Selection dialog box, enter a position number in pixels in the Top field to move the selection vertically or enter a number in the Left field to move the selection horizontally.

1 *Outline Selection tool*

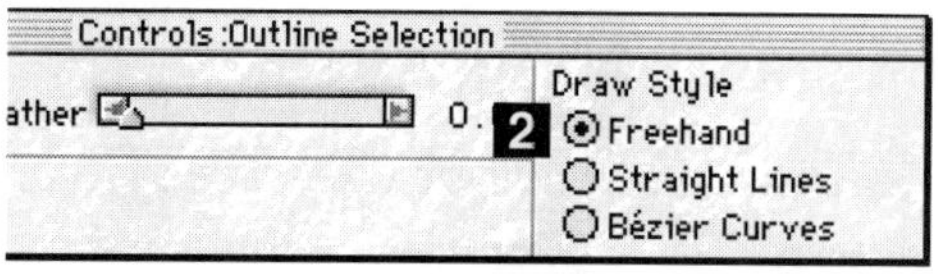

Freehand path

Regular path **3** *Path stroke*

Straight Lines path

To draw a freehand path:

1. Choose the Outline Selection tool **1**.
2. On the Controls: Outline Selection palette, click the Draw Style: Freehand button **2**.
3. Press and drag a selection area on your picture.
4. To complete the shape, drag back toward the starting location or just release the mouse. The shape will close automatically, and it will be listed on the Objects: P. List palette with the next higher path number.

To create a path stroke **3**, hold down Control while drawing the path. Don't crisscross or close the path while you draw it. If you use a pressure sensitive tablet to create a path stroke, the path width will vary with stylus pressure.

To draw a straight lines path:

1. Choose the Outline Selection tool **1**.
2. On the Controls: Outline Selection palette, click the Draw Style: Straight Lines button.
3. Click on your picture. An origin marker will appear.
4. Continue clicking to place other corner points. They will automatically be connected by straight lines. Press and hold the mouse to see a "rubber band" preview of the line as you move the mouse or stylus.
5. To complete the shape manually, drag back toward the starting location.
   or
   To close the shape automatically, press Return or choose the Path Adjuster (arrow) tool (A).

   The new path will be listed on the Objects: P. List palette with the next higher path number.

You can't delete points from a completed Bézier curve path.

To draw a Bézier curve path:

1. Choose the Outline Selection tool **1**a, then click the Draw Style: Bézier Curves button on the Controls: Outline Selection palette **1**b.
   or
   Press "P".
2. Press and drag on your picture in the direction in which you want the first curve segment to go, then release the mouse or lift the stylus. A control point will appear.
3. Continue pressing and dragging to create more points and handles.
4. To close the path, press and drag over the original starting control point. The new path will be listed on the Objects: P. List palette with the next higher path number and with a pen icon next to its name.

To delete the last created control point, press Delete. Repeat to delete other points on the path.

Don't leave the curved path open. If you do, next time you use the Outline Selection tool you will add to this open path rather than create a new path.

1a *Outline Selection tool*

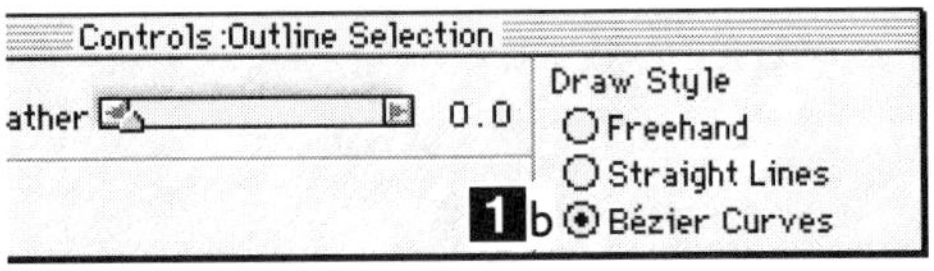

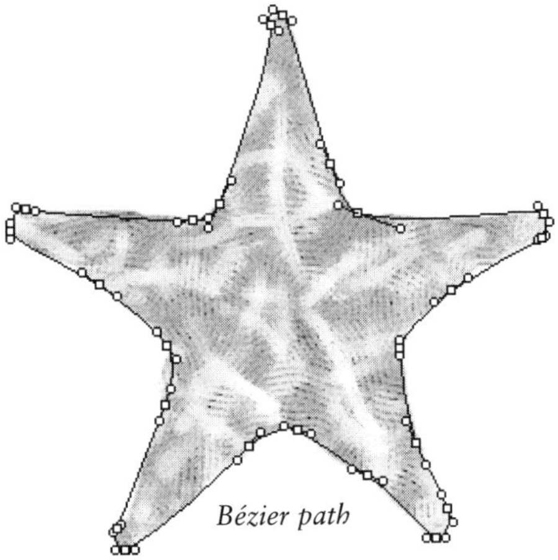

Bézier path

To convert a freehand path into a Bézier curve path:

1. Click the path name on the Objects: P. List palette.
2. Choose Tools > Selections > Convert to Curve. The path will now have control points and handles and the path name on the Objects: P. List palette will have a pen icon next to it.

To reshape Bézier curves

- **Click the pen icon next to the path name on the P. List palette to show/hide the path's control points and handles. Turning on the pen icon automatically selects the Outline Selection tool. Turning the pen icon off automatically selects the Path Adjuster tool.**
- **Use the Outline Selection tool or the Path Adjuster tool to adjust the handles or to move the control points along the path.**
- **To convert a curved control point into a corner point or vice versa, hold down Control and drag one of its handles.**

The **Magic Wand** command usually selects *adjacent* pixels that are similar in hue, saturation or value to the pixel you click on in the image window. To select similar *non-adjacent* pixels by color, choose Edit > Select All or create a selection using the Rectangular Selection tool before you choose the Magic Wand command, or use the Color Mask command instead (page 107).

To create a Magic Wand (color) selection:

1. *Optional:* Choose Edit > Select All.
2. Choose Edit > Magic Wand.
3. Click on a color or shade in the image window.

   or

   Drag across an area of varying color to select a wider range of colors.

   The color bars in the Magic Wand dialog box will reflect the hue, saturation, and value range in the selection.
4. *Optional:* Hold down Shift and click or drag on adjacent pixels in the picture to add to the selection. If you chose Select All before you chose the Magic Wand command, you can add similar, non-adjacent pixels.
5. *Optional:* To widen or narrow the hue, saturation, or value range in the selection, press and drag either end of the H, S, or V color bar. Shorten the bar to narrow the range. Try moving the V slider first.
6. Click OK or press Return. The selection will display as a moving marquee and a new Wand Group will be listed at the top of the P. List palette.

To remove the Magic Wand selection after clicking OK, click the Wand Group name at the top of the Objects: P. List palette, then click Clear. You can't Undo the Clear command.

Rodney Alan Greenblat

The first pass over the boy's sweater with the Magic Wand selected only the dark stripes. After moving the Value slider slightly to the right...

...the entire sweater is selected.

Each text character created in Painter is listed on the P. List palette as a separate path. If you fill or paint text paths, you'll be painting on the background layer within the confines of the character shapes, but **the text path will actually be separate from its fill.**

If you turn your text into a floater, you'll be able to paint or fill it without altering the background. Reshape, move, or rotate your text paths first, though.

To create a text selection:

1. Choose the Text tool (T) **1**.
2. Move the Point Size slider on the Controls: Text Selection palette to the desired point size **2**.
3. Choose from the Font pop-up menu. If the font you want isn't on the menu, choose Other, choose a font **3**, then click OK.
4. *Optional:* Move the Tracking slider to adjust the spacing between letters **4**.
5. Click in the image window where you want the text to appear.
6. Enter the text. (Press Delete to delete characters one at a time. To delete all the characters at once, hold down Shift and click their path names on the Objects: P. List palette, then click Clear.)
7. *Optional:* Choose the Floating Selection tool, then Option-click one of the characters to convert all the characters into one floater.

Like any other element in Painter, text is bitmapped. To create standard PostScript type, import your painting in QuarkXPress or Illustrator and add the type there. Create Painter-ly text, of course, in Painter.

Text tips

- **Unfortunately, you can't preview text before it appears in the image window. You can create it, delete it before you paint it, then create it again, etc. until it has the size and tracking that you like. You can resize text using the Effects > Orientation > Scale command.**
- **To fill text paths, see page 112. To stroke text paths, see page 79.**
- **Use the Path Adjuster tool to select and move multiple text paths at once or to move individual text paths closer together or further apart (drag inside the text path). Or use the arrow keys on the keyboard to move them one pixel at a time. Group text paths to make it easier to move them as a unit.**

1 *Text tool.*

To produce this illustration, our own Woody Grain surface texture was applied using the Color Overlay command (Opacity 50%, Hiding Power). Then the type was added, turned into floaters, and the Color Overlay command was applied to each word several times (Paper Grain, Opacity 100%, Dye Concentration).

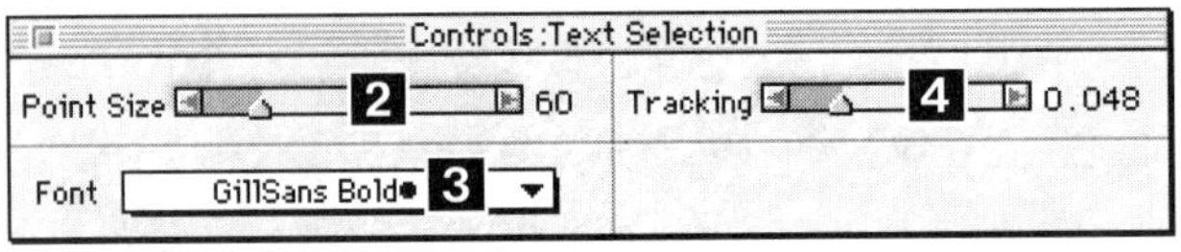

Rodney Alan Greenblat

Rodney Alan Greenblat's interactive stories on CD — Dazzeloids and Rodney's Wonder Window — have won wide acclaim for their humor, invention and artistry. He writes and illustrates, as well as composes and records the soundtrack for his CDs. He's also written and illustrated several children's books, including Uncle Wizmo's New Used Car, Aunt Ippy's Museum of Junk, and the upcoming Thunder Bunny.

Greenblat starts an illustration with a traditional media pencil-and-paper sketch. He scans the sketch, traces over it and refines the shapes in FreeHand, and then imports his FreeHand EPS files into Painter as selections, where he fills them with color using the Paint Bucket tool and applies brush strokes using charcoal and colored pencil brushes. Greenblat, whose background is in traditional painting and sculpture media, loves the painterly look that he achieves using Painter. (Look at Rodney Alan Greenblat's work in the color section.)

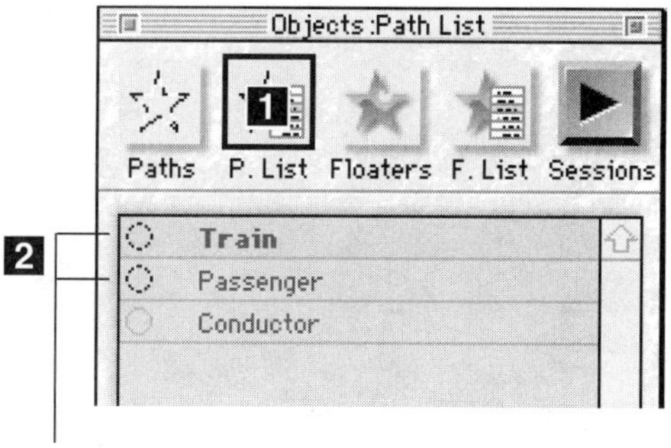

These two paths are displayed as selections.

When a path's selection icon on the Objects: P. List palette (the circle next to the path name) is dashed, the path is displayed in the image window as a marqueed selection. When the selection icon is solid, the path is displayed in the image window as a solid outline (not a selection). More than one path can be displayed as a selection at one time.

To display a path as a selection:

1. Click the P. List icon on the Objects palette **1**.
2. Click the leftmost selection (circle) icon **2**.
   or
   Click the path name on the palette, then press Return.

Click the dashed circle again or press Return again to deactivate the path.

If you choose Edit > Deselect to deselect a path, and then paint with the second or third Drawing button chosen, the path will still function as a selection.

Choose Edit > Reselect to reselect a path, or just click on the path name.

If path handles are visible (the Path Adjuster tool is selected) and you choose the Deselect command, only the path's handles will disappear.

To rename a path, double-click the path name, type in the Name field, then click OK.

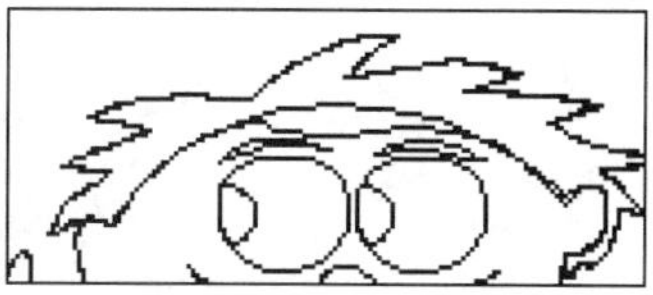

An unselected path.

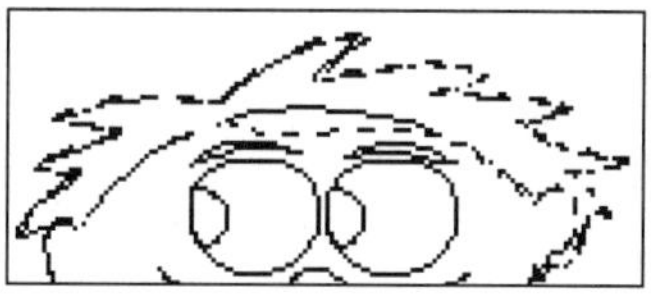

The same path displayed as a selection.

Rodney Alan Greenblat's Springing (detail)

To choose editing and display options for a path:

1. Make sure the path is displayed as a selection: On the Objects: P. List palette, the selection (circle) icon next to the path name should be dashed. Click on it, if necessary.
2. Click a Drawing (pencil) button on the extended Objects: P. List palette **1**.
3. Click a Visibility (eye) button **2**.

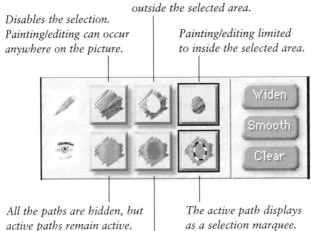

Tips

- **You can also choose Drawing and Visibility options from the bottom left corner of the image window at any time, or from the Controls palette when the Path Adjuster tool or the Outline Selection tool is selected.**
- **A warning prompt will appear if all of a document's paths are deselected and you attempt to work on the picture while the third Drawing button is selected. Click on the first Drawing button to work on the picture.**
- **If you click on a path name on the Objects: P. List palette, the third Drawing and Visibility buttons will select automatically.**

1 DRAWING BUTTONS

Painting/editing limited to outside the selected area.

Disables the selection. Painting/editing can occur anywhere on the picture.

Painting/editing limited to inside the selected area.

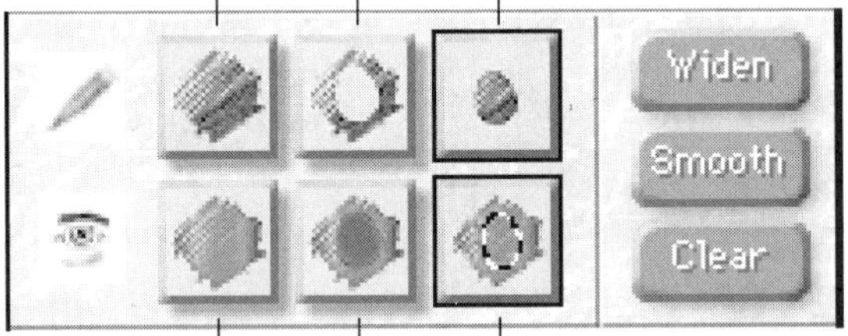

All the paths are hidden, but active paths remain active.

The active path displays as a selection marquee.

A mask covers the selected or unselected area, depending on which Drawing button is currently selected.

2 VISIBILITY BUTTONS

Path Adjuster tool

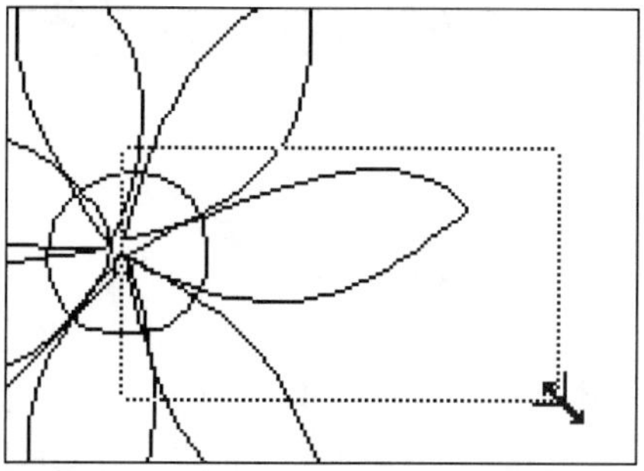

Hold down Shift and drag a corner handle to resize a selection proportionally.

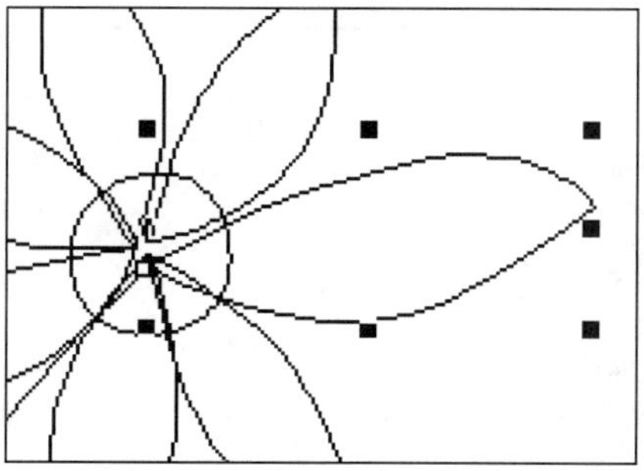

Rodney Alan Greenblat (detail)

The following operations will modify a path's outline, but not the path's contents.

To move, resize, or rotate a path:

1. Choose the Path Adjuster tool (A).
2. To **move** the whole path, press and drag inside it.
   or
   To **resize** the path, click on its edge, then drag any of the path's handles. Hold down Shift while dragging to resize proportionally.
   or
   To **rotate** the path, hold down Command and drag a corner handle.
   or
   To **copy** the path, hold down Option and drag inside it. (To copy and paste a selection, see page 86.)

To resize a selection path and its contents (and turn the path into a floater), use the Effects > Orientation > Scale command. If you apply the Scale command when all the document's paths have solid outlines, you'll resize your entire picture and turn it into a floater.

You can't Undo this.

To add to or subtract from a selection:

1. Make sure the selection is active (see page 75).
2. Choose the Outline Selection tool.
3. To add to the selection, position the cursor over the selection, then hold down Command and drag to define an additional selection area, ending at your starting point.
   or
   To subtract from the selection, hold down Shift and, starting from right on one edge, drag across the shape, and end right on the opposite edge.

To add or subtract from a path that is part of a group, you have to temporarily take the path out of its group. (Open the group list, drag the path name out of the list, then drag it back over the group when you're finished.)

Outline Selection tool

To subtract from a selection, drag precisely from edge to edge.

You can't Undo a path deletion.

To delete a path and its contents:

1. Choose the Path Adjuster tool.
2. Click on the path in the image window.
3. Press Delete.

or

1. Click the path name on the Objects: P. List palette. (Hold down Shift and click to select multiple paths.)
2. Click Clear.

Path Adjuster tool

Outline Selection tool

To delete the contents of a path:

1. Click the path name on the Objects: P. List palette to activate the path.
2. Choose any tool except the Path Adjuster.
3. Press Delete. The path will fill with the current paper color 3.

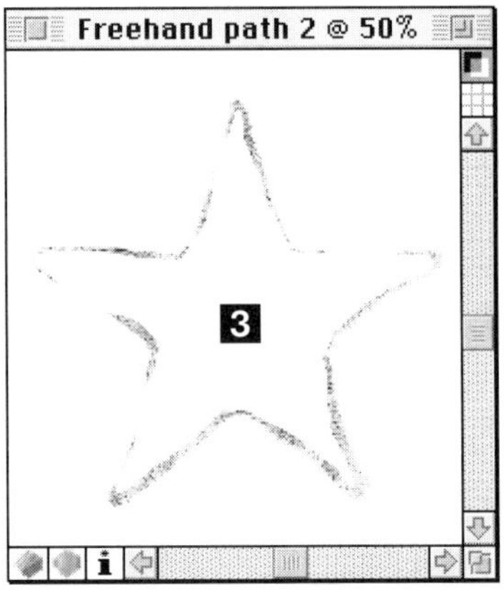

The path's contents are deleted.

To feather a selection:

1. Choose the Path Adjuster tool or the Outline Selection tool.
2. Click the second Visibility (eye) button on the Controls palette or on the Objects: P. List palette so you'll be able to see the feather.
3. Move the Feather slider on the Controls palette to the right.

The feather will be saved with the path when you save your document and if you save the path in a Paths library. The Controls: Outline Selection palette Feather slider will automatically reset to zero when you reopen the document.

Click Smooth on the P. List palette to smooth the corners of a selection. Click Smooth again to smooth more.

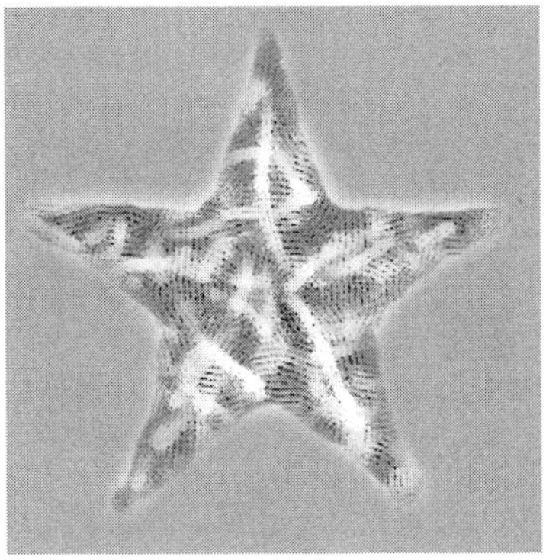

A feathered selection.

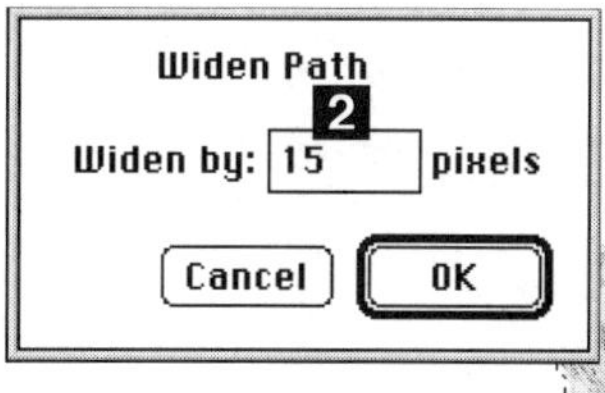

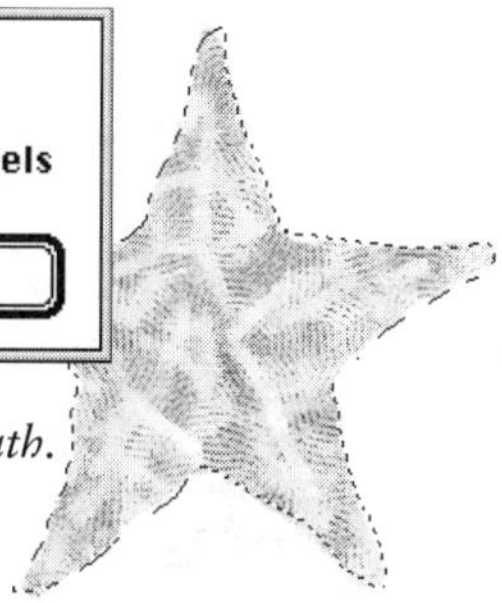

The original path.

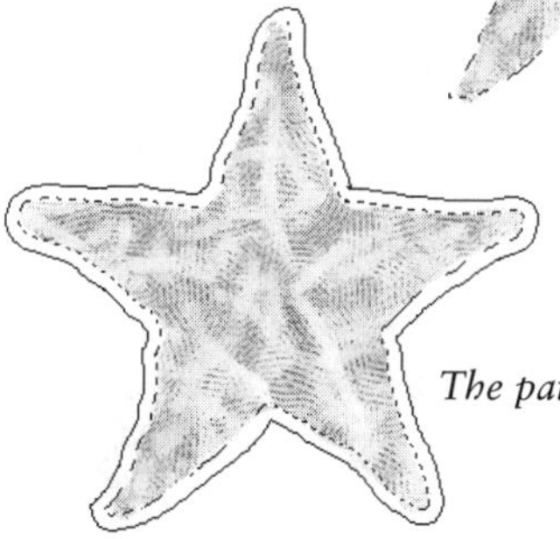

The path widened.

To widen or shrink a selection:

1. On the Objects: P. List palette, click on the name of the path that you want to widen, then click Widen.
2. Enter the number of pixels by which the path will be widened **2**. Enter a negative number to shrink the path.
3. Click OK. The widened path will be listed on the P. List as a separate path from the original, but with the same name and number.

To stroke a selection:

1. Choose a brush, variant, and Primary color for the stroke.
2. Click on the first, second, or third Drawing button on the P. List palette to stroke both sides, outside, or inside the selection, respectively.
3. Choose Tools > Selections > Stroke Selection.

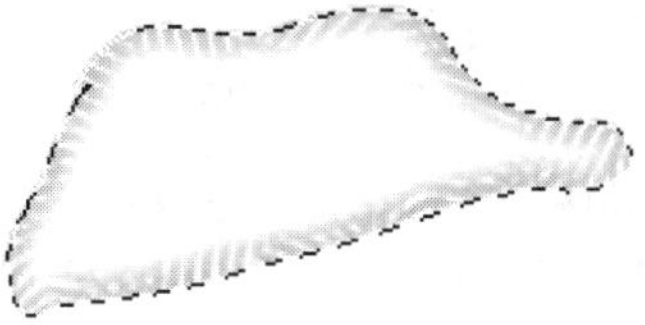

A selection stroked with a Chalk variant, grainy method subcategory.

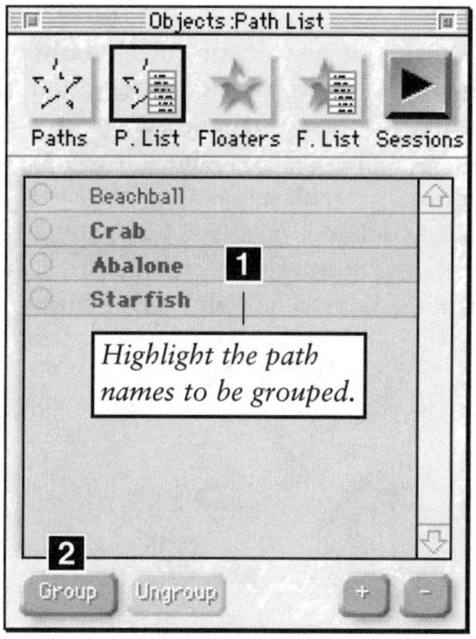

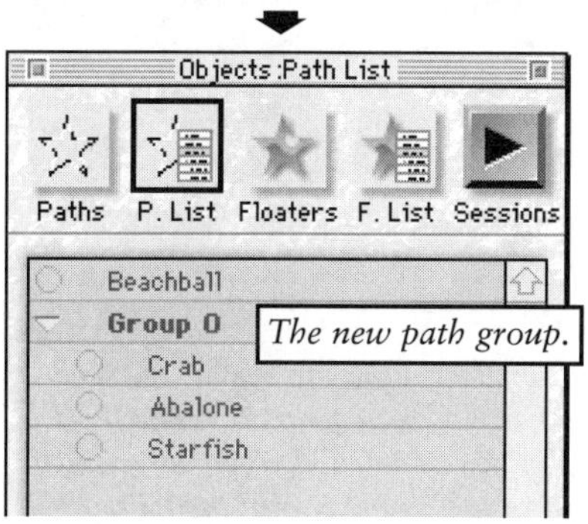

Grouped paths can be moved or resized as a unit.

To group paths:

1. Hold down Shift and click the names of the paths you want to group on the Objects: P. List palette **1**.
   or
   To select all the paths, click on a path name, choose the Path Adjuster tool, then choose Edit > Select All (⌘-A).
2. Click Group **2**. The word "Group" followed by the next sequential group number will appear on the path list.

To display the individual path names, click the arrowhead next to the group name so the arrowhead points downward. Click the arrowhead again to close the group list.

To edit a path group:

1. Make sure the group list on the Objects: P. List palette is closed (click the arrowhead next to the group name if it's not).
2. Click the group name.
3. Choose the Path Adjuster tool (A) **3**.
4. Do any of the following:

   Drag inside any of the grouped paths to **move** the whole group.

   Drag any path handle to **resize** the whole group. Hold down Shift while dragging to preserve the paths' original proportions.

   To **remove** a path from a group but keep the path, drag the path name away from the group list.

   To **delete** a grouped path altogether, click on its name, then click Clear. (To delete a whole group, close the group list, then click Clear.) You can't Undo either operation!

   To **add** a path to a group, make sure the group list is open on the Objects: P. List palette (the arrowhead should point downward), then drag the path name under the group name.

To ungroup paths:

1. Click the group name on the Objects: P. List palette.
2. Click Ungroup. The group name will disappear and the names of the previously grouped paths will be highlighted.

3 *Path Adjuster tool*

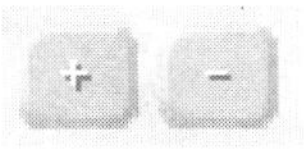

The + and – buttons on the P. List palette

Create a negative path

The + button makes a selection positive, the default setting for a selection (black dashed marquee). The – button makes a selection negative (red dashed marquee). When a selection is negative, areas where it overlaps the selection immediately behind it (listed immediately below it on the P. List palette) are uneditable. In other words, only the visible areas of the selection behind it are editable.

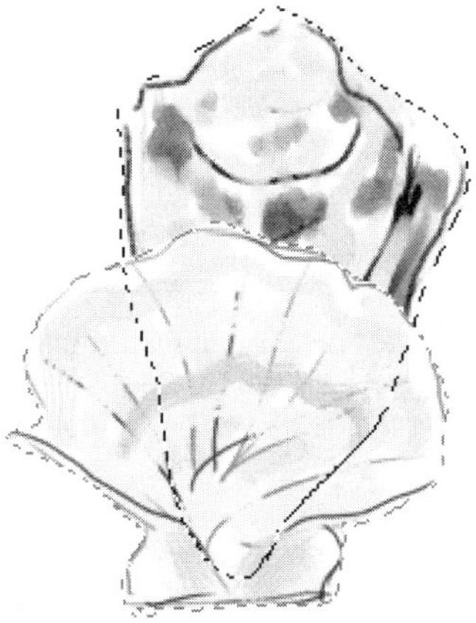

The clam shell has a negative path; the shell behind it has a positive path. With the third Drawing button selected, painting effects will be limited to the visible part of the taller shell.

1 *Path Adjuster tool*

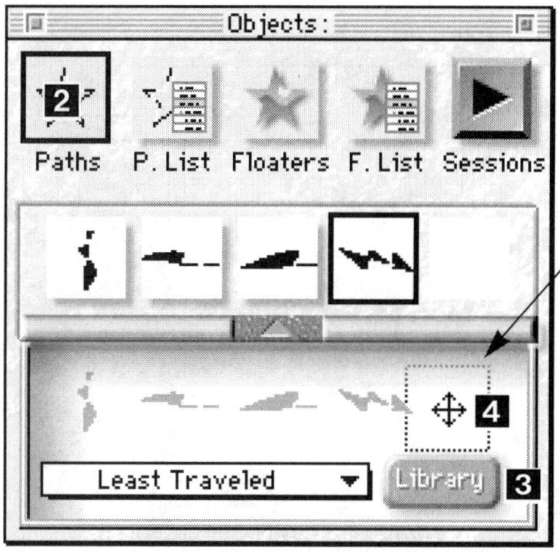

To save a path in a Paths palette library:

1. Choose the Path Adjuster tool (A) **1**.
2. Click the Paths icon on the Objects palette **2**.
3. *Optional:* To place the path in other than the currently open library, click Library in the Paths palette drawer **3**, locate and highlight the library you want to open, then click Open.
4. Press and drag the path shape from the image window into the open Objects: Paths palette drawer or onto the drawer front **4**.
5. Enter a name in the Save Path dialog box.
6. Click OK. An icon for the saved path will appear on the Objects: Paths palette, and the name you entered will appear on the pop-up menu in the palette drawer.

To edit a Paths library, see page 16.

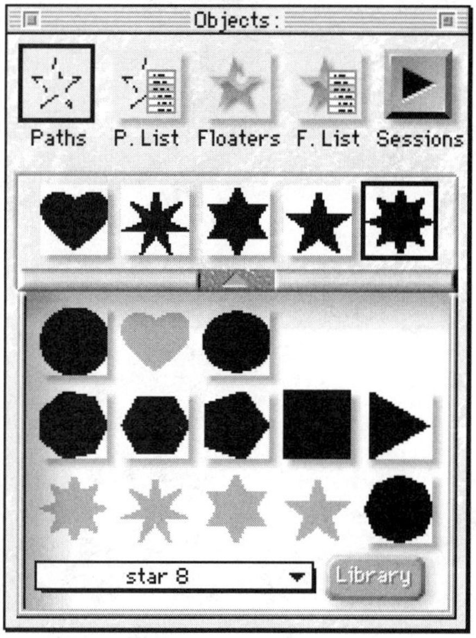

The preformed paths in the Painter Paths library.

To retrieve a path from the Paths palette:

1. Click the Paths icon on the Objects palette.
2. If the path you want to retrieve is not in the currently open Paths library, click Library, locate the library you want to open, then click Open.
3. Drag a path icon from the Paths palette drawer front or drawer onto the picture. The path appear as a selection in the image window.

To retrieve a path to the same position in the same document from which you saved it to the Paths palette, drag the path's icon onto the drawer front, then double-click it. This won't work if you changed the document's resolution or canvas size after the path was originally saved.

If you save a path as an EPS file, you can then open it in an illustration program.

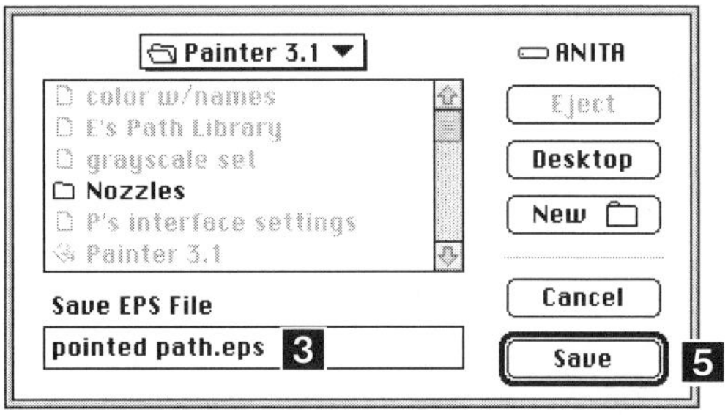

To save a path as an EPS file:

1. If the path you want to save as an EPS is already in the image window, turn it into an active selection by clicking its circle icon on the Objects: P. List palette.

   If the path is saved in a library but is not in the image window, drag it into the image window now.
2. Choose Tools > Selections > Save Selection as EPS.
3. Enter a name for the file **3**.
4. Choose a location in which to save the file.
5. Click Save **5**. The path will be saved as a separate file (not in a Paths library).

As of this writing, 3.1 Painter EPS files can't be opened in Illustrator 5.

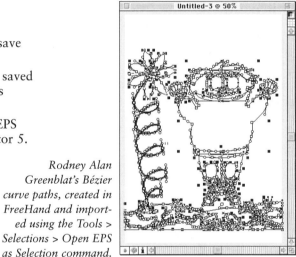

Rodney Alan Greenblat's Bézier curve paths, created in FreeHand and imported using the Tools > Selections > Open EPS as Selection command.

After choosing Tools > Selections > Convert to Selection.

To import an Illustrator, FreeHand, or other EPS file in Painter as a selection:

For an Illustrator file, save it in the Illustrator 5 format in Illustrator. For a FreeHand file, save it in the Illustrator format in FreeHand. In Painter, create or open a file, choose Tools > Selections > Open EPS as Selection, then double-click the EPS file you want to open. Closed paths will become selections in Painter. Open paths will remain as Bézier curve paths and will not become selections.

Floaters 6

David Humphrey, ***Blond Again*** *(detail).*

Floaters

A floater is a shape that floats above the background pixels. Floaters add enormous flexibility to picture-making because you can repaint, restack, move, or feather a floater or change its opacity or composite method without affecting the background. Floaters can be grouped, and each floater has its own mask.

Floaters will remain floating if you save your file in the RIFF or Photoshop 3.0 format. If you save your file in any other format, floaters will automatically be merged into the background. To drop a floater, see page 95.

Painter supplies a few pre-made floaters, but you'll probably want to create your own and save them in a Floaters library. Any selected area of a painting can be turned into a floater.

To create a floater:

1. Create a selection using the Text tool, Oval Selection tool, Outline Selection tool, or Rectangular Selection tool.
2. Choose the Rectangular Selection tool or the Floating Selection tool **2**.
3. Hold down Option and click inside the selection to copy it and leave the background intact **3**a.
   or
   Click inside the selection to cut the selection out of the background **3**b.

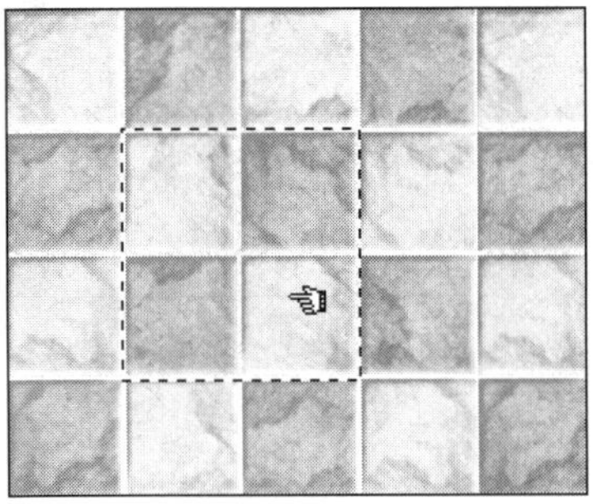

3b *If you click on a selection with the Floating Selection tool without holding down Option, you'll cut a hole in the background.*

Painter floaters ↔ Photoshop layers

Now you can make a round trip without losing layers or floaters. If you save a Painter 3.1 file with floaters in the Photoshop 3.0 file format and then open it in Photoshop, each floater will be assigned its own layer. If you open a Photoshop 3.0 file in Painter 3.1, each layer will become a floater.

Rectangular Selection tool   *Floating Selection tool*

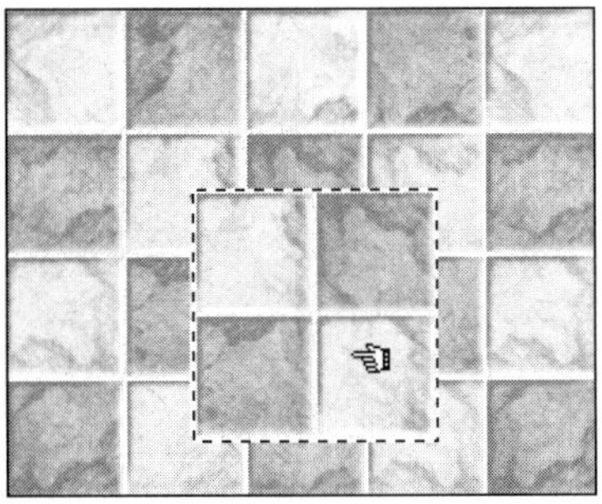

3a *If you click on a selection with the Floating Selection tool while holding down Option, you'll copy background pixels and you won't cut a hole in the background.*

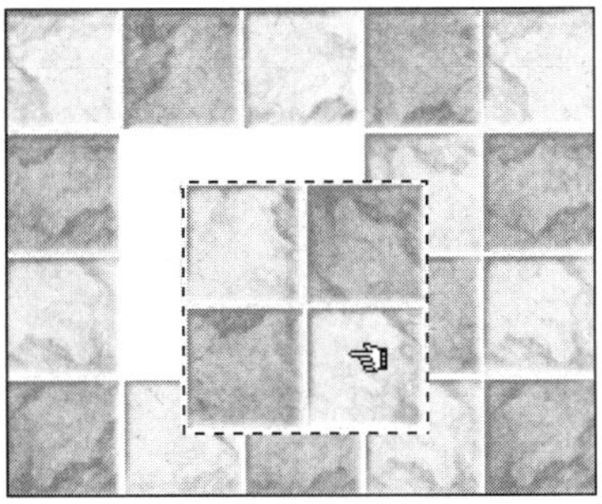

If you move the floater, you'll reveal the hole.

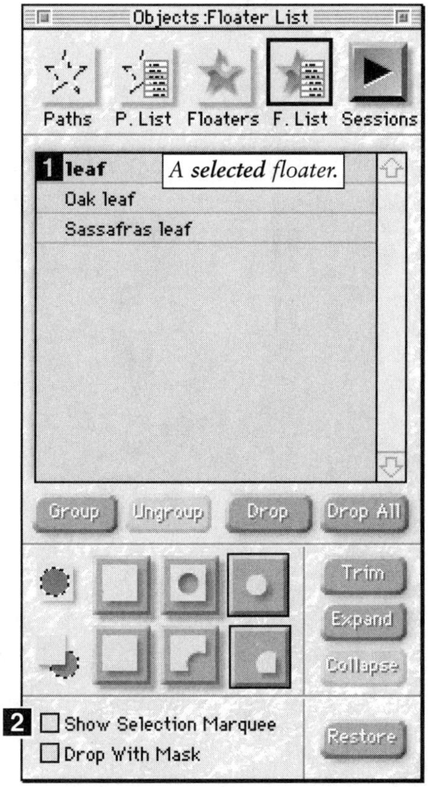

If there is a floater in your image window, its name will appear on the Objects: F. List palette. When a floater is selected, its name is highlighted. **You can only modify a floater if it is selected, and only one floater or floater group can be selected at a time** (though you can highlight more than one floater name at a time).

To select a floater or a floater group:

Click on the name of the floater on the Objects: F. List palette **1**.

or

Choose the Floating Selection tool, then click on the floater in the image window.

To hide the floater marquee, uncheck the Show Selection Marquee box on the Objects: F. List palette (⌘-Shift-H) **2**.

A deselected floater is uneditable, but it still floats.

To deselect a floater:

Click on the blank area below the floater names on the Objects: F. List palette.

or

Choose the Floating Selection tool or the Rectangular Selection tool, then click outside the floater in the image window.

To delete a floater group, make sure the group list on the Objects: F. List palette is closed.

To delete a floater or a floater group from a document:

1. Click on the name of the floater or floater group on the Objects: F. List palette that you want to delete.

   or

   Choose the Floating Selection tool, then click on the floater or floater group in the image window.
2. Press Delete.

We can't figure out why the Scale command is accessed from the Orientation submenu. (You can also resize a selection using this command. It will turn your selection into a floater.)

To resize a floater:

1. Click on the name of the floater that you want to resize on the Objects: F. List palette.
2. Choose Effects > Orientation > Scale.
3. Enter the amount you want to enlarge or shrink the floater in the Horizontal and/or Vertical Scale fields **3a**. Uncheck the Constrain Aspect Ratio box if you don't want to preserve the selection's original proportions.
   or
   Press and drag any of the floater's handles in the image window **3b**.
4. *Optional:* Check the Preserve Center box to resize the selection from its center.
5. Click OK or press Return.

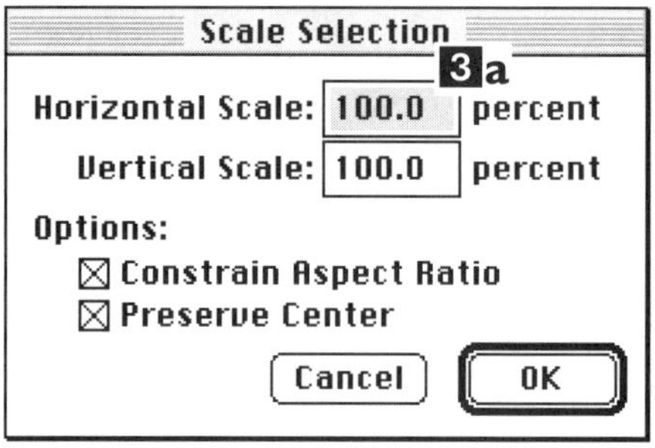

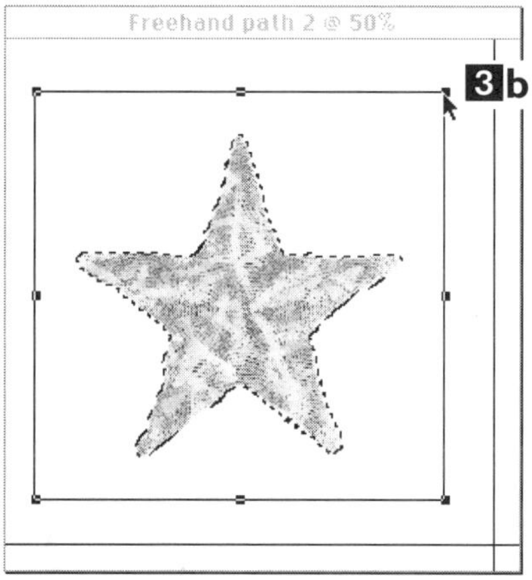

With the Scale Selection dialog box open, you can resize a selection by dragging any of its handles.

To copy a floater in the same file:

1. Choose the Floating Selection tool.
2. Hold down Option and drag the floater in the image window.

If the resolution of the original image is higher than the resolution of the destination image, the floater will increase in size when pasted, and vice versa.

To copy a floater to a different file:

1. Choose the Floating Selection tool.
2. Choose Edit > Copy (⌘-C).
3. Click in the destination image window.
4. Choose Edit > Paste > Normal (⌘-V).

If you Copy and Paste a selection, it will become a floater.

If you copy a large image to the Clipboard, copy a small area when you're finished so the Clipboard contents don't occupy a large chunk of memory.

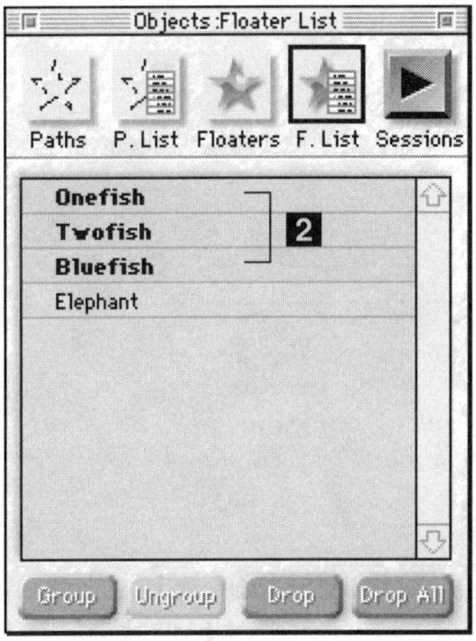

Grouped floaters can be moved easily as a unit, yet can still be edited individually. A floater group can be saved in a Floaters library.

To group floaters:

1. Open the Objects: F. List palette.
2. Hold down Shift and click on the names of the floaters you want to group **2**.
3. Click Group.
4. *Optional:* To rename the group, double-click the group name, enter a name, then click OK.

When you group floaters, each floater stays on its original layer.

Shortcuts

To open/close the Objects palette: (⌘-5).

To open the F. List palette: Double-click the Floating Selection tool.

To add a floater to a group:

1. If the group list isn't open, click the arrowhead next to the group name (it should point downward).
2. Drag the name of the floater you want to add under the group name.

To combine all the floaters in a group into one floater:

1. Click on the floater group name on the Objects: F. List palette.
2. Click the Collapse button on the extended Objects: F. List palette.

To remove a floater from a group:

Drag the floater name upward or downward out of the open group list.

To select one floater in a group:

1. If the group list isn't open, click the arrowhead next to the group name (it should point downward). **1**.
2. Click on the name of the floater you want to modify **2**.

To ungroup a floater group:

1. Click the floater group name on the Objects: P. List palette.
2. Click Ungroup.

To move a floater or a floater group manually:

1. Click on the floater name or floater group name on the Objects: F. List palette. For a floater group, close the group list (the arrowhead should point to the right) **1**.
2. Choose the Floating Selection tool or the Rectangular Selection tool.
3. Drag the floater in the image window.

   Note: If you dragged the floater from the Objects: Floaters palette, it won't make a hole in the background when you move it. But if you just created the floater by selecting an area of the background without holding down Option and you drag the floater for the first time, you'll create a hole in the background. If you want to refill the hole, choose Undo immediately, then recreate the floater.

Press any arrow key to move a selected floater one pixel at a time.

Rectangular Selection tool

Floating Selection tool

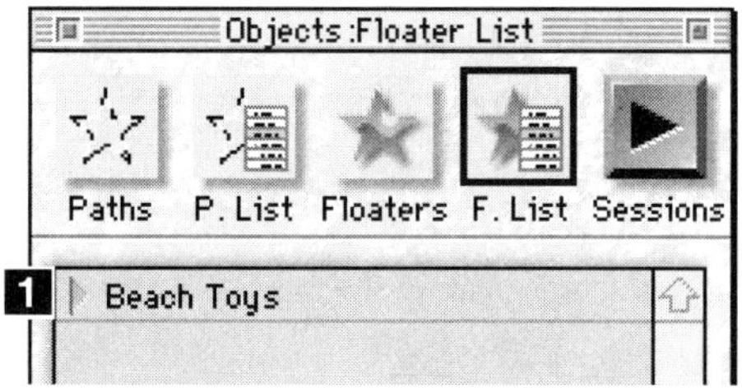

To move a floater or a floater group using a dialog box:

1. Double-click the floater name on the Objects: F. List palette.
2. Enter a higher number in the Position: Top field to move the floater downward or enter a lower number to move the floater upward.

   Enter a higher number in the Position: Left field to move the floater to the right or enter a lower number to move the floater to the left.
3. Click OK or press Return.

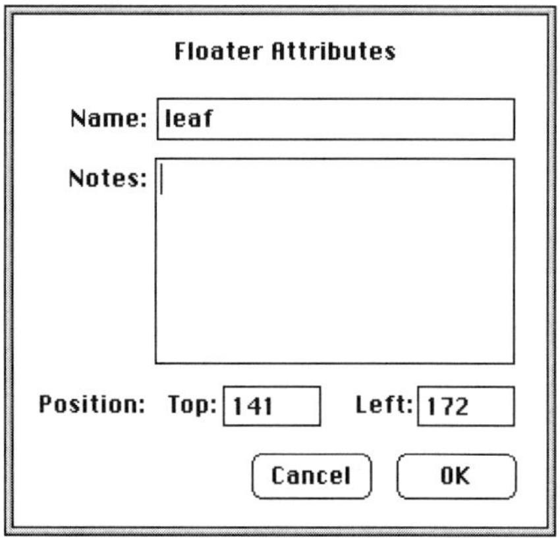

Floating Selection tool

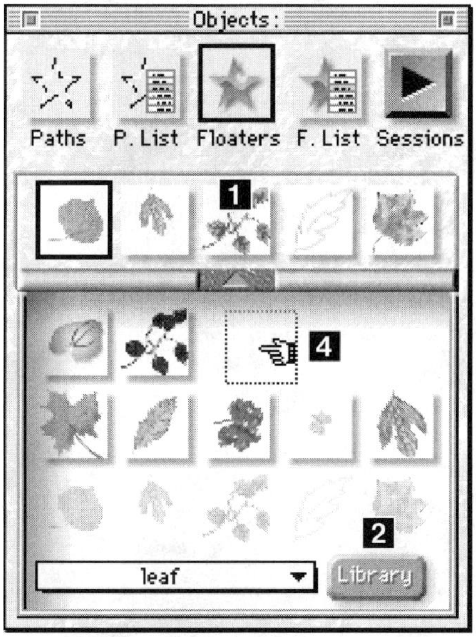

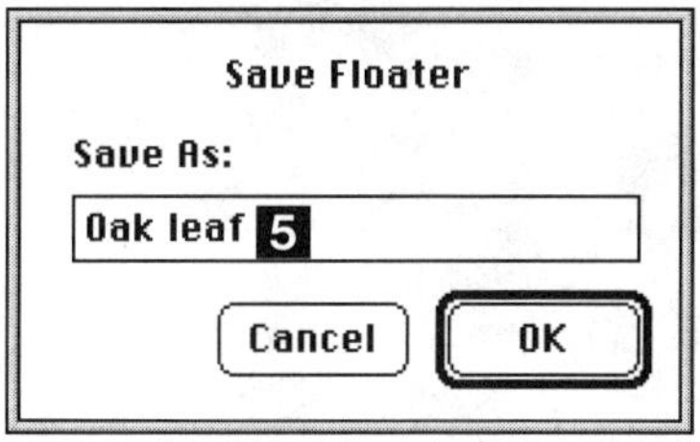

If you save a floater in a floaters library, its icon will appear on the Objects: Floaters palette and you'll be able to drag it into any open image window.

To save a floater or a floater group to the Floaters palette:

1. Click the Floaters icon on the Objects palette **1**.
2. *Optional:* To add a floater to a library that isn't currently open, click Library in the Floaters palette drawer **2**, locate and highlight the library you want to open, then click Open.
3. Choose the Floating Selection tool (F).
4. Drag a floater or a floater group onto the Floaters palette drawer or drawer front. The floater will be removed from your document **4**.
   or
   Hold down Option while dragging to save a copy of the floater.
5. Enter a name for the floater **5**.
6. Click OK. A thumbnail of the floater will appear on the Floaters palette.

To rename a floater, double-click its name on the Objects: F. List palette, enter a name, then click OK.

To create or edit a floater library, see the instructions on pages 15-16.

When you retrieve a floater from the Objects: Floaters palette, it takes on the resolution of the file it is placed into.

To retrieve a floater from the Floaters palette:

1. If the floater you want to retrieve is not in the currently open library, click Library in the Objects: Floaters palette drawer, then locate and double-click the name of the library that contains the floater you want to retrieve.
2. Drag the floater icon from the drawer front or drawer into the image window.

Ways to modify a floater:

You must select a floater before you can modify it. To select a floater, click on it in the image window with the Floating Selection tool or click the floater name on the Objects: F. List palette.

- **Paint** using any technique except Wet Paint. Modifications will be restricted to the selected floater. To paint on the background behind the floater, first deselect the floater.
- Choose the Floating Selection tool, then change the floater's **Opacity**, **Feather** amount, or **Composite Method** using the Controls: Floating Selection palette. (Or press keypad keys to choose 10% opacity increments: 1=10%, 2=20%, etc.)

  Note: You can only feather up to what the "Floating selection pre-feather" amount setting (General Preferences dialog box) was when the floater was created. To feather beyond that amount, first click the Expand button to enlarge the floater area to accommodate a wider feathered edge. (To view the feather, place the floater over a colored background.)
- Click **Trim** on the Objects: F. List palette to shrink the floater area to the minimum area needed to contain the floater and its mask.
- Choose Effects > Orientation > **Scale** to resize the floater or Effects > Orientation > **Rotate** to rotate it. Both commands cause slight blurring.
- **Mask** part of a floater with White paint using a Masking brush variant or a non-Masking brush at 100% opacity with the Mask method category and the third Floater Visibility button selected (top row). Click Restore on the Objects: F. List palette to remove masking brush strokes from a floater. Floater masks are discussed in depth on pages 108-110.

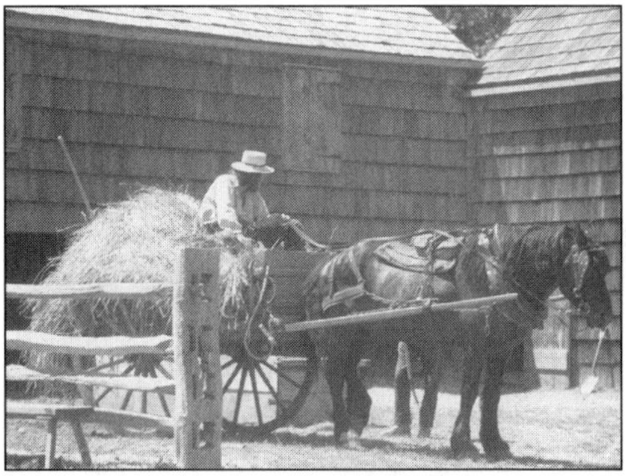

To produce the image below, first this entire picture was selected and turned into a floater (Option-click method to make a copy)...

Then Painter's "tri-weave" texture was applied to the floater using the Express Texture command. Finally, the Hard Light Composite Method was chosen on the Controls: Floating Selection palette and the Opacity slider was lowered to reveal some of the underlying pixels.

A text selection turned into a floater and feathered using the Controls: Floating Selection palette.

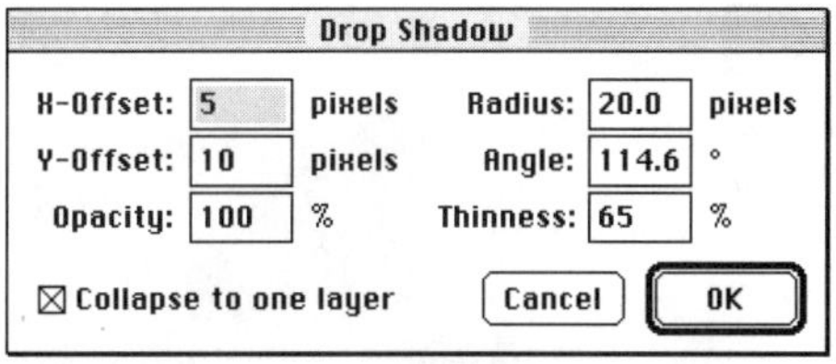

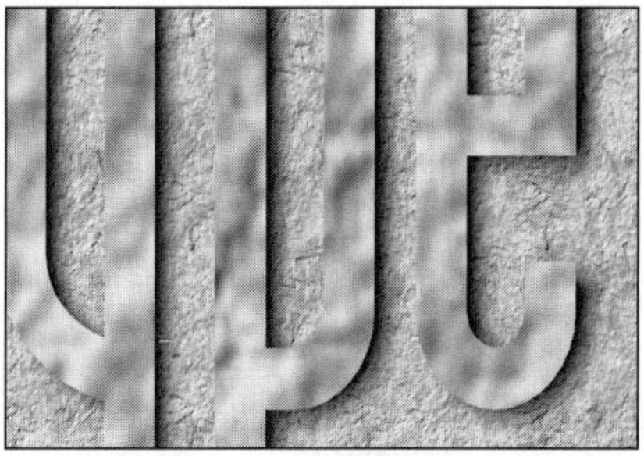

We placed text over Ray Rue's Yellow Quartz texture, turned it into a floater, filled it with the background texture using Color Overlay, enlarged it, and then applied the Create Drop Shadow command.

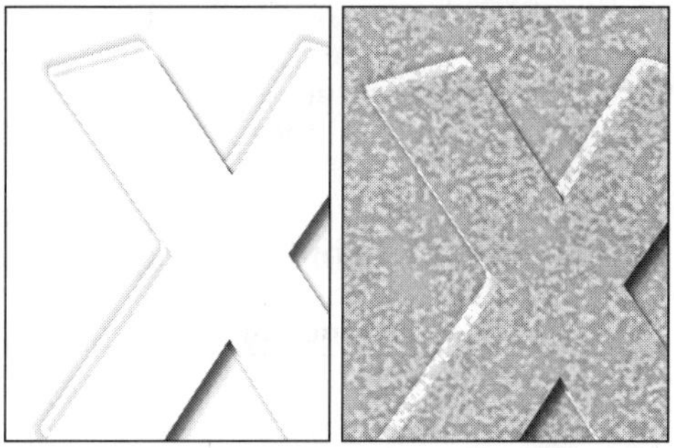

To produce this embossed effect, a drop shadow was added to a text floater and dropped. Then a second shadow was added using negative Offset numbers and dropped. A paper texture was applied via Color Overlay to the floater and then to the background. Finally, the upper left shadow's mask selection was activated and lightened via the Equalize command.

And of course you can easily hand paint your own shadows behind a floater if you don't like the uniformity of Painter's drop shadows. Try using the Airbrush.

A drop shadow can be part of the original floater or a separate floater on its own. You can't preview the Drop Shadow effect.

To add a drop shadow to a floater:

1. Click on the floater or floater group name on the Objects: F. List palette.
2. Choose Effects > Objects > Create Drop Shadow.
3. Do any of the following:

   Enter higher **Offset** values to create a greater illusion of depth. You can enter negative Offset numbers.

   Enter an **Opacity** value for the darkest part of the shadow.

   Enter a **Radius** value for the width of the shadow.

   Enter an **Angle** for the direction of the shadow. 0° is horizontal, 90° is vertical.

   Enter a **Thinness** percentage for the amount of softness on the edge of the shadow.
4. Check the **Collapse to one layer** box if you want the shadow to become part of the floater.

   Uncheck the **Collapse to one layer** box if you want the shadow to be separate from the floater. If you choose this option you'll be able to adjust the shadow's opacity, color, or position, or delete the shadow altogether. The floater and its shadow will become a floater group, which will be listed on the Objects: F. List palette as "[floater name] and Shadow."
5. Click OK or press Return.
6. *Optional:* If you unchecked the "Collapse to one layer box" when you created the drop shadow, you can adjust the shadow's opacity. Choose the Floating Selection tool, click the shadow name on the Objects: F. List palette, then move the Opacity slider on the Controls: Floating Selection palette.

The intensity of the Composite Methods effect will be affected by the current Controls: Floating Selection palette Opacity slider setting. Composite Methods won't actually alter underlying pixels until the floater is dropped.

Floating Selection tool

To combine a floater with underlying pixels:

1. Choose the Floating Selection tool.
2. Select the floater (click on the floater in the image window or click on the floater name on the Objects: F. List palette).
3. Choose from the **Composite Method** pop-up menu on the Controls: Floating Selection palette.

   Gel: Underlying pixels are tinted with the floater's color.

   Colorize: The underlying pixels' hue and saturation are replaced by the floater's hue and saturation. Underlying luminosity values are preserved.

   Reverse-Out: Underlying pixels turn into their opposite value and complementary hue.

   Shadow Map: Makes the highlight areas of the floater transparent so the background shows through. Darker areas of the floater remain, creating a shadow effect.

   Magic Combine: Floater pixels are replaced by underlying pixels, except for floater pixels that are lighter than underlying pixels.

   Pseudocolor: Translates floater and underlying luminosity values into hues on the color spectrum (darks at the Red end, lights at the Cyan end).

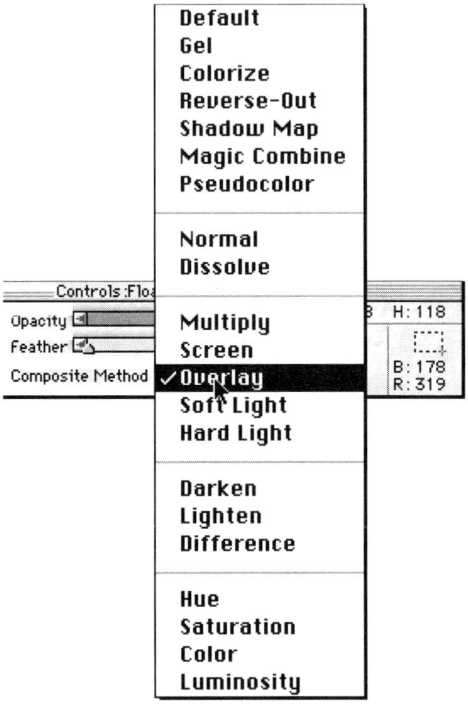

Fractal Design's method for filling type with imagery

Turn an entire photograph or painting into a floater, choose the Magic Combine Composite Method for it, deselect the floater, create type, then fill the type with Black.

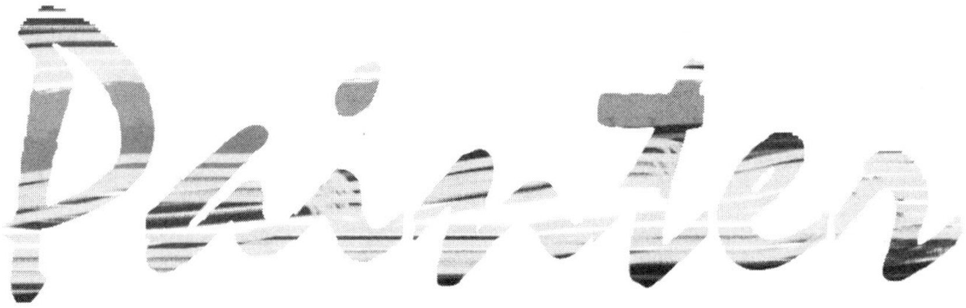

Photoshop modes on Painter's Controls: Floating Selection palette Composite Method pop-up menu (Painter 3.1):

NORMAL:

Like Painter's default Composite Method.

DISSOLVE:

Combines the floater and underlying pixels to create a stippled texture. The higher the opacity, the more solid the color.

MULTIPLY:

Floater pixels and underlying pixels combine to produce a darker color. Similar to Painter's Shadow Map.

SCREEN:

Bleaches the inverse of the floater color and the underlying color.

OVERLAY:

Multiplies (darkens) dark pixels and screens (lightens) light pixels. Preserves luminosity (light and dark) values.

SOFT LIGHT:

Floater pixels that are lighter than underlying pixels are lightened. Floater pixels that are darker than underlying pixels are darkened. Subtle light effect.

HARD LIGHT:

Floater pixels that are lighter than the underlying pixels are lightened. Floater pixels that are darker than the underlying pixels are darkened. Harsh light effect.

DARKEN:

Underlying pixels that are lighter than the floater pixels are modified; underlying pixels that are darker than floater pixels are not.

LIGHTEN:

Underlying pixels that are darker than the paint color are modified; underlying pixels that are lighter than floater pixels are not.

DIFFERENCE:

Subtracts the underlying pixel color from the floater color, or vice versa, depending on which is brighter.

HUE:

Underlying pixel's hue is replaced with floater's hue. Saturation and luminosity values aren't modified. Similar to Painter's Colorize mode.

SATURATION:

Underlying pixels' saturation is replaced with floater's saturation. Underlying hue and luminosity values aren't modified.

COLOR:

Underlying pixels' hue and saturation are replaced with floater's hue and saturation. Underlying luminosity values aren't modified.

LUMINOSITY:

Underlying pixels' luminosity values are replaced with floater's luminosity values. Underlying hue and saturation values aren't modified.

Floaters are listed on the Objects: F. List palette in front-to-back order. Follow these instructions to change the stacking position of any floater.

To move a floater frontward or backward:

Drag the name of the floater you want to restack up or down on the Objects: F. List palette **1**.

or

Click on the name of the floater you want to move on the Objects: F. List palette and choose the Floating Selection tool. Then, on the Controls: Floating Selection palette, click **Front** to make the floater the frontmost floater, or click **Back** to make it the backmost floater, or click the right arrow to move the floater forward one layer at a time, or click the left arrow to send the floater backward one layer at a time **2**.

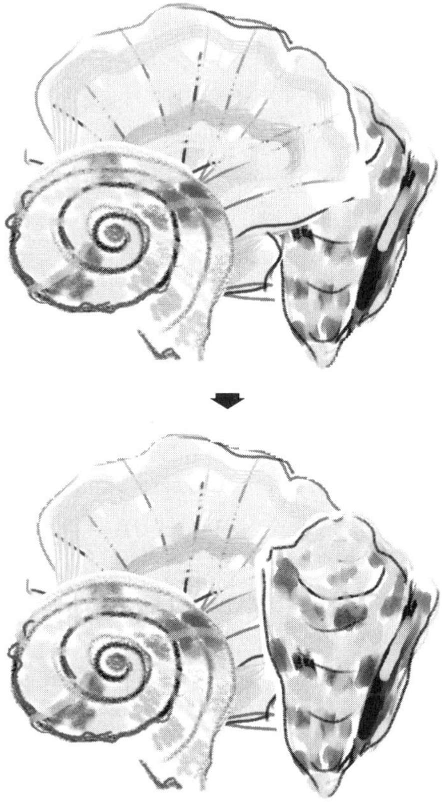

The clam shell moved to the back.

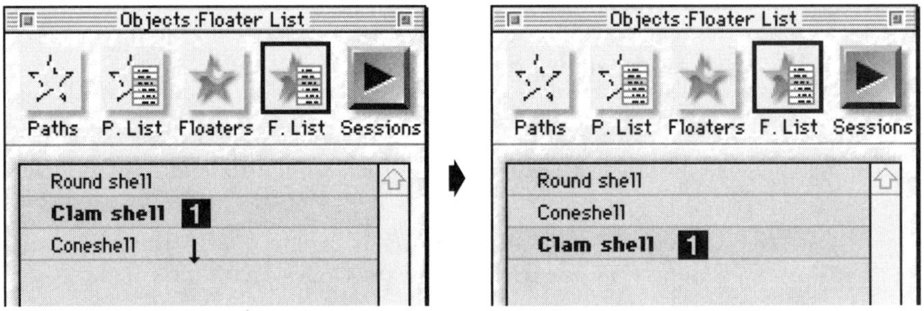

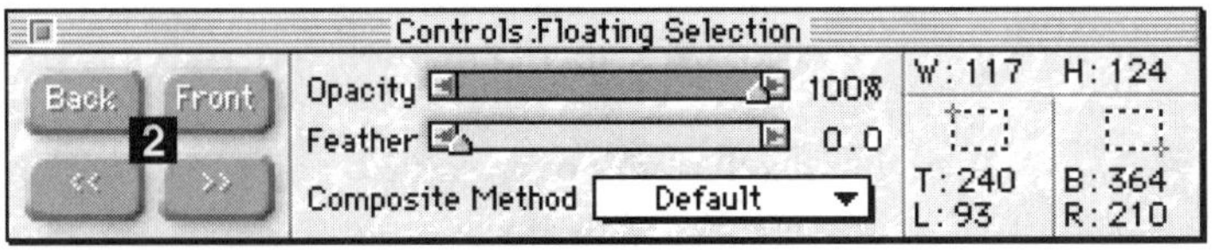

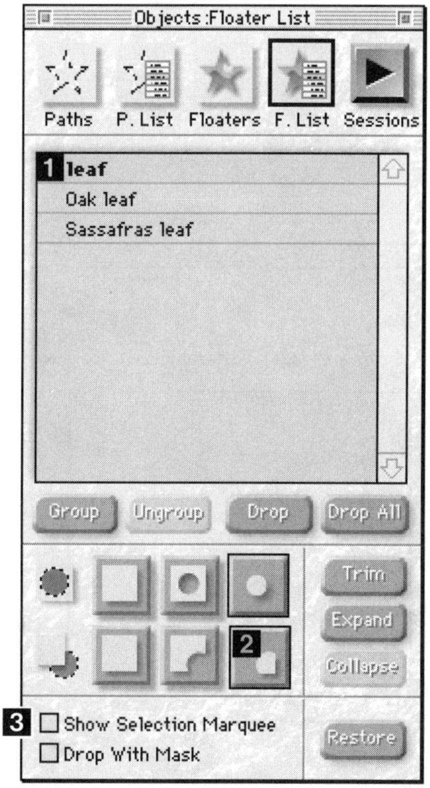

To hide a floater:

On the Objects: F. List palette, click on the name of the floater that you want to hide **1**.

and

Click the third Image Mask Visibility button on the expanded palette **2**.

and

Uncheck the Show Selection Marquee box **3**.

- To redisplay the floater, click the first Image Mask Visibility button. To redisplay the selection marquee, check the Show Selection Marquee box.
- Make sure there are no active selections on the Objects: P. List palette that may be masking the floater.

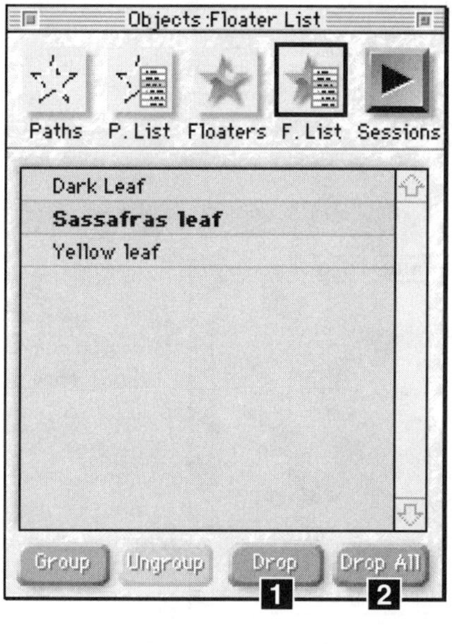

Save your document in the RIFF or Photoshop 3.0 file format to save it with floaters. Before dropping your floaters, you might want to save a copy of the original document with its floaters under another name using the Save As command and then drop the floaters into the background in the new, open document.

To drop a floater(s) into the background:

To drop one floater or one floater group, click its name on the Objects: F. List palette, then click Drop **1** or choose Edit > Drop (⌘-Shift-D).

or

Click Drop All **2** to drop all the documents' floaters at once.

Follow these instructions to save a floater's outline as a path if the floater originated from the Floaters palette. If you drop a floater that was created in the current document, its outline will be saved as a path automatically, whether the Drop with Mask box is checked or unchecked.

To drop a floater and save its outline as a path:

1. Click the name of the floater on the Objects: F. List palette that you want to drop **1**.
2. Check the Drop with Mask box **2**.
3. Click the third Floater Mask Visibility button **3**. What you see in the image window is what will drop.
4. Click Drop **4**.
5. On the Objects: P. List palette, click the third Visibility (eye) button. The mask group name will appear on the list.
6. To ensure mask groups from subsequently dropped floaters don't become part of the same mask group, convert the active Mask Group into a selection by pressing Return (the name will become blue).

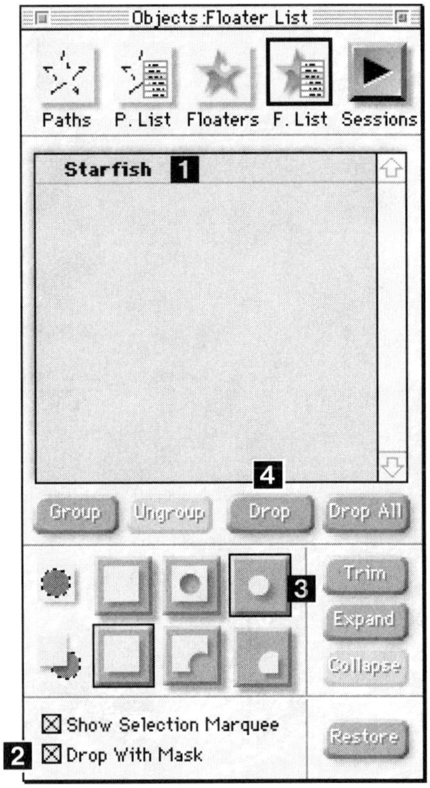

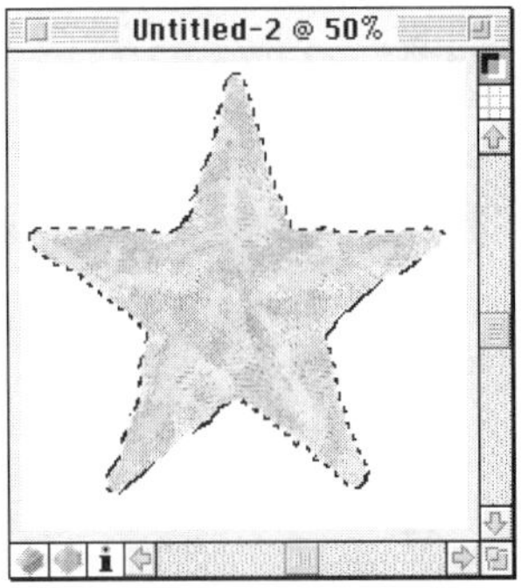

Activate the floater you want to drop.

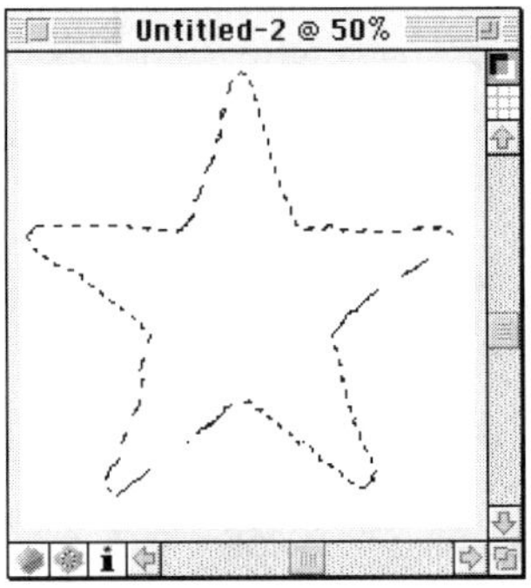

The floater mask converted into a selection path. A selection path has a black dashed-line marquee; a mask representation path has a green marquee.

The Image Hose

The Image Hose is a brush that sprays imagery. The imagery that you fill the Hose with is called the nozzle. A nozzle can be built from floaters or movie frames. To paint with the Image Hose, see the instructions on the next page.

To create an Image Hose nozzle from floaters:

1. Create a new document.
2. Move the floaters you want to put in the nozzle into the image window **2**: Drag them from the Objects: Floaters palette or copy and paste them from another document. Use the Outline Selection tool to create floaters out of non-rectangular elements.
3. Click the F. List icon on the Objects palette.
4. For any floater group, click a floater name in the group, then click Collapse.
5. Click Trim for each floater.
6. If you want to spray images in a sequence (like from small to large or from one particular image to the next), organize the floater names on the F. List from top to bottom in that order. (Choose a Sequential variant when you're ready to use the Image Hose.)
7. Hold down Shift and click on the names of the floaters you want to load into a nozzle.
8. Click Group.
9. With the group name still highlighted, choose Tools > Image Hose > Make Nozzle From Group.
10. Choose File > Save.
11. Enter a name for the nozzle.
12. Leave the Type as RIFF, open a nozzle folder, then click Save.
13. Close both image windows.

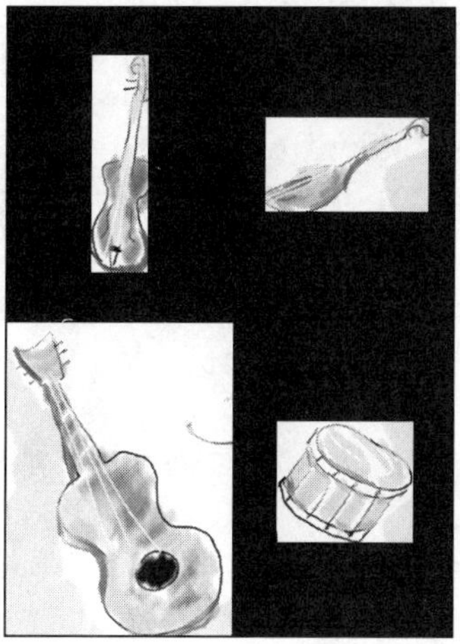

This is what an actual nozzle file looks like.

To make a nozzle from a movie

Open the movie file, choose Tools > Image Hose > Make Nozzle from Movie, choose File > Save, choose RIFF from the Type pop-up menu, open a folder in which to store the nozzle, then click Save.

To paint using the Image Hose:

1. Choose the Brush tool from the Tools palette.
2. Click the Nozzle icon on the Brush Controls palette **2**.
3. Click Load (⌘-L) **3**.
4. Locate and highlight the name of the nozzle file you want to use, then click Open (or just double-click the nozzle file name).
5. Choose the Image Hose brush from the Brushes palette.
6. Choose a variant. **Small**, **Medium**, and **Large** refer to the space between elements, not the size of the elements.

   3 Rank R-P-D stands for Randomness, Pressure, and Directionality. If you choose this variant, you can use the Brush Controls: Nozzle palette to adjust the R-P-D settings for the nozzle file.

   Random Linear: Elements are sprayed in random order where you drag.

   Random Spray: Elements are randomly placed in random order. To make the placement more random, move the Dab Location: Placement slider on the Advanced Controls: Random palette to the right.

   Sequential Linear: Elements are sprayed sequentially (1-2-3, 1-2-3) in a uniform pattern based on the top-to-bottom order of elements on the Objects: F. List palette when the nozzle was created.

   Directional: The direction in which the mouse or stylus is moved determines which elements are sprayed.
7. Click or drag on your picture.

Nozzle-load shortcut: If no nozzle is loaded and you try to paint with the Image Hose brush, you'll get a warning prompt. Click Load Nozzle, then locate and double-click the name of the nozzle you want to use.

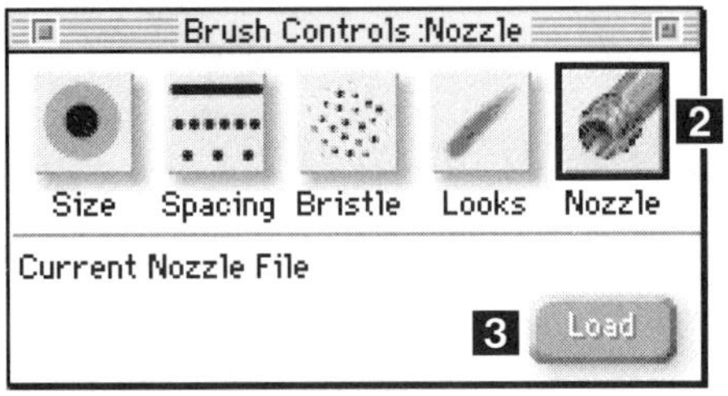

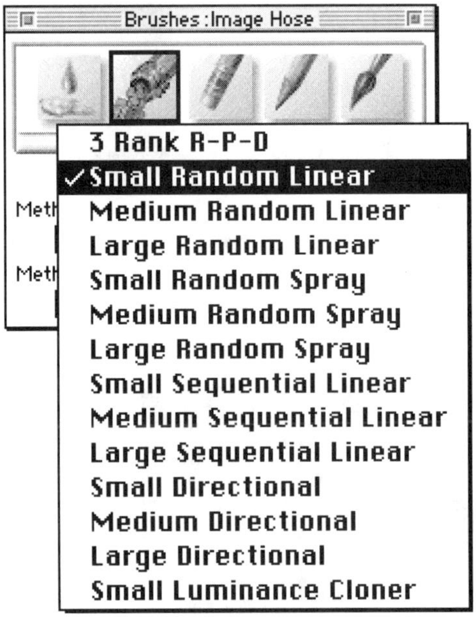

What is the Image Hose resolution?

Nozzle elements are stored at 72 ppi, but they will take on the resolution of the document they are sprayed into. The nozzle elements will change size if their resolution doesn't match the resolution of the file they are sprayed into. For example, if the nozzle resolution is lower than the document resolution, the nozzle elements will appear smaller when they're placed in the document.

Our favorite Image Hose effect: the Opacity slider on the Advanced Controls: Sliders palette pushed up to Random.

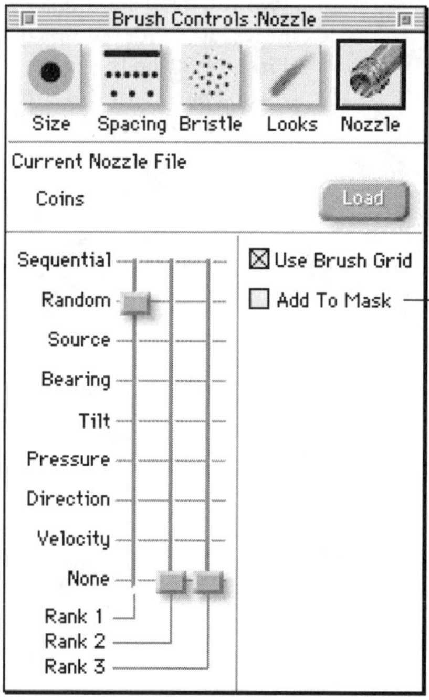

*Check the **Add to Mask** box to create a mask for the Image Hose elements so they can be selected or protected during further image editing or painting.*

To fine-tune the Image Hose:

Do any of the following:

- Adjust the **spacing** between elements using the Brush Controls: Spacing palette Spacing/Size or Min Spacing slider. Use the Brush Controls: Size palette Size slider to increase element spacing if the Spacing palette sliders are at their maximum settings. You can't change the size of the Image Hose elements themselves.
- Adjust the **opacity** using the Controls: Brush palette.
- Move the Grain slider to the left on the Controls: Brush palette to **tint the Image Hose elements with the current Secondary color.**
- To make a **Random Spray** variant spray more unpredictably, move the Brush Controls: Size palette Size slider or the Advanced Controls: Random palette Dab Location slider to the right.
- Adjust a variety of settings on the Advanced Controls: Sliders palette.
- Adjust settings on the expanded Brush Controls: **Nozzle** palette. The default nozzle settings conform to the variants. For example, for a Sequential variant, the Sequential option will be selected. Adjust these sliders to produce non-default variants. The Bearing, Tilt, and Pressure sliders don't work with a mouse. Adjust the Rank 1, Rank 2, Rank 3 sliders for the 3 Rank R-P-D variant. Check the **Use Brush Grid** box to spray elements on a horizontal/vertical grid if it was built into the nozzle file when it was created.

Artistic ideas often arise from unexpected sources. "I discovered this technique quite by accident," says Ray Rue, "when I took a carrots nozzle I had designed for a vitamin screen and put the setting on Small Directional. The result immediately suggested scales to me, and the dragon illustration soon followed."

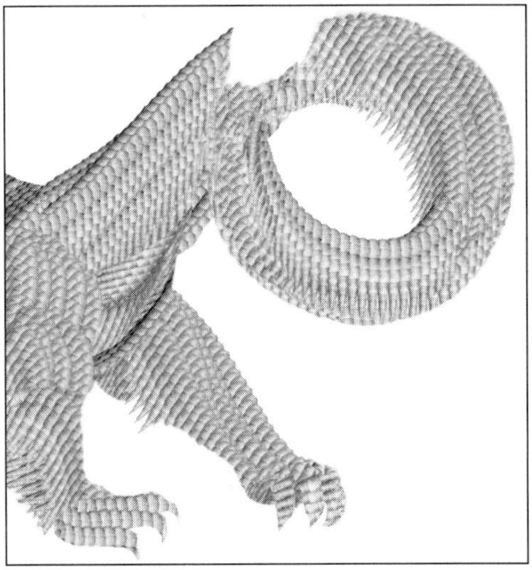

Starting to paint the dragon with the Image Hose.

The final image by Ray Rue.

Have you done something spectacular with the Image Hose? We'd like to see it! Our mailing address is listed at the bottom of page 193.

Peter Lourekas,
Figure & Shroud.

Peter Lourekas, ***Simi.***

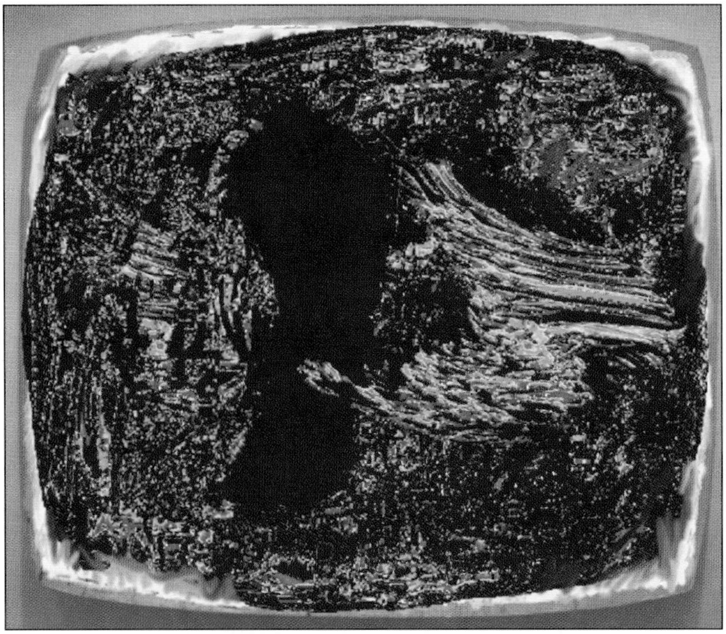

Ron Gorchov,
Clone of Herophile.

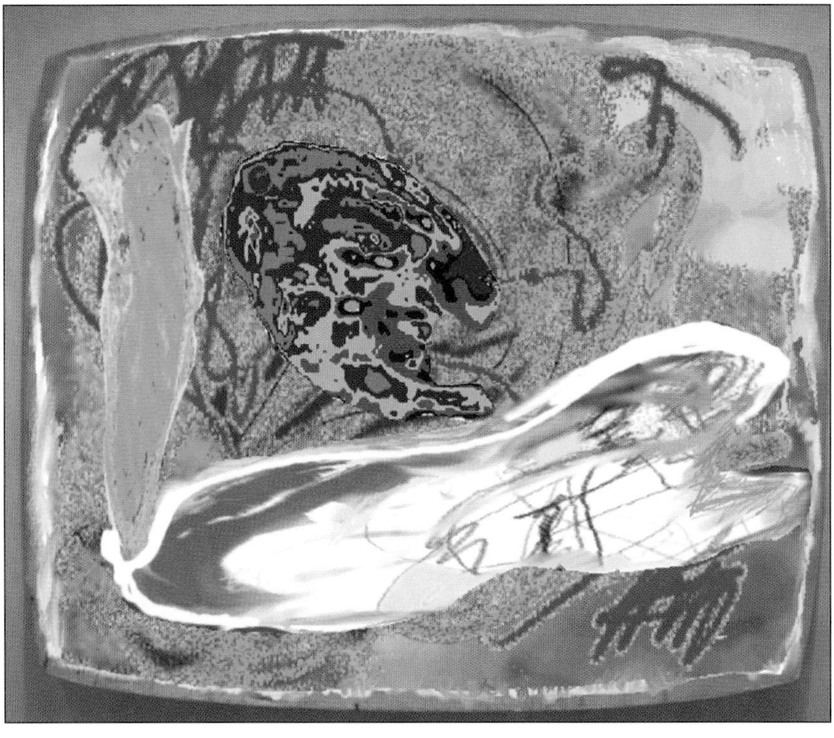

Ron Gorchov,
Low Comedy II.

Ron Gorchov, ***Knossos.***

Ron Gorchov,
Year of the Boar.

David Humphrey,
Yearbook.

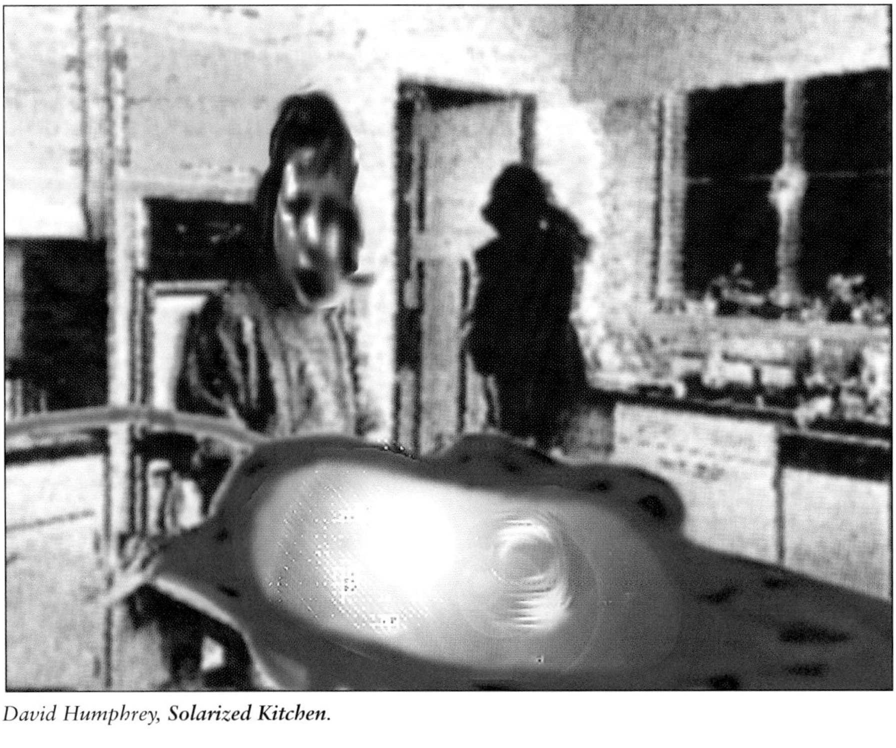

David Humphrey, ***Solarized Kitchen.***

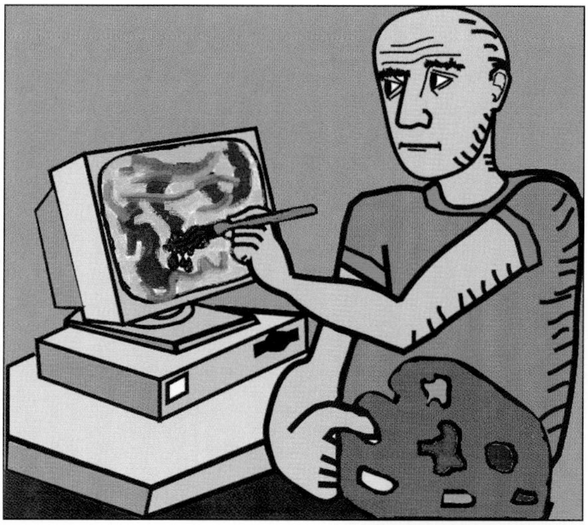

Phil Allen

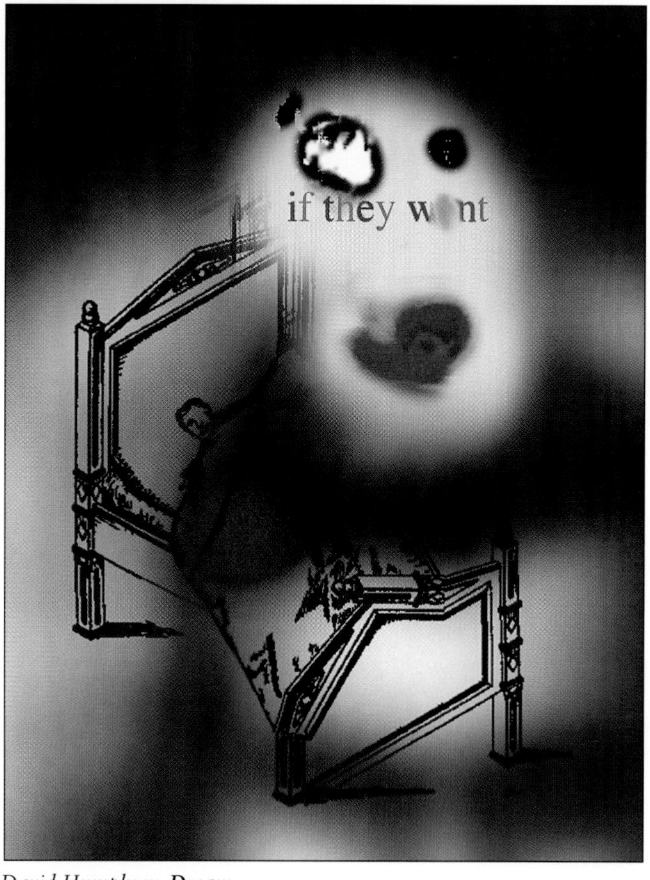

David Humphrey, ***Dream.***

David Humphrey, ***Blond Again.***

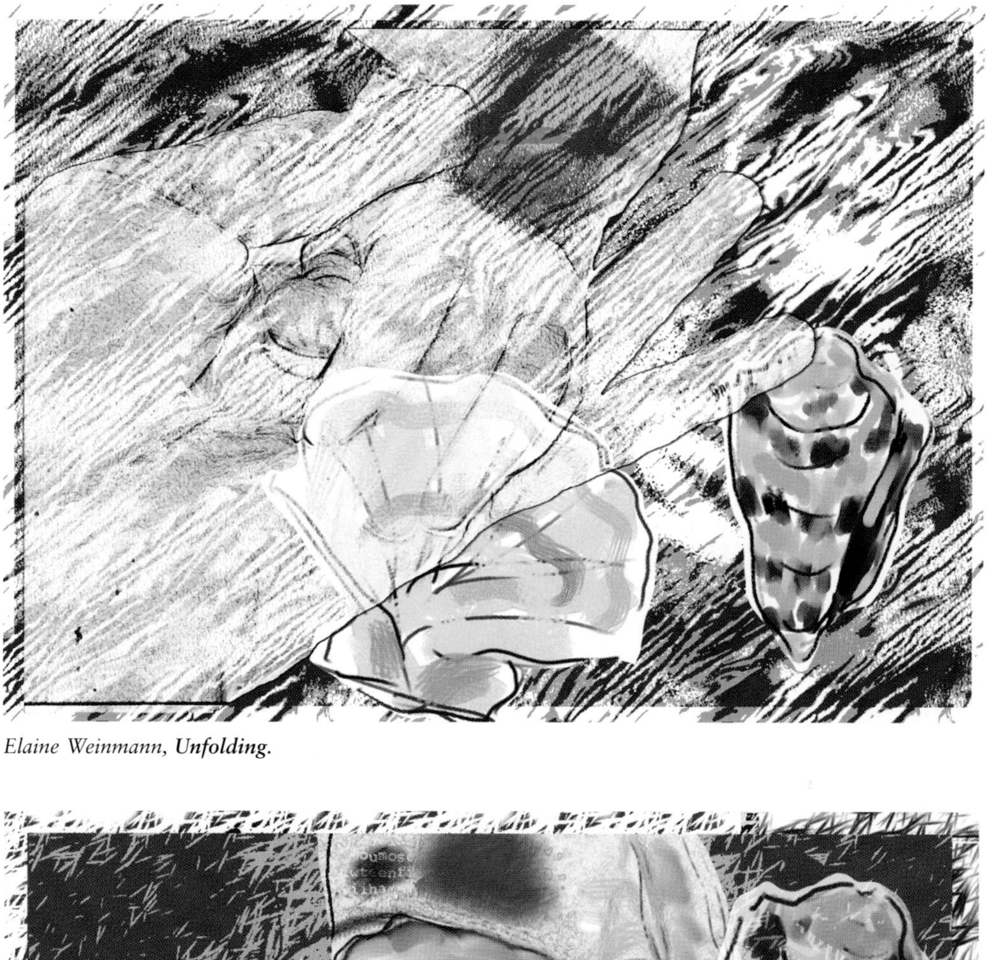

Elaine Weinmann, ***Unfolding.***

Elaine Weinmann, ***Synthesis.***

Rodney Alan Greenblat.

*Rodney Alan Greenblat, **Springing**.*

*Diane Margolin, **Self Portrait**.*

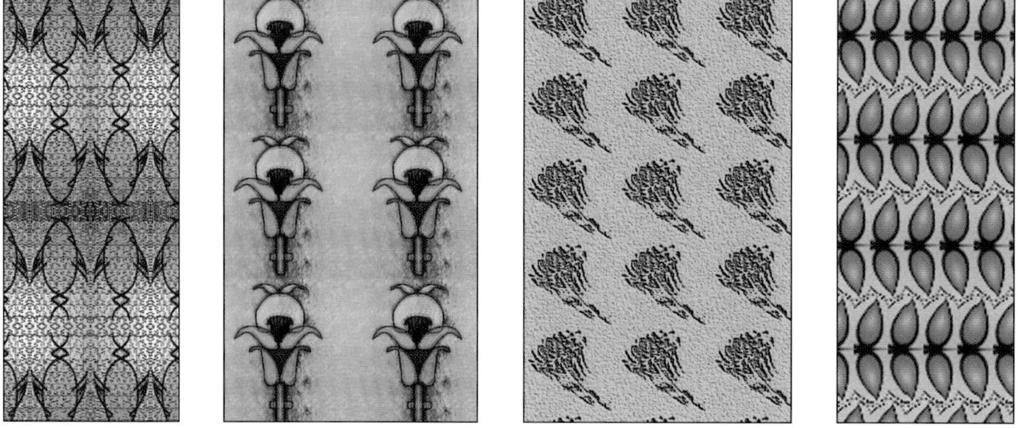

Patterns and textures by Diane Margolin.

Diane Margolin, ***Nicky and Zoe.***

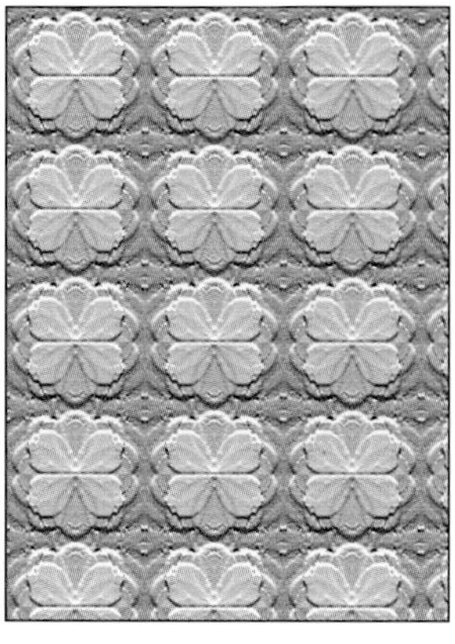

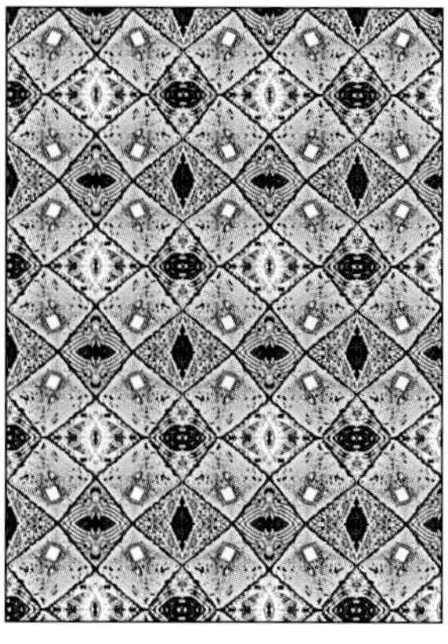

Fabric Effects, Inc.

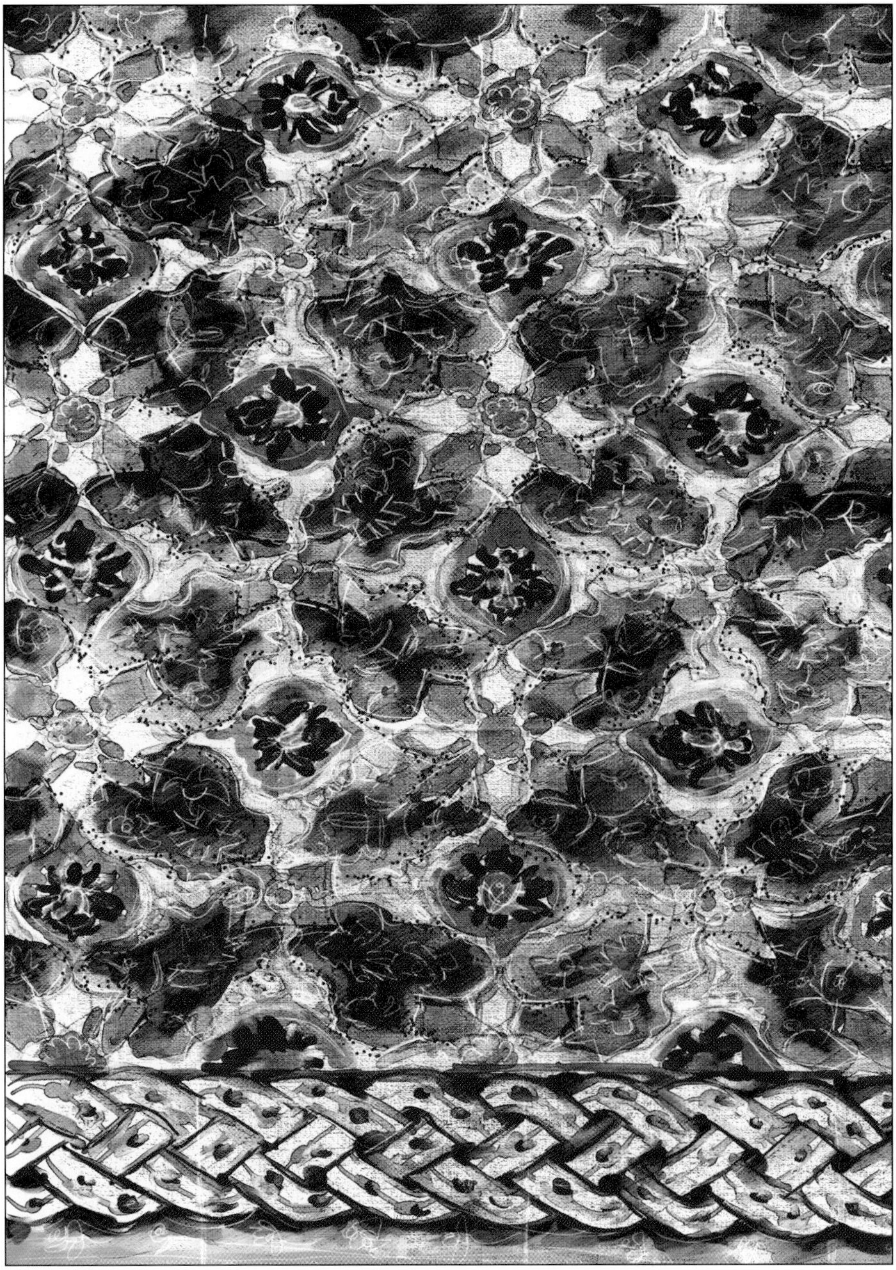

Fabric Effects, Inc.

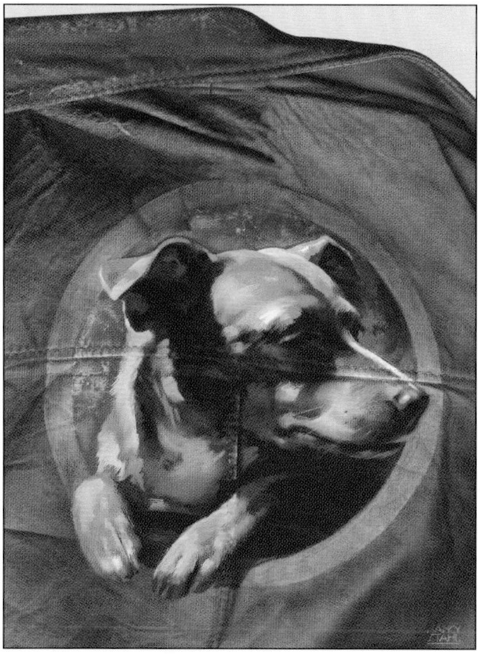

Nancy Stahl, **Jacket**.

Jaime Davidovich.

Nancy Stahl, **Island Woman**.

*Nancy Stahl, **Greenish Head**.*

Ray Rue, ***Minotaur.***

Ray Rue, ***Arc Library.***

Masks 7

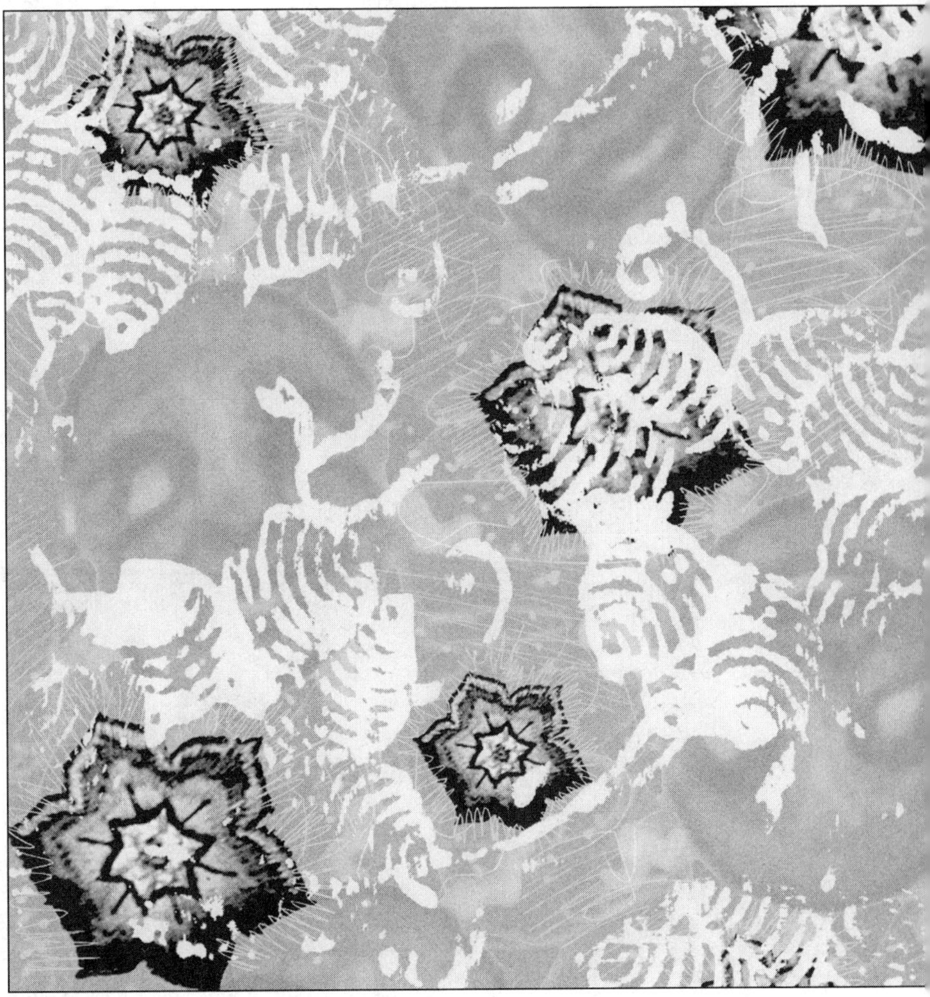

Fabric Effects, Inc.

Masks

Normally, areas that are covered with a mask are protected from editing. You can create a mask using a Masking brush variant or using any non-Masking brush at 100% opacity with the Mask method category selected. Or, using special Mask commands, you can create a mask based on a color, on a range of colors, on image luminosity values, or on a paper texture. Masks are accessed from the Objects: P. List palette. You can also display a selection path as a mask. In the image window, a mask representation path will have a green dashed marquee to distinguish it from a selection path, which has a black dashed marquee. Floater masks are discussed at the end of this chapter.

To create a mask from a selection:

1. Create a selection. Don't use the Rectangular Selection tool.
2. Click the P. List icon on the Objects palette.
3. Click the second Visibility (eye) button on the extended P. List palette. The selection now displays with color around it.
4. To limit paint strokes to outside the masked area, click the second Drawing button or choose the second Drawing icon from the lower left corner of the image window **4a**.
   or
   To limit paint strokes to inside the selection, click the third Drawing button or choose the third Drawing icon from the lower left corner of the image window **4b**.

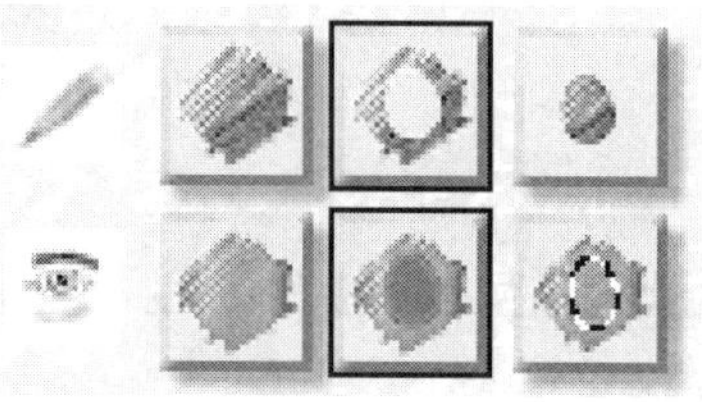

Photoshop masks ↔ Painter masks

If you open a Photoshop file in Painter 3.1 with a mask in channel #2 (grayscale) or channel #4 (RGB), the mask will become part of the Painter file, but it won't be listed on the Objects: P. List palette right away. Click the third Visibility (eye) button to make the mask name appear on the P. List palette.

If you save a Painter file with an active selection marquee in Photoshop 3.0 format (check the Save Mask Layer box in the Save As dialog box) and then open the file in Photoshop, the mask will appear in channel #4. Any Painter paths will appear on Photoshop's Paths palette.

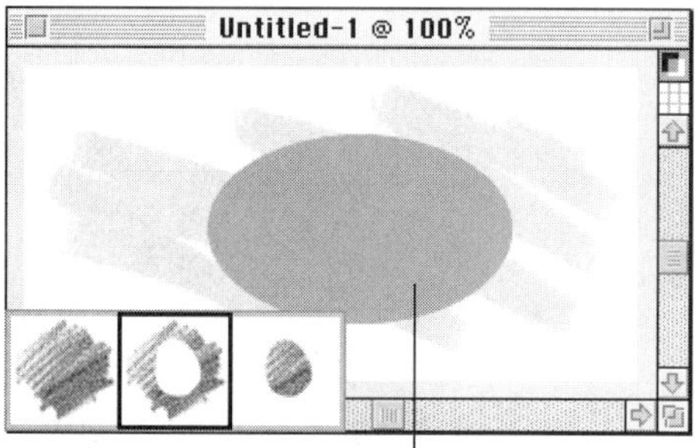

4a *With the second Drawing button selected, the mask protects the selected area.*

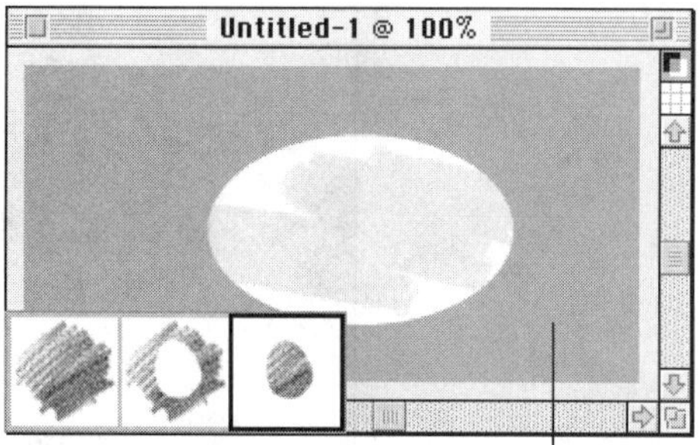

4b *With the third Drawing button selected, the mask protects the unselected area.*

The default Masking brush variants

Grainizer: Large, grainy strokes that reveal paper texture.

Big Masking Pen: Large, anti-aliased, solid circular strokes, clean swipe of mask color. Doesn't reveal paper texture.

Masking Airbrush: Soft spray, default opacity 23%.

Masking Chalk: Smaller version of Grainizer.

Masking Pen: Smaller version of Big Masking Pen.

Single Pixel Masking: Single pixel line. Choose a large display size for your picture when you work with this variant.

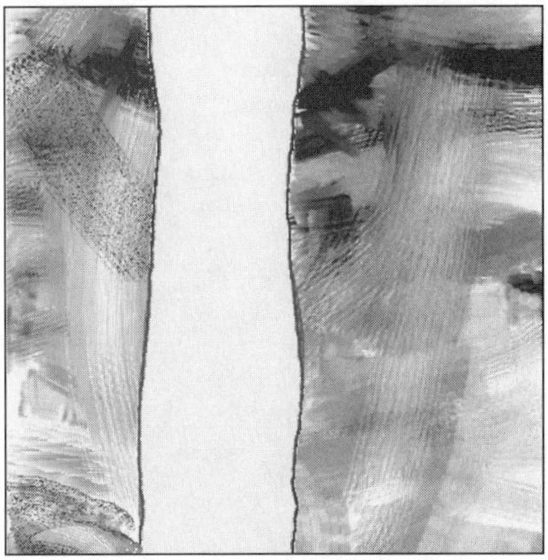

A tree trunk is masked to protect it from gestural brush strokes painted outside it.

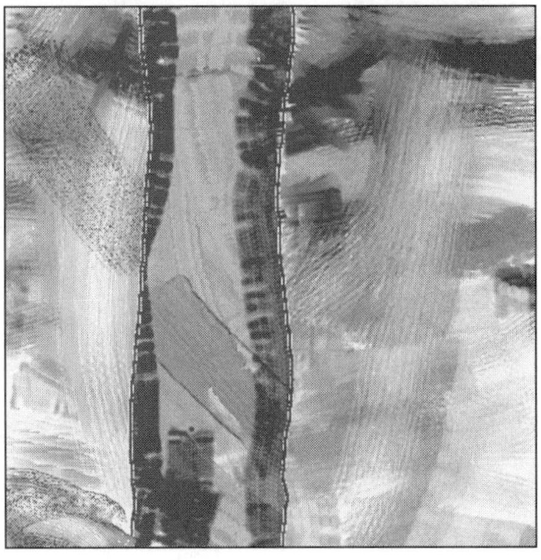

To create a mask using a brush:

1. Click the P. List icon on the Objects palette.
2. Check the Transparent Mask box at the bottom of the extended P. List palette.
3. Choose the Brush tool.
4. Choose the Masking brush and one of its variants (see box at left).
   or
   Choose a non-Masking brush, choose the Mask method category, and set the Controls: Brush palette Opacity slider to 100%.
5. Make sure the second Drawing (pencil) button and the second Visibility (eye) button are selected on the extended P. List palette.
6. Paint with Black as the Primary color to create the mask.
   or
   Paint with White as the Primary color to remove the mask.
   or
   Paint with a shade between Black and White to create a partial mask. (You can also use the Opacity slider on the Controls: Brush palette to change the mask opacity.)

   Reverse these colors if the third Drawing button is selected.

   The new mask group name will appear on the P. List palette if you click the third Visibility button on the P. List palette to make the mask into a selection, or if you choose the Oval Selection, Path Adjuster, or Outline Selection tool. The mask will have a green dashed marquee when the third Visibility (eye) button is selected. Beware: If you press Return, the mask group will become a selection (black dashed marquee), and if you press Return again, it will become a non-active path.

To reshape a selection using a masking brush:

1. Activate a mask group or a path selection using the Objects: P. List palette.
2. Choose a Masking brush variant or choose the Mask method category for any non-Masking brush.
3. Click the second Drawing button on the Objects: P. List palette.
4. Choose the Brush tool.
5. Paint with Black as the Primary color to add to the mask. (Make sure the Opacity slider on the Controls: Brush palette is at 100%.)
   or
   Paint with White as the Primary color to remove the mask.
   or
   Paint with a gray shade between Black and White to create a partial mask. (You can also use the Opacity slider on the Controls: Brush palette to change the mask opacity.)

   Reverse these colors if the third Drawing button is selected.
6. Click the third Visibility (eye) button on the Objects: P. List palette to view the mask as a selection. A new mask group will appear on the P. List palette. The original path won't be modified.
7. *Optional:* Press Return to turn the mask representation into a selection. The selection marquee will turn into a black dashed line and the selection name will be listed in blue on the P. List palette.

To modify a mask group

Click the mask group name on the P. List palette, press Return to activate the selection, then follow any of the instructions on pages 79-80.

The original image.

After applying a mask to the area around the figures and then choosing the Feather Mask command.

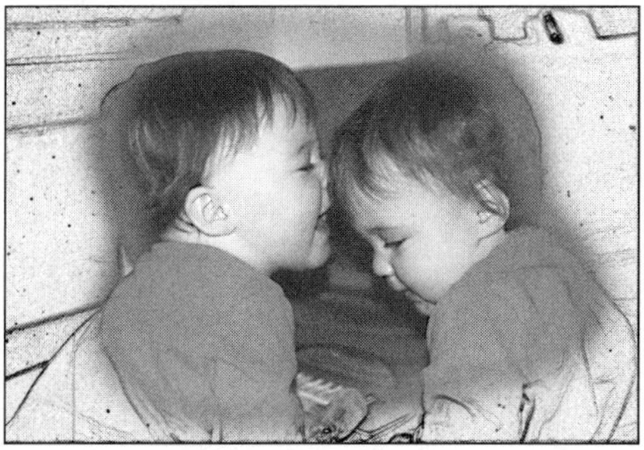

After importing the image and its mask into Photoshop and applying Photoshop's Find Edges filter.

To switch the masked and non-masked areas:

Choose Edit > Mask > Invert Mask (⌘-Shift-I).

Note: If you invert the mask and then click the third Visibility (eye) button, you will create a new Mask Group.

You can apply the Feather Mask command to a mask group after it is created, whether it is displayed as a selection or as mask color. If you subsequently apply brush strokes or Effects menu commands, you'll reveal the soft transition between the masked and unmasked areas.

Note: If you apply the Feather Mask command to an active path, the path will automatically become a mask group, but if you then convert the mask into a selection (by pressing Return or choosing Tools > Selections > Convert to Selection), the feather will disappear. To create a feather on a path selection that won't disappear, see page 78.

To feather a mask:

1. Make sure the mask is active.
2. Click the second Visibility (eye) button on the extended Objects: P. List palette to see the feather effect.
3. Choose Edit > Mask > Feather Mask.
4. Enter the number of Pixels for the Feather.
5. Click OK or press Return.

To remove a mask:

1. Click the name of the mask group that you want to remove on the Objects: P. List palette.
2. Choose Edit > Mask > Clear Mask.
   or
   Click Clear on the P. List palette.

Switch Masked/Non-Masked; Feather, Remove a Mask

Use the Auto Mask command to create a mask based on paper texture, luminosity, or the current Primary color.

To create an Auto Mask:

1. Choose Edit > Mask > Auto Mask.
2. Choose a masking method from the **Using** pop-up menu:

   Paper Grain creates a mask based on the raised and lowered parts of a texture. Click Invert to reverse the masked and non-masked areas.

   3D Brush Strokes creates a mask in a clone based on highlights and shadows of 3D modeled strokes in the source picture. The clone must have been produced using strokes, and the Apply Surface Texture command applied to it with 3D Brush Strokes chosen from the Using pop-up menu.

   Original Mask creates a mask in a clone based on the mask in the source picture. Use to copy the source image mask into the clone image's mask layer.

   Image Luminance creates a mask based on the the picture's light and dark values. Shadow areas will receive a 100% mask; highlight areas won't be masked. High contrast pictures create well defined mask areas.

   Original Luminance uses the lights and darks in the source picture to create a mask in a clone.

   Current Color masks color areas in the picture that match the current Primary color. Use the Dropper tool to grab a color from the picture first.
3. Click OK or press Return.
4. Click the second Visibility (eye) button on the extended P. List palette to display the mask color.
5. Click the second Drawing (pencil) button to paint around the mask or click the third Drawing button to paint inside the mask.

To make the Mask Group name appear on the P. List palette, click the third Visibility (eye) button.

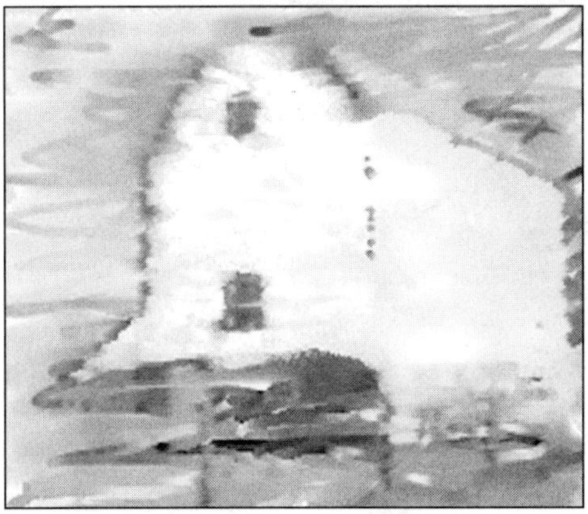

The barn is masked (the white area).

To create a mask based on a color in the picture:

1. Choose Edit > Mask > Color Mask.
2. Click on a color in the image window. The H(ue), S(aturation) and V(alue) extent sliders will calibrate automatically based on that color's HSV values.
3. Do any of the following:

   Press and drag in the preview window to preview other areas of the picture.

   Move the H Extent slider to the right to add colors close in **hue** to the chosen color or to the left to narrow the hue range.

   Move the S Extent slider to the right to add colors close in **saturation** to the chosen color or to the left to narrow the saturation range.

   Move the V Extent slider to the right to add colors close in **value** to the chosen color or to the left to create more abrupt transitions.

   Move the H, S, or V **Feather** slider to the right to soften the transition between the masked and unmasked areas.
4. Click OK or press Return.
5. Click the second Visibility button to display the mask in the image window.
6. Click the second Drawing button to make the unmasked areas editable.

   or

   Click the third Drawing button to make the masked areas editable.

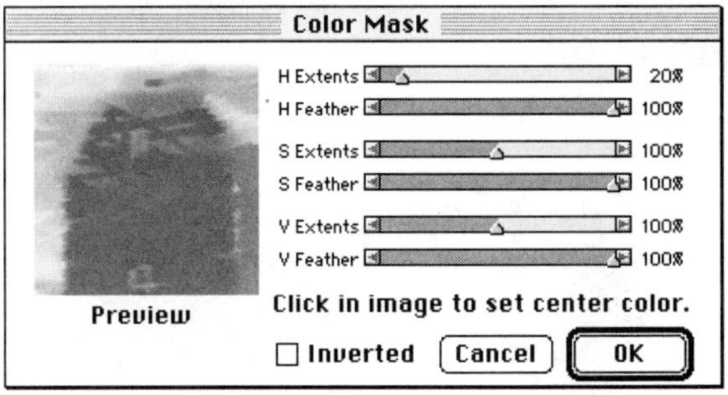

Floaters and their masks

Every floater automatically has a mask that matches its shape. You can mask part of a floater itself or disable the mask altogether. To display and edit a floater's mask, use the Floater Mask Visibility buttons (top row of buttons on the extended Objects: F. List palette). To contro! how the floater interacts with a mask or a neighboring selection, use the Image Mask Visibility buttons (bottom row of buttons).

THE FLOATER MASK VISIBILITY BUTTONS

Icon for the row of Floater Mask Visibility buttons.

The Floater Mask Visibility buttons

With the floater active, click the **Masking Disabled** (first button) to disable the floater mask. The floater's original background displays within the masked area.

***Masking Disabled** button.*

Click the **Masked Inside** (second button) to mask the floater itself. Use a Masking brush variant or use any non-Masking brush at 100% opacity with the Mask method category selected to modify the floater's mask. Paint with White as the Primary color to add to the mask and hide more of the floater. Paint with Black as the Primary color to remove parts of the mask (and reveal areas of the floater's original background or restore areas that you may have inadvertently painted out using White). If parts of the floater become exposed as you apply masking brush strokes, beware — you're actually masking parts of the floater.

***Masked Inside** button. The floater itself is masked. The background picture will show through the current masked area.*

Click the **Masked Outside** (third button) to mask the floater's background, but not the floater shape itself. This is the default setting when a floater is active. With this button selected, painting with a masking brush with White will remove parts of the floater and painting with a masking brush with Black will expose the floater's original background.

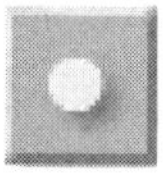

***Masked Outside** button, the default visibility mode. Only the floater is visible, not its background.*

Whatever is visible, including the mask or original background of the floater, will drop into the background if you click the Drop button.

THE FLOATER MASK VISIBILITY OPTIONS

Masking Disabled button. The floater and its original background are visible.

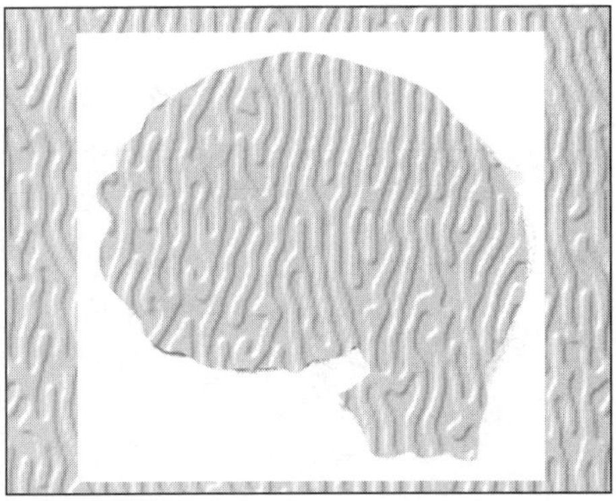

Masked Inside button. The floater is masked.

Masked Outside button. The floater's background is masked.

To unmask parts of a floater that you may have inadvertently covered:

1. Click the third Floater Mask Visibility button so you'll be able to see the floater as you draw with a masking brush.
2. Choose the Brush tool.
3. Choose a Masking brush variant.
   or
   Choose the Mask method category for any non-Masking brush.
4. Choose Black as the Primary color to remove parts of the mask and reveal parts of the floater that may have been inadvertently covered. Be careful not to paint outside the floater shape.
   or
   Choose White as the Primary color to hide parts of the floater's original background.

To remove masking brush strokes and restore the original floater mask, click Restore on the Objects: F. List palette.

Mask part of a floater with a background selection:

1. Create or activate a selection path. Don't use the Rectangular Selection tool.
2. Position a floater so it partially overlaps the selection.
3. Click the **Masked Inside** Visibility button (second button on the bottom row) of the extended Objects: F. List palette to display only parts of the floater that don't overlap the selection.

   or

   Click the **Masked Outside** Visibility button (third button on the bottom row) to display only parts of the floater that overlap the selection.

Click the Masking Disabled (first) button to have the floater be unaffected by any active background selection.

THE IMAGE MASK VISIBILITY BUTTONS

Icon for the row of Image Mask Visibility buttons.

***Masking Disabled** button. This is the default image mask visibility mode. The whole floater is visible.*

***Masked Inside** button.*

***Masked Outside** button.*

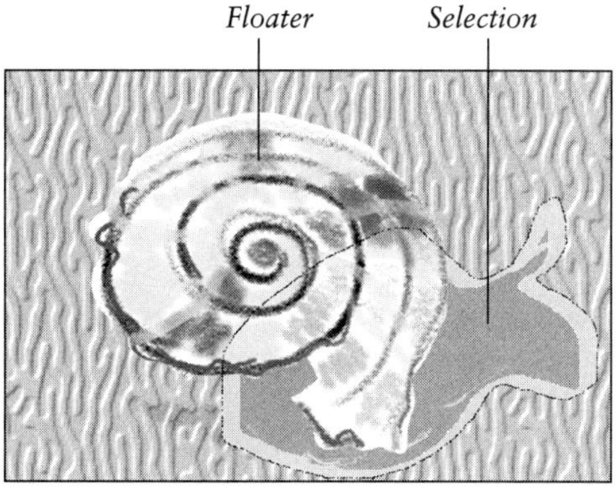

Masking Disabled.

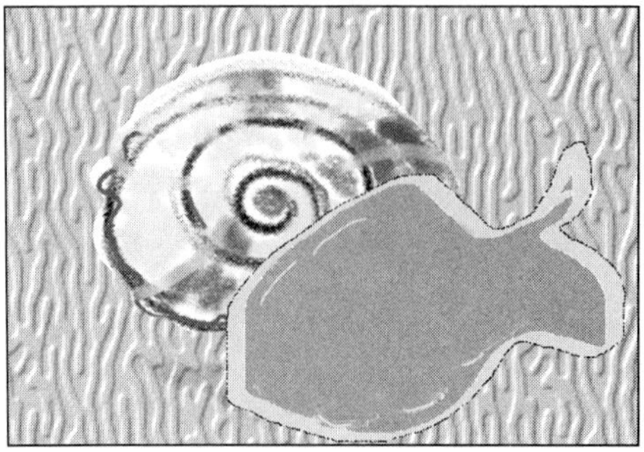

***Masked Inside.** Only parts of the floater that don't overlap the selection are visible.*

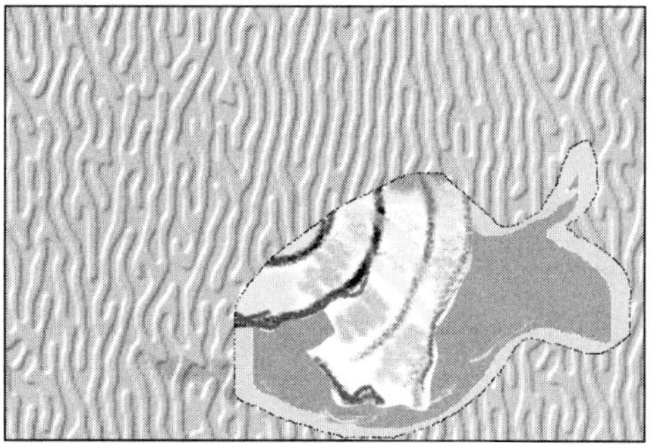

***Masked Outside.** Only parts of the floater that overlap the selection are visible.*

Fills 8

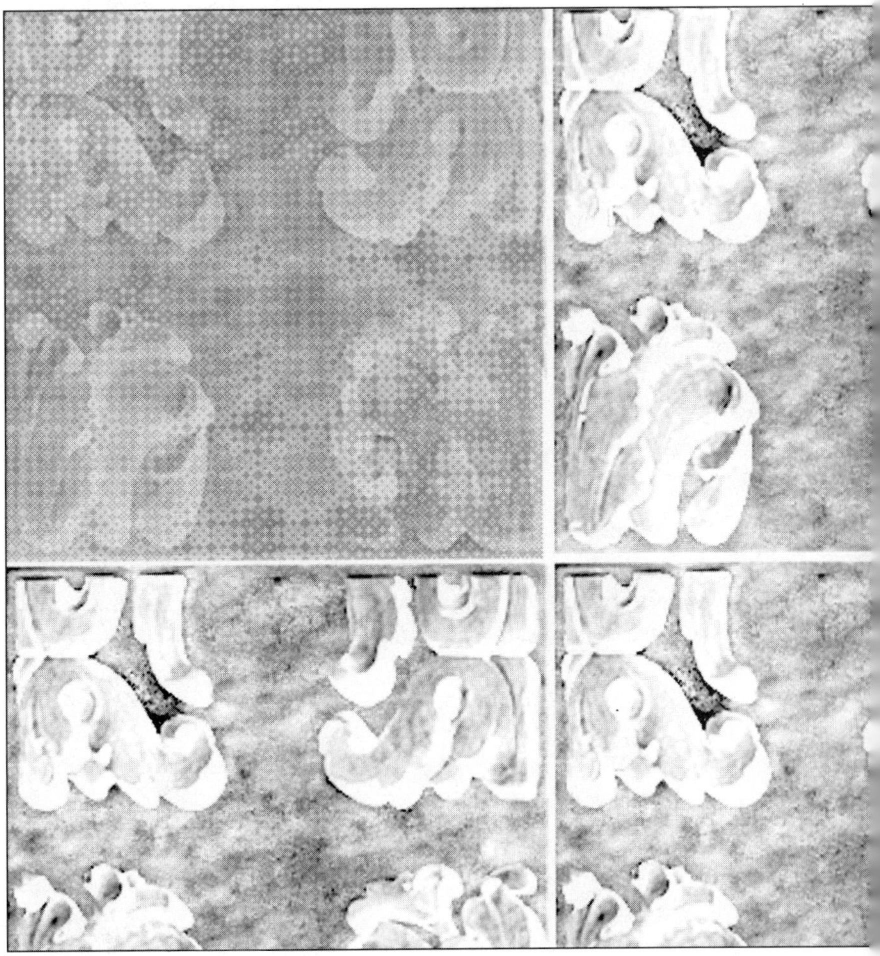

If there is no selection in your picture, the Paint Bucket will fill adjacent pixels whose color is similar to the color you click on. If the picture is blank, the Paint Bucket will fill it entirely with color.

If you click inside or outside a selection or click on an active floater with the Paint Bucket tool, color will fill only that area.

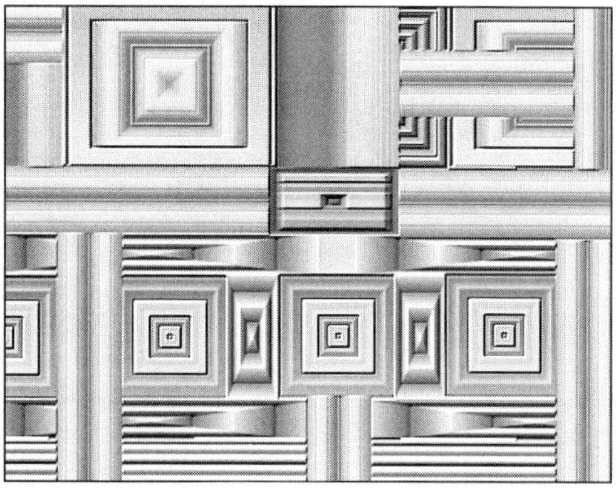

Ray Rue produced this texture using gradations.

To fill with a color, a gradation, or a weaving using the Paint Bucket tool:

1. *Optional:* Create a selection or activate a floater to restrict the fill.
2. Choose a Primary color (see page 22), a gradation (see page 113), or a weave (see page 116).
3. Choose the Paint Bucket tool.
4. Click What to Fill: Image on the Controls: Paint Bucket palette.
5. Click the correct Fill With: button (Current Color, Gradation, or Weaving), if it is not already selected.
6. Click on the area of your picture you want to fill.
   or
   Press and drag to marquee the area you want to fill.

Paint Bucket tool

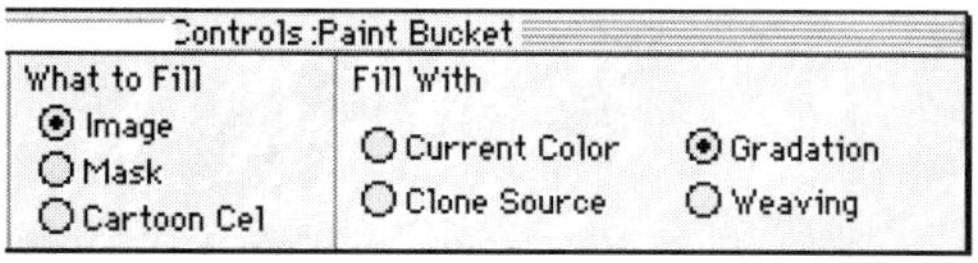

Using the Fill command, you can apply a color, gradation, or weaving at any opacity.

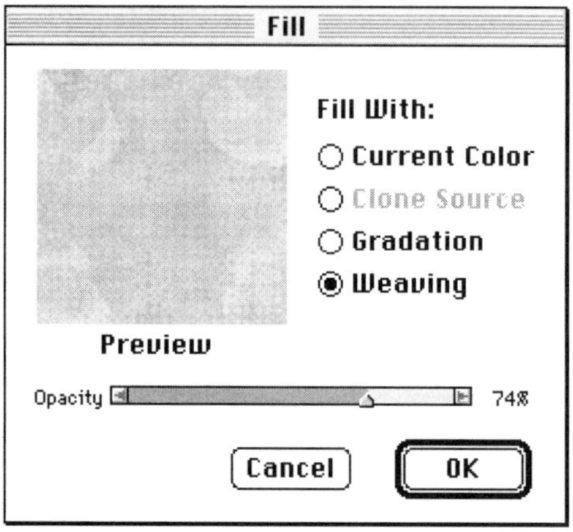

To fill with a color, a gradation, or a weaving using the Fill command:

1. *Optional:* Create a selection or activate a floater to restrict the fill.
2. Choose a Primary color (see page 22), a gradation (see page 113), or a weave (see page 116).
3. Choose Effects > Fill (⌘-F).
4. Click Current Color, Gradation, or Weaving. You can choose a different color, gradation or weave from the Art Materials palette while the dialog box is open.
5. Choose an Opacity.
6. Click OK or press Return.

Bernice Mast

Gradations

Use the Art Materials: Grads palette to choose a gradation Type (pattern) and an order for the gradation's colors. Once you choose a gradation, you can use either fill method described on page 112. To capture a gradation from a painting or create a gradation using a dialog box, follow the instructions on the next page.

To choose a gradation:

1. Click the Grads icon on the Art Materials palette **1**.
2. Click a gradation on the drawer front or in the drawer. To create a gradation that uses the current Primary and Secondary colors at the time you use the gradation as a fill, click the Two-Point icon **2**, then choose Primary and Secondary colors (front and back color rectangles on the Colors palette). Tear off the Colors palette from the main Art Materials palette to preview colors as you choose them.
3. Click a gradation Type (linear, radial, spiral, or circular) **3**.
4. Do any of the following:

   To change the **angle** of the gradation, click on the rotation ring or drag the little red ball **4a**. (To loosen or tighten a spiral gradation, hold down ⌘ while dragging the red ball).

   To change the **order** of the colors, click a different Orders button on the expanded Grads palette **4b**.

   To **save** a modified gradation, click Save on the Grads palette, enter a *new* name, then click OK. **Once a gradation is saved in a Grads palette library, it can't be edited.** If you save a Two-Point gradation, the colors in the palette icon for the gradation won't change, but the gradation will always be applied with the current Primary and Secondary colors.
5. Follow either set of instructions on page 112 to use the gradation as a fill.

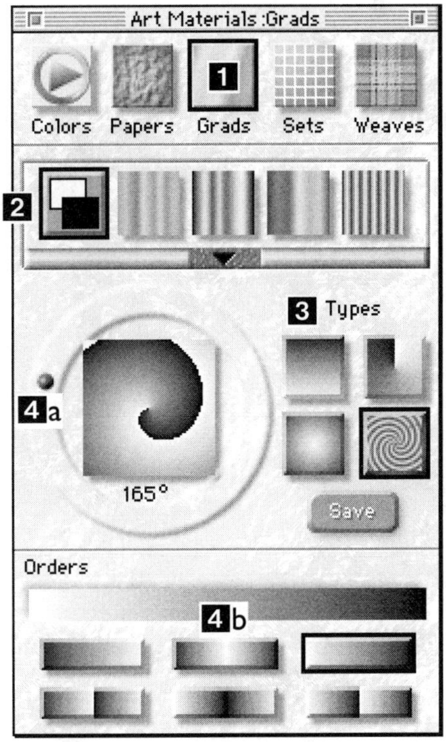

Help!

You clicked on the preview square, and now the gradation is rotating aimlessly. Click on the rotation ring to stop it.

To capture a gradation from a painting:

1. Paint a gradation.
2. Choose the Rectangular Selection tool.
3. Create a skinny horizontal or vertical selection **3**. Only the topmost or leftmost row of pixels will be used.
4. Choose Tools > Gradations > Capture Gradation.
5. Enter a name for the gradation.
6. Click OK or press Return. A thumbnail of the gradation will appear on the Grads palette drawer front **6**.

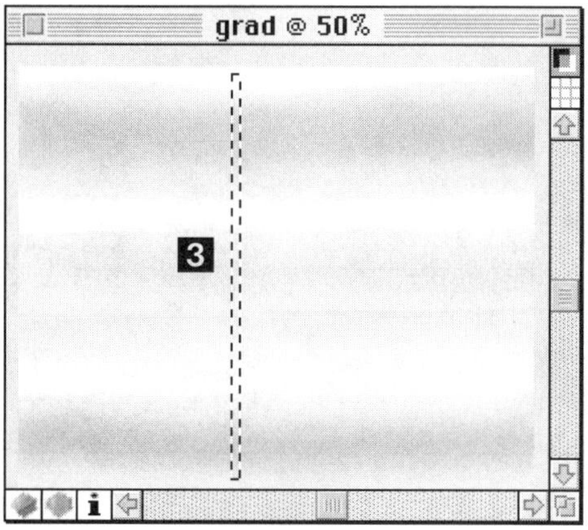

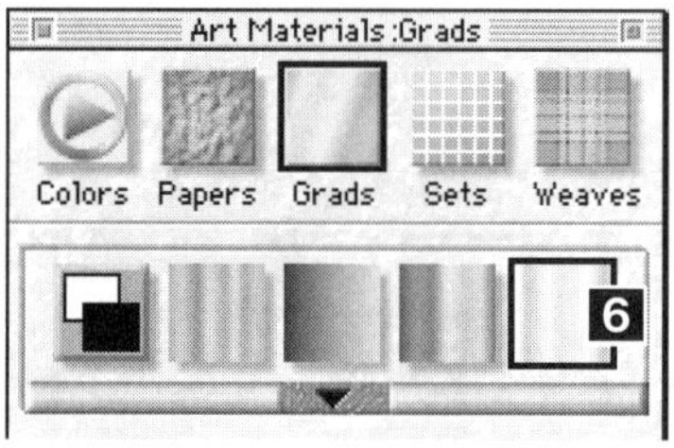

A captured gradation.

To create a gradation using a dialog box:

1. Tear off the Colors palette from the Art Materials palette so you can preview the gradation on the Grads palette and choose colors at the same time.
2. Choose Tools > Gradations > Edit Gradation.
3. Do any of the following:

   To **change a color**, click a marker under the color bar, then choose a color from the Colors palette.

   To **add a color**, choose a Primary color, then Option-click inside the bar.

   To **remove a color**, click its marker, then press Delete.

   To **change the location of a color**, drag its marker.

   To manually **adjust the blending** of colors at the currently selected marker point, check the Linear box, then move the Color Spread slider.

   To **choose a different color space** for a segment, click a square box above it. RGB is the default. Click on a marker to close the pop-up menu.
4. Click OK or press Return.
5. *Optional:* To save the gradation, click Save on the Art Materials: Grads palette, enter a name, then click OK.

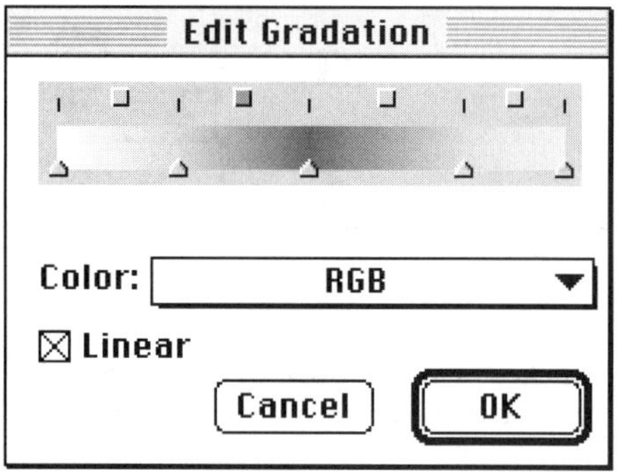

Capture a Gradation; Create a Gradation

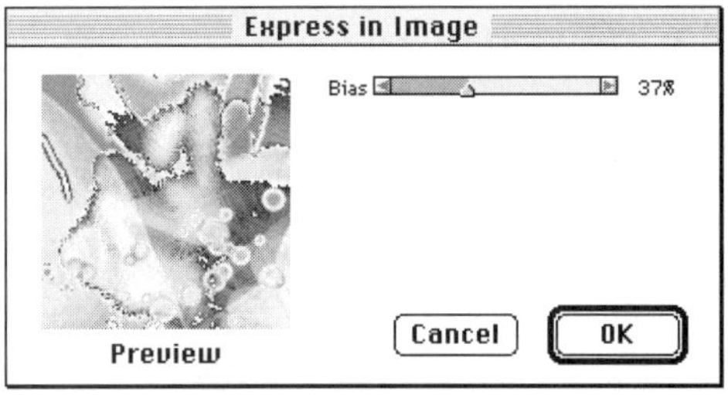

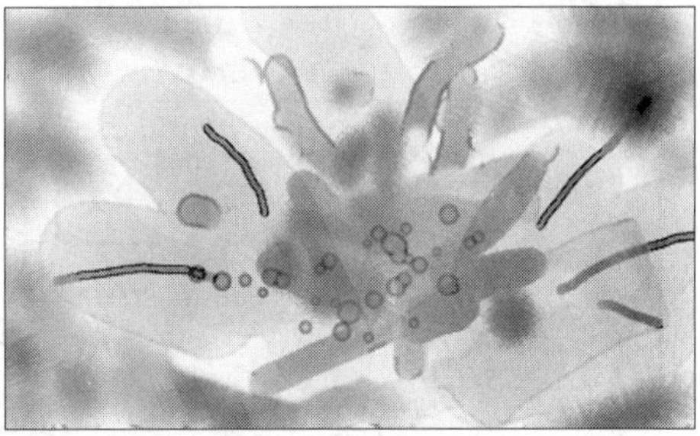

The original image.

After applying the Express in Image command using the captured gradation shown on the previous page and three different Bias percentages:

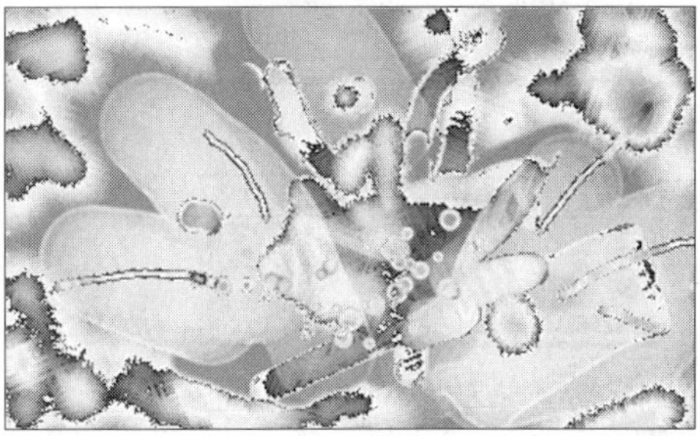

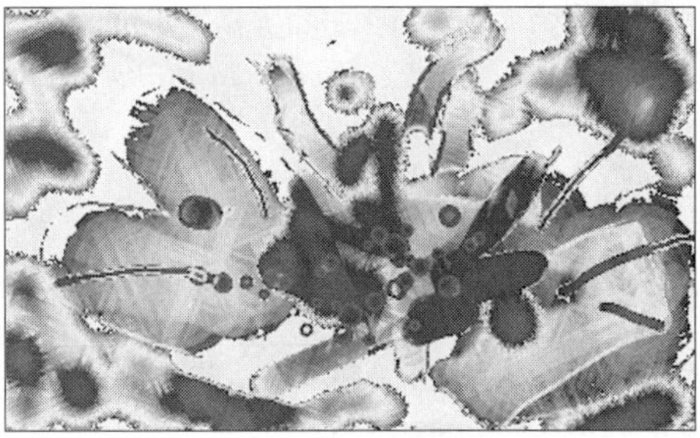

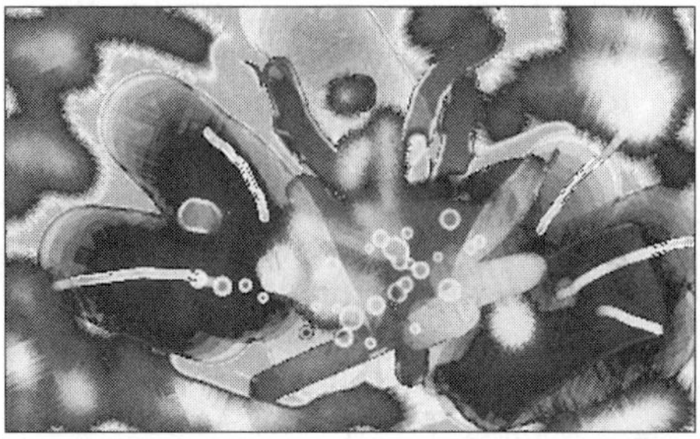

The Express in Image command replaces colors in a picture with colors that match them in luminance value in the currently selected gradation.

You can't preview different gradations with the Express in Image dialog box open — you have to close and reopen it.

To recolor a picture using a gradation:

1. *Optional:* Select part of a picture to restrict the effect to that area.
2. Click a gradation on the Art Materials: Grads palette.
3. Choose Tools > Gradations > Express in Image.
4. Move the Bias slider to cycle gradation colors through the picture's luminance values. (0% and 100% produce the same result.)
5. Click OK or press Return.

If you want to try out a different gradation, first choose Edit > Undo (⌘-Z). Try clicking a different Order button on the expanded Grads palette (the bottommost buttons), and then reapply the Express in Image command.

To create or edit a gradation library, see the instructions on pages 15 and 16.

Weaves

You can choose a preset weave pattern from the Weaves palette or you can customize a weave pattern and save it. Once you select a weave, use the Paint Bucket tool or the Fill command to apply it to a selected area.

To choose or modify a weave:

1. Click the Weaves icon on the Art Materials palette [1].
2. Click a weave pattern on the drawer front or in the drawer [2]. To display a different weave library, click Library in the Weaves palette drawer, locate and highlight the Weaves library you want to open, then click Open.
3. If you're happy with the weave design, follow either set of fill instructions on page 112.

   or

   To modify the weave design before using it as a fill, follow the remaining steps.
4. Close the drawer on the Weaves palette and expand the palette.
5. Do any of the following:

   Move the **Horizontal** and/or **Vertical Scale** sliders [5]a or click the left or right Scale arrow to adjust the width or height, respectively, of the whole pattern. Each increment increases or reduces the scale by 100%.

   To change the thickness of the threads (not the spaces between them) for a three-dimensional pattern, adjust the Scale, then move the Horizontal and/or Vertical **Thickness** sliders or click the left or right arrow.

   Click the **Fiber Type** button [5]b to switch between the two-dimensional and three-dimensional versions of the pattern. (You'll need to make Scale and Thickness adjustments to preview a 3-D Fiber Type.)

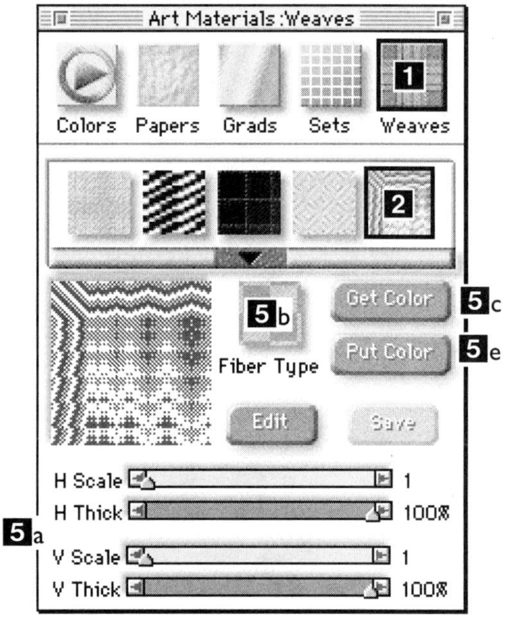

The original color set for Painter's Satin Diamonds weave.

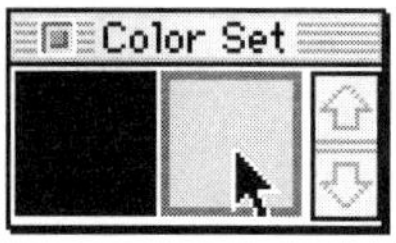

[5]d *Hold down Option and click a color to replace it with the currently selected Primary color.*

To see the Glass Distortion command applied to a weave, see page 149.

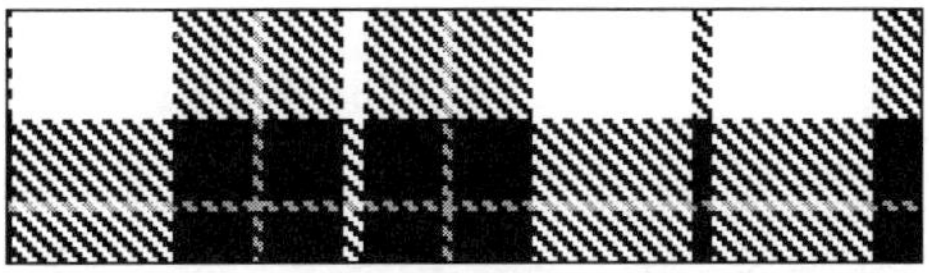

Painter's original Scottish Tartan Brodie B&W.

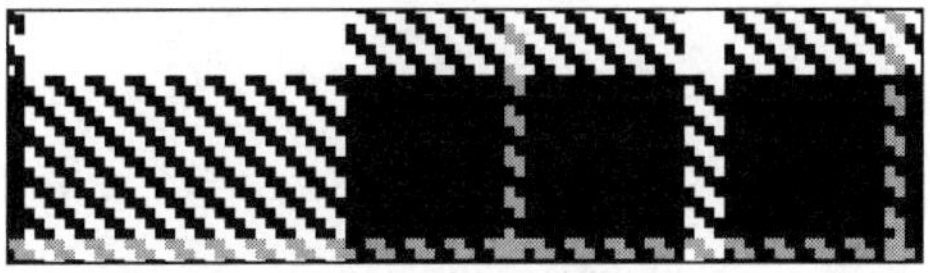

Same weave, Horizontal and Vertical Scale enlarged to 2 (a 100% increase).

To **recolor** the weave, click Get Color **5c**. The Color Set palette for the weave will open. Choose a Primary color from the Art Materials: Colors palette, then hold down Option and click the swatch on the Color Set palette that you want to replace **5d**. Click Put Color on the Weaves palette **5e**. Repeat for any other colors you want to change.

6. *Optional:* To save the weave in the currently open weaves library, click Save, enter a new name for the pattern, then click OK. An icon for the modified weave will appear on the Weaves palette. (If you don't enter a new name, the modified weave will replace the original.)
7. Follow either set of instructions on page 112 to use the weave as a fill. If you use the Fill command, you can choose an opacity for the weave.

To create or edit a weaves library, see the instructions on pages 15-16.

To design for loom weaving, see the instructions in Painter Technical Note #4 on the Painter 3 Extras CD. You'll use the Edit Weaving dialog box, opened by clicking Edit on the Art Materials: Weaves palette.

Ray Rue

Ray Rue is a self-taught artist who creates interactive multimedia art for Arc Studios International using Painter's brushes, Image Hose, lighting effects, and various plug-ins, like Kai's Power Tools and Paint Alchemy. He creates his own trompe-l'oeil wood, metal, and stone textures that he incorporates into his images. Rue is also an illustrator, published poet and non-fiction author, muralist, actor, director, stage designer, and Elvis impersonator. We're not kidding.

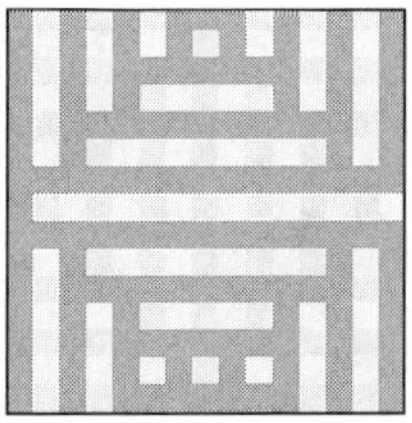

To create an inlaid wood texture (right), Ray Rue filled rectangles in Painter's Shadow Op Art weave (above) with his own light or dark wood texture.

Rue's parquet texture.

Patterns

Are you a textile or wallpaper designer? You'll love the Define Pattern command. As you paint over one edge of your document, the pattern repeats at the opposite edge, creating a perfect wrap-around effect.

The Capture Pattern command automatically sets up a source/clone relationship, the source being the captured pattern. You can use a captured pattern as a fill in any document, including the source document.

Once a file has been saved as a pattern, it can be opened again and reused as a pattern.

To create a wraparound pattern:

1. Create a new document, and enlarge the image window so you'll be able to draw on and off the edge of the image.
2. Choose Tools > Patterns > Define Pattern.
3. Choose the Brush tool.
4. Draw with any brush. The Image Hose works beautifully.
5. *Optional:* To use the new pattern as a fill, follow the steps on the next page.

To recolor the pattern, move the Hue slider in the Effects > Tonal Control > Adjust Colors dialog box.

To reposition the pattern tiling, hold down Shift and Space bar and drag in the image window. (If the Grabber tool happens to be selected, just hold down Shift.)

To see how the wraparound effect works, draw from the inside the "live" picture area to far outside it, or vice versa.

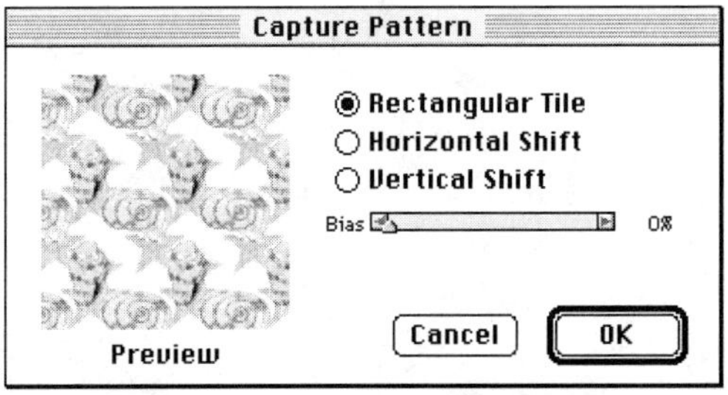

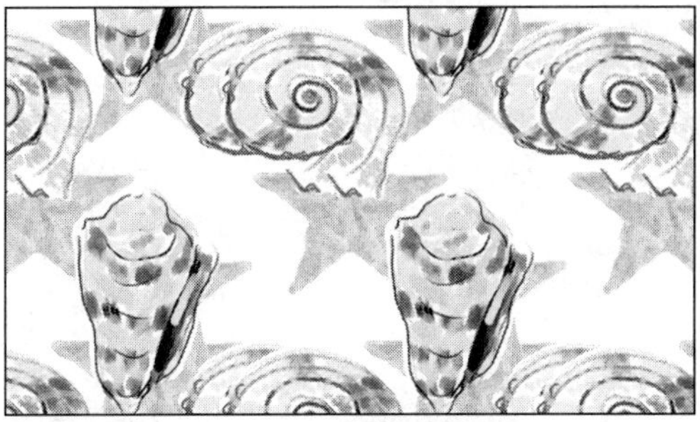

The original pattern shape.

The "batik" effect.

To create a batik effect

Follow steps 1-6 at right , then choose Black as the Primary color, choose the Paint Bucket tool, click What to Fill: Mask and Fill with: Clone Source, and click in the new image window. Then choose a different Primary color and the Brush tool, click the second Drawing button and the first Visiblity button on the Objects: P. List palette, and paint with a non-Masking brush.

If for some unknown reason you get an error message when you try to use the Paint Bucket, click What to Fill: Image, click on the image, choose Edit > Undo, then use the Paint Bucket again, Mask and Clone Source options.

To capture a pattern from a picture:

1. Open or create a picture to use as a pattern tile. You can use a wrap-around pattern (previous page).
2. To use the whole picture as a pattern tile, choose Edit > Select All (⌘-A).
   or
   To use part of a picture as a pattern tile, use the Rectangular Selection tool to create a selection (hold down Control if you want to create a square selection).
3. Choose Tools > Patterns > Capture Pattern.
4. Choose Rectangular Tile, Horizontal Shift, or Vertical Shift. If you choose either Shift option, you can then move the Bias slider to stagger the tiles.
5. Click OK. A new clone image window will open.
6. Open or create a larger document to fill with the pattern. Be sure to leave the source document open so you can clone the pattern from it.
7. *To fill using the Paint Bucket:*
   Choose the Paint Bucket tool, click the What to Fill: Image button on the Controls: Paint Bucket palette to fill the entire image and click the Fill With: Clone Source button to fill the image with the clone source, then click in the image window.
   or
   To fill using the Fill command:
   (To restrict the pattern to a selection, create an active selection.) Choose Edit > Fill, click Pattern, choose an Opacity percentage, then click OK.
   or
   To paint the pattern in strokes:
   Choose the Brush tool, choose any Cloners brush variant or choose a non-cloning brush and the Cloning method category, then paint on the picture.

Capture Pattern

Since most Painter strokes are anti-aliased, a normal fill technique might leave small white gaps between the fill and the line work. The cartoon cel fill method prevents this problem. Before you can use the cartoon cel fill method, though, you must create a mask to protect your line work. The Auto Mask command is perfect to use for this step.

If you use the Lock out color method (next page) without using the cartoon cel fill method, areas may fill incompletely, leaving tiny white dots.

To fill using the cartoon cel method:

1. Choose the Brush tool.
2. Choose the Scratchboard Tool variant of the Pen brush or any other hard-edged, non-anti-aliased brush.
3. Choose Black as the Primary color.
4. Draw **closed** line work shapes. **If there is a break in a line work shape, the fill color will leak outside it.**
5. Choose Edit > Mask > Auto Mask.
6. Choose Image Luminance from the Using pop-up menu.
7. Click OK or press Return. A mask is now protecting the black line work.
8. Choose a Primary color from the Art Materials: Colors palette or the Color Set palette.
9. Choose the Paint Bucket tool.
10. On the Controls: Paint Bucket palette, click What to Fill: Cartoon Cel.
and
Click Fill With: Current Color.
11. Click inside any of the line work shapes in the image window.

Click the second Visibility (eye) button on the Objects: P. List palette to display the mask. Don't click the third Visibility button — you'll lose the mask. The mask will save with the file, even if you remove or erase its matching line work shape. Click Clear on the Objects: P. List palette if you want to remove the mask.

Circles indicate areas to be filled.

Phil Allen

***Paint Bucket** tool*

The areas are filled.

Cartoon Cel Fill Method

If you plan to use the Auto Mask feature to protect your line work, black lines will be fully protected, but non-black lines will be only partially protected because Image Luminance determines the level of masking (full for black to none for white). Use the following method in conjunction with the cartoon cel fill method (instructions on the previous page) to protect (lock out) non-black line work or any solid color areas.

Dropper tool

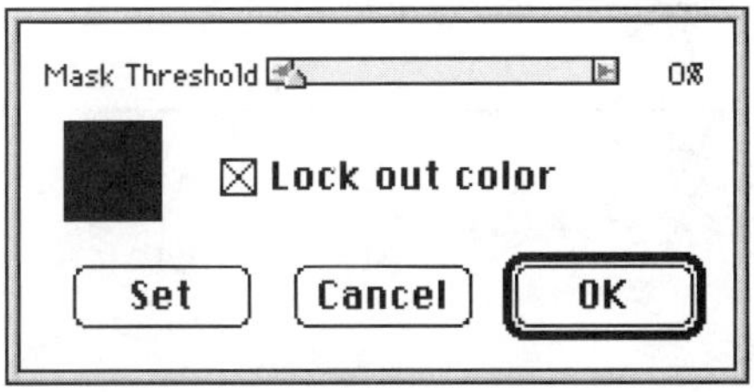

To lock out a color:

1. Choose the Dropper tool (D), then click on the color in the picture that you want to protect.
2. Double-click the Paint Bucket tool.
3. Click Set to place the current Primary color in the color preview square. The "Lock out color" box will become checked automatically.
4. If the color you want to protect isn't Black, move the Mask Threshold slider to about 15 percentage points above the Lock out color's Value (V) percentage reading on the Colors palette. Readjust this slider to a higher percentage later if the whole image fills in.
5. Click OK or press Return.
6. Follow the cartoon cel fill instructions on the previous page.

To change the Lock out color, choose another Primary color, then click Set.

To turn off the Lock out color feature, double-click the Paint Bucket tool and uncheck the "Lock out color" box.

Importing line art from Illustrator

Save the file in Illustrator 5 format in Illustrator. In Painter, create or open a file, then choose Tools > Selections > Open EPS as Selection. Closed Illustrator paths will become selections in Painter. Open paths will remain as Bézier paths and will not become selections. Both types of paths will be listed on the Objects: P. List palette.

An alternate route via Photoshop:

Open the Illustrator file in Photoshop and save it in the Photoshop 2.5 or 3.0 format. Open the file in Painter 3.1, then choose Edit > Mask > Auto Mask. Choose the Image Luminance option, then click OK. Your black line work will now have a protective mask. Use the cartoon cel fill method or any paintbrush to apply color.

Open line work shapes can be filled using the cartoon cel method if the gaps are first closed using a mask.

To protect open line work for filling:

1. If your image does not contain line work, choose the Brush tool, choose the Scratchboard Tool variant of the Pen brush, choose Black as the Primary color, then paint your line work shapes.
2. Choose Edit > Mask > Auto Mask.
3. Choose Image Luminance from the Using pop-up menu.
4. Click OK or press Return. A mask is now protecting the black line work.
5. Choose the Mask method category for the current brush.
6. Click the second Visibility button on the extended Objects: P. List palette (bottom row).
7. Use Black as the Primary color and draw on the line work shapes to close the gaps. (Use White if you need to remove the mask.)
8. Click the first Visibility button on the Objects: P. List palette to hide the mask.
9. Follow the instructions on page 120 to fill using the cartoon cel method.

If you have filled an area with color, don't use the Auto Mask command again — the filled areas will be partially masked. If you want to redo the mask, click the third Visibility button on the Objects: P. List palette, click Clear, choose Black as the Primary color, then choose Edit > Mask > Auto Mask (Using: Current Color).

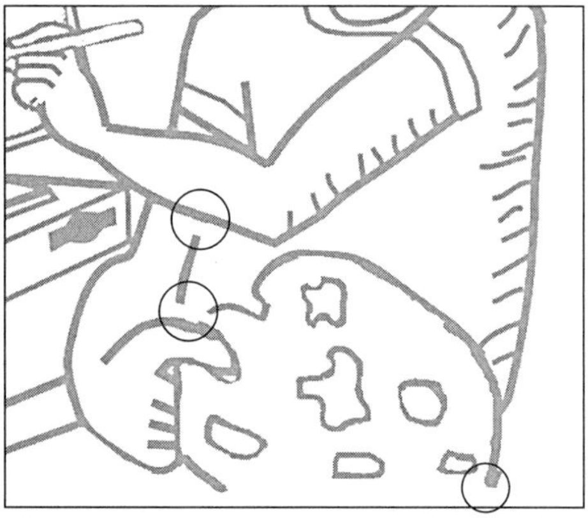

Phil Allen (detail)

The black lines are now protected by a mask after applying the Auto Mask command using Image Luminance, but the open shapes need to be closed before they can be filled.

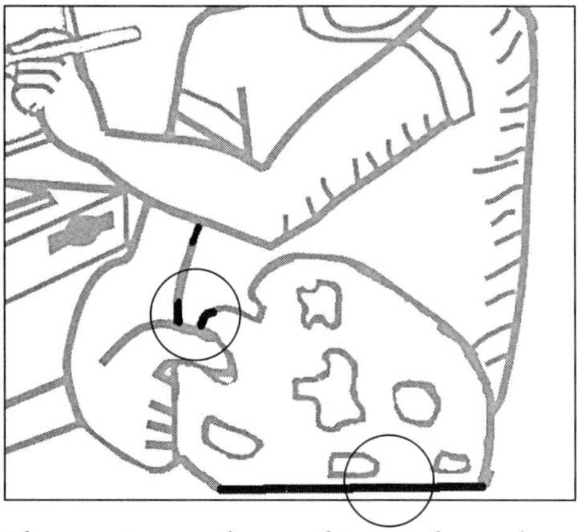

The same image after touching up the mask. Dark gray is used here only to make our point clear — normally you won't be able to differentiate between the Auto Mask and the painted mask.

An alternate method

Create the line work as closed shapes first, follow steps 2 through 4 at left, choose the Eraser method category for your brush, then erase where you want the shape to be open — the eraser won't remove your original line work mask.

Cloning 9

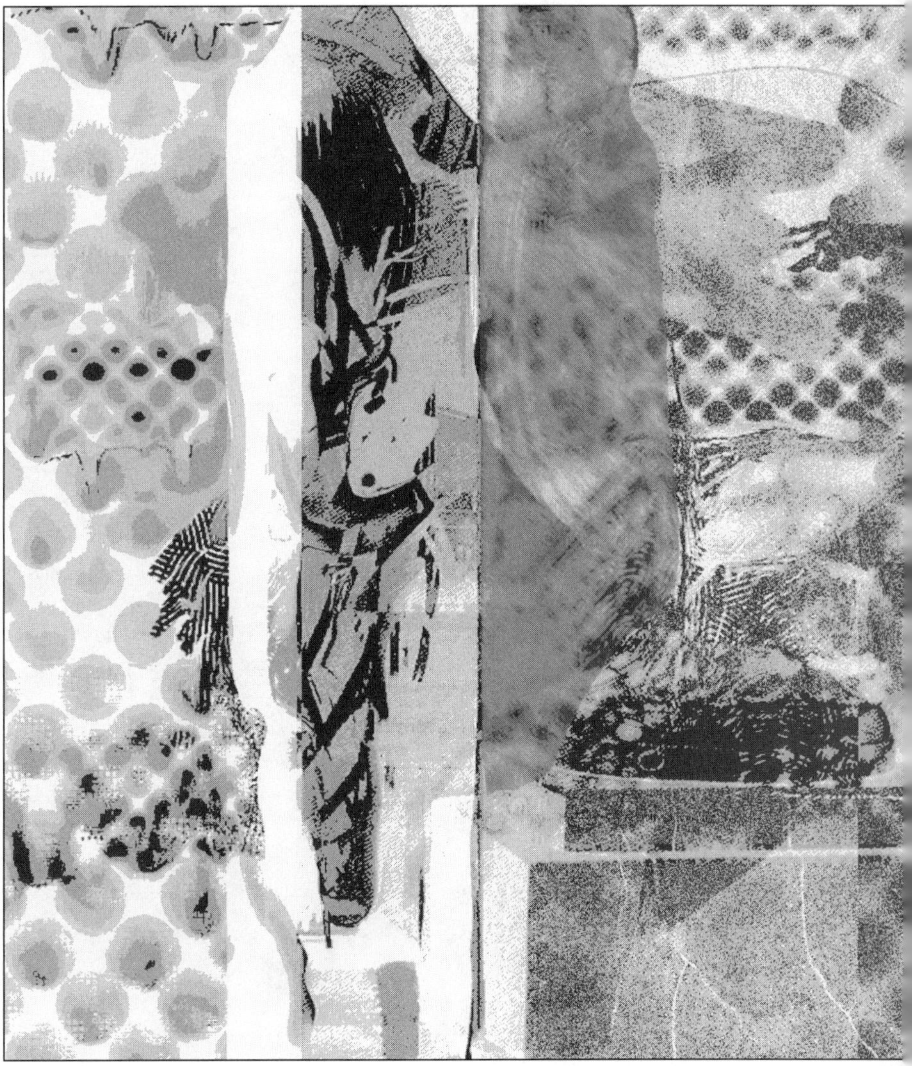

Peter Lourekas (detail).

Cloning

Use the Clone command to recreate an entire document exactly as the original. Or use a Cloners brush variant to clone all or part of the source image in its original colors, stroke by stroke, in different media — as a pencil sketch, an oil painting, or a watercolor, for example. When you use a Cloners brush variant, you determine stroke direction, number of strokes, opacity, and graininess. Another reason to clone a document is so that if you modify the clone, you'll have the option to use the Straight Cloners variant like an eraser to restore areas from the source image.

Other cloning features include the Tracing command, which you can turn on to trace over a ghosted version of the clone, the Auto Clone command, which does the brush stroking for you, and the Auto Van Gogh command, which automatically recreates an image in quasi-Van Gogh style.

To clone a whole picture exactly:

1. Open the picture you want to clone (the source document).
2. Choose File > Clone. The cloned image will appear in a new image window.

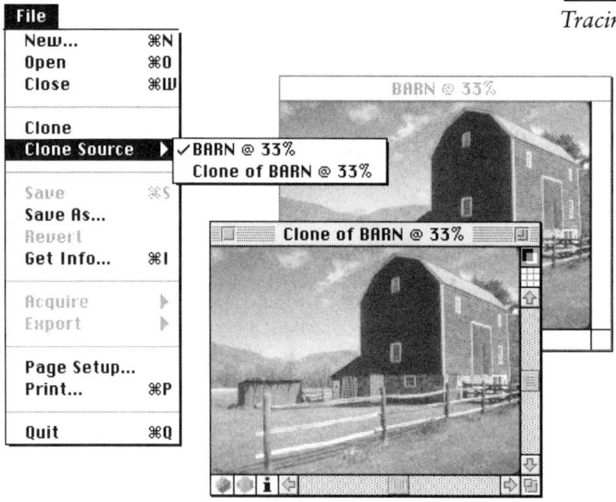

To trace a picture's contours

Clone the image (File > Clone). With the clone image active, choose Edit > Select All (⌘-A) and press Delete. Turn on Tracing Paper (Canvas menu), then draw using a fine point brush, like the Sharp Pencil variant of the Pencils brush or the Fine Point variant of the Pens brush (Cover or Buildup method category).

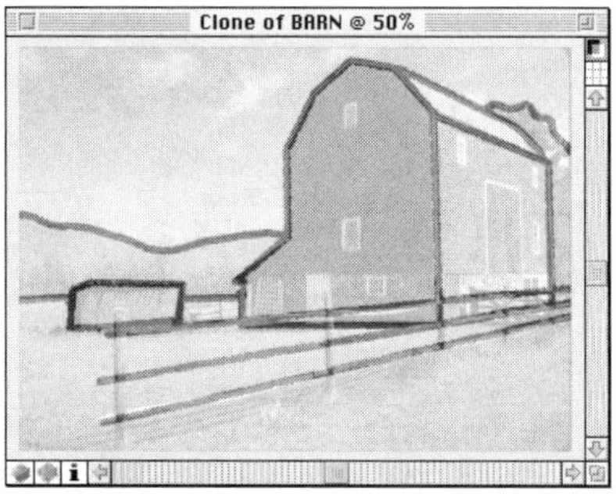

Tracing contours, Tracing Paper turned on.

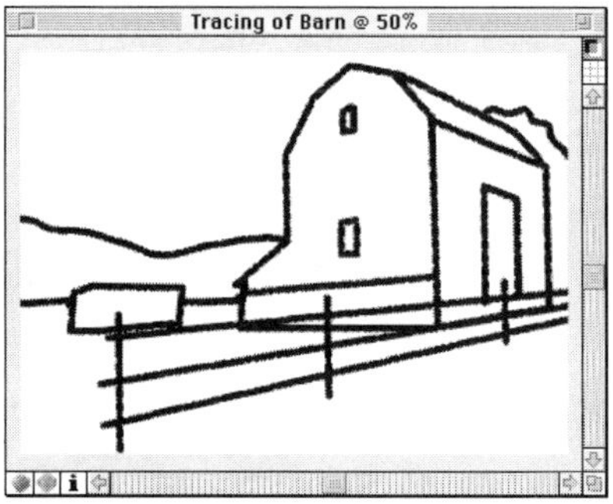

Tracing Paper turned off.

Cloning tips

- **If you close the source or the clone document, the source/clone link will be broken. To reestablish the source/clone link, open both documents, click in the clone image window, then choose the source document name from the Clone Source submenu under the File menu.**
- **To clone from a second source document, open it and choose its name from the Clone Source submenu under the File menu.**
- **To clone more randomly, move the Clone Location sliders and check the Random Clone Source box on the Advanced Controls: Random palette (see page 64). To add random color, raise the Color Variability setting (Colors palette).**
- **To restore part of the source document in the clone, use the Straight Cloner variant. To restore the entire source image, choose Edit > Select All, press Delete, then click on the image with the Paint Bucket tool (What to Fill: Image and Fill with: Clone Source options selected).**

To clone manually using brush strokes:

1. Open the document you want to clone (the source document).
2. Choose File > Clone.
3. *Optional:* With the clone image active, choose Edit > Select All, then press Delete if you don't want to paint on the existing image.
4. Choose the Brush tool.
5. Choose a Cloners brush variant.
   or
   Choose a non-Cloners brush and check the Use Clone Color box on the expanded Art Materials: Colors palette. Don't choose the Cloning method category.
6. *Optional:* Turn on Tracing Paper to display a light, non-editable version of the image behind your paint strokes. Click the Tracing Paper icon in the upper right corner of the clone image window or choose Canvas > Tracing Paper (⌘-T).

   Note: For Tracing Paper to work, the source and clone documents must have the same dimensions and resolution, as in these instructions.
7. *Optional:* To establish a custom source point for cloning, activate the source image window, then hold down Control and click on the area of the source image that you want to clone.
8. Draw in the clone image window. Try drawing short brush strokes at first. If you turned on Tracing Paper, turn it off occasionally to monitor your progress. (Just choose the command again or click the icon.)

Choose a different method category or subcategory for the Cloners brush. If you find the Buildup method category causes strokes to darken too quickly, choose the Cover method category instead. Choose a Grainy method subcategory to reveal the current paper texture under your strokes.

Clone Manually

To clone from a specific source point in the same or another image:

1. Choose a Cloners variant or choose the Cloning method category for a non-Cloners brush.
2. Hold down Control and click on the area you want to clone.
3. Draw brush strokes in the same or another image window where you want the cloned imagery to appear.

To produce this illustration for a CD cover, Johanna Gillman cloned a photograph of a woman behind a guitar figure.

Nadine Markova

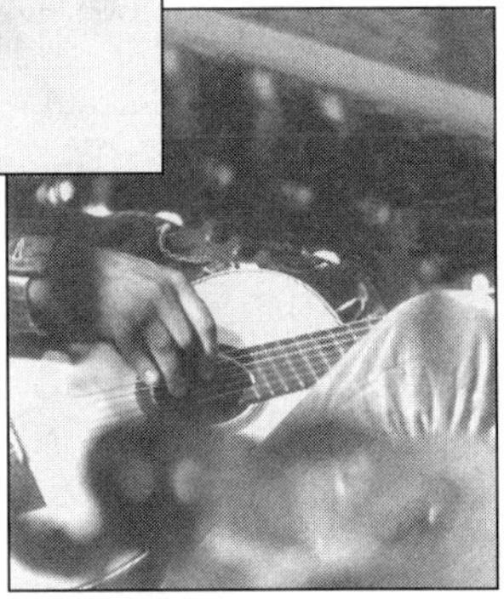

An example of Straight cloning from one document to another.

The Cloners brush variants

There are two main Cloners brush variant types — Single Cloners and Multi or Rake Cloners — and of course they produce different kinds of strokes. (The Single, Multi, and Rake Stroke Types are chosen from the Brush Controls: Spacing palette.) Except for the Straight Cloner and Soft Cloner variants, the Cloners brush variants clone in different media than the source picture.

The Single Stroke Type Cloners brush variants (Chalk, Pencil Sketch, Felt Pen, Melt, Driving Rain, and Impressionist)

Chalk. (The original image is on page 128.)

Melt

Pencil Sketch

Oil Brush

match colors from corresponding areas in the source document. A continuous stroke with any of these variants will duplicate the source picture's color and detail, though in different media.

When you use a Multi or Rake Stroke Type Cloners brush variant (Hairy Oil Brush, Hard Oil, Oil Brush, or Van Gogh), the first sampled color is maintained for the full length of the stroke, so it's best to draw short brush strokes with these variants. Non-Cloners brushes also follow this rule of Single versus Multi or Rake Stroke Type when the Use Clone Color box is checked and brush strokes are applied to a clone image.

To clone in the same media as the source picture, use the Straight Cloner variant or use the Cloning method category for any non-Cloners brush. Only the brush shape will vary. (Choose a Grainy submethod category to reveal texture as you clone.) Choose the Soft Cloner variant to create a soft, airbrushed clone.

Some Cloners method subcategories

Hard Cover. Semi-anti-aliased strokes that cover existing color. The source document is reproduced cleanly.

Soft Cover. Soft, anti-aliased strokes that cover existing color. The source document is reproduced cleanly.

Grainy Hard Cover, Grainy Soft Cover. Semi-anti-aliased and anti-aliased, respectively. Strokes reveal the current paper texture. **Grainy Flat** also reveals paper texture.

Drip. Distorts the image by pushing color around and produces a wet, crumbly surface texture.

To compare Cloners brush variants

Choose Tools > Brushes > Brush Look Designer, draw a brush stroke in the preview window, then note the preview as you choose other Cloners variants from the Brushes palette.

Cloners Brush Variants and Method Subcategories

The Auto Clone command clones automatically, dab by dab, in the Cloners brush variant of your choice. Painter does the brush stroking — you just sit and watch! You can clone right over an existing photograph to make it look more painterly or you can clone onto a blank canvas.

To clone automatically:

1. Open the image you want to clone.
2. *Optional:* To clone onto a blank canvas, choose File > Clone, choose Edit > Select All, then press Delete.
3. Choose the Brush tool.
4. Choose a Cloners brush variant, method category and method subcategory. If you choose a Grainy method subcategory, choose a paper texture from the Art Materials: Papers palette.
   or
   Choose any non-Cloners brush (don't choose the Cloning method category) and check the Use Clone Color box on the Art Materials: Colors palette.
5. Choose Effects > Esoterica > Auto Clone.
6. To stop the auto cloning, click in the clone image window.

To clone different areas of your picture using different brush sizes or variants, create a selection before you choose the Auto Clone command. Try using a smaller brush for details, like facial features.

To add more variety and create a less "machine made" look, interrupt the auto cloning, choose a different variant, brush size (Brush Controls: Size palette), or paper texture, then resume auto cloning.

Use the Straight Cloner or Soft Cloner variant at a very low opacity to restore some detail from the original image.

To clone using a recorded brush stroke

Choose the Brush tool, choose a non-Cloners brush, choose Tools > Record Stroke and draw a stroke. Activate the clone image window, choose a Cloners brush variant (or choose a non-Cloners brush and check the Use Clone Color box on the Art Materials: Colors palette), then choose Tools > Auto Playback. Click in the image window to stop the Auto Playback.

The original image.

(close-up)

Auto Clone with Hard Oil Cloner variant

(close-up)

Artists brush, Auto Van Gogh variant, Record Stroke, Auto Playback.

(close-up)

Artists brush, Auto Van Gogh variant, Effects > Esoterica > Auto Van Gogh.

Let's be honest. Van Gogh Cloning techniques will produce a clone in Impressionistic-like dabs or strokes, but it won't be a Van Gogh.

To produce a "Van Gogh" clone:

1. Open the document you want to clone (the source document).
2. Choose File > Clone.
3. With the clone image window active, choose Edit > Select All (⌘-A).
4. Press Delete.
5. Use any one of the following three methods:

   To draw the brush strokes yourself, choose the Artists brush and the Van Gogh variant, check the Use Clone Color box on the Art Materials: Colors palette, then draw short, "Impressionistic" strokes.

   or

   To clone automatically in little orzo-shaped strokes, choose the Artists brush and the Auto Van Gogh variant, choose Tools > Record Stroke, draw one stroke, then choose Tools > Auto Playback. Click in the image window to stop the playback.

   or

   To render the clone automatically, but in strokes that follow the forms and lights-and-darks of the source image more closely, choose the Artists brush and the Auto Van Gogh brush variant, then choose Effects > Esoterica > Auto Van Gogh.

To produce an embossed or line art clone:

1. Open the document you want to clone (the source document).
2. Choose File > Clone.
3. With the clone image window open, choose Edit > Select All.
4. Press Delete.
5. If you want to emboss the clone, choose a Primary color from the Art Materials: Colors palette or from the Color Set palette, choose Edit > Fill, click Current Color, then click OK.

   To produce a line art rendering, leave the clone blank.
6. Choose Effects > Surface Control > Apply Surface Texture.
7. Choose 3D Brush Strokes or Original Luminance from the Using pop-up menu.
8. Do any of the following optional steps:

   Move the Shiny slider to the right to emphasize the highlights.

   Click a different Light Direction button to change the angle of the cast light.

   Drag the light source dot to another part of the sphere.

   Move the Amount, Brightness, and Conc[entration] sliders to lighten or darken.

   Move the picture in the preview window.
9. Click OK.

For a beautiful effect, choose a non-Cloners brush and the Cloning method category, move the Controls: Brush palette Opacity slider way down to 2 or 3 percent, then stroke lightly over the clone to restore some of the source image color. Or just use the Soft Cloner variant of the Cloners brush.

Embossed clone

To remove gray shades in a line art clone, move the Picture slider and the Brightness or Exposure slider to the right. A line art clone works very well as a starting sketch, over which you can apply colored brush strokes. The Straight Cloners variant was applied to this picture in broad brush strokes to restore a few details from the source document.

And a third variation: A picture cloned using the Auto Van Gogh variant of the Artists brush and the Auto Van Gogh command, then texture added via Apply Surface Texture (3D Brush Strokes).

Effects Menu 10

*Ray Rue, **Arc Library**.*

The Tonal Control commands

Use the **Adjust Colors** dialog box to change the dominant color cast, saturation, or value (brightness) of an entire picture or of a selection.

To change a picture's hues, saturation, or brightness:

1. Choose Effects > Tonal Control > Adjust Colors (⌘-Shift-A).
2. Choose from the **Using** pop-up menu:

   Uniform Color: Adjusts colors without applying a paper texture.

   Paper Grain: Adjusts colors and applies the current paper texture.

   Mask: Adjusts the non-masked area when the second Visibility button is selected.

   Image Luminance: Adjusts color based on light and dark values in the image. Produces subtler effects. Move the Hue slider before moving the other sliders.

   Original Luminance: Adjusts color in a clone based on light and dark values in the source image.
3. Move the **Hue Shift** slider to shift the picture's colors along the color wheel.

   Move the **Saturation** slider to adjust color intensity.

   Move the **Value** slider to lighten or darken the picture.
4. *Optional:* Click Reset at any time to restore the original settings.
5. Click OK or press Return.

Beware of oversaturating a picture if it's going to be printed. Choose Effects > Toning Controls > Printable Colors to force the picture's colors into the printable range.

Move the Saturation slider to the left to make a photograph look hand tinted. Move the Saturation slider all the way to the left to turn a color picture into a grayscale picture.

ABOUT THE EFFECTS MENU COMMANDS

- Effects menu (image editing) commands don't work on the Wet Paint layer. To dry brush strokes on the Wet Paint layer, choose Canvas > Dry (⌘-D).
- If the dialog box has a preview window, you can press and drag inside it to display a different part of the picture. Most commands preview in the dialog box, but not in the picture, unfortunately.
- You can restrict any Effects menu command to a selection, including text, or to an active floater. To image edit the whole picture, make sure no selection is active before you choose the command.
- To adjust a clone, make sure the clone window is active and the clone source document name is selected from the File > Clone Source submenu before choosing the Effects menu command.
- **Shortcuts:**

  ⌘-/ to reopen the last opened Effects menu dialog box.

  ⌘-; to reopen the second-to-last opened Effects menu dialog box.

  ⌘-. to cancel a command while it's processing.
- You can choose from the Art Materials: Colors palette or the Art Materials: Papers palette while any of these dialog boxes are open: Adjust Colors, Adjust Selective Colors, Color Overlay, Dye Concentration, Apply Surface Texture, Apply Screen, Glass Distortion.
- Plug-ins are accessed from the Effects menu (see page 180).
- When adjusting with the Using: Mask option, not all sliders work predictably.

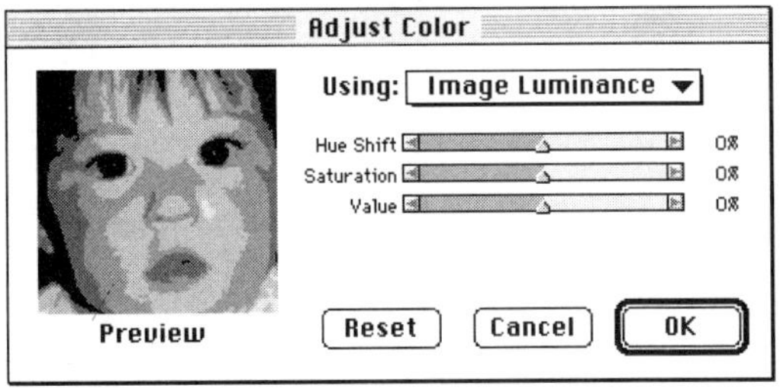

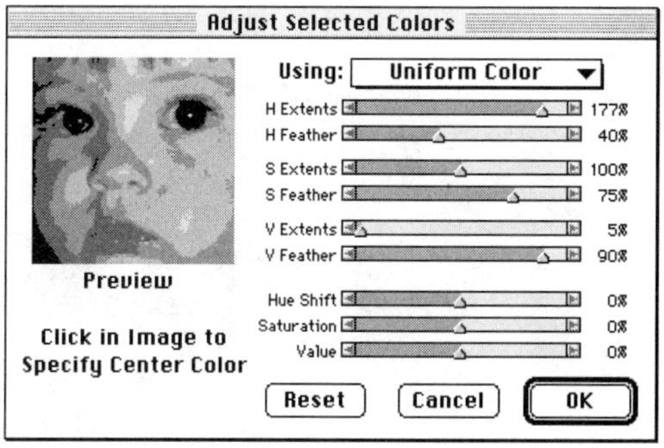

To adjust selected colors:

1. Choose Effects > Tonal Control > Adjust Selected Colors.
2. Click on the color in the image window that you want to adjust.
3. Choose from the **Using** pop-up menu:

   Uniform Color shifts colors with the base color being at the center of the slider. No paper texture is added.

   Paper Grain adjusts color *and* adds a paper texture.You can choose a different paper texture from the Art Materials: Papers palette while the Adjust Selected Colors dialog box is open. Use only the Hue Shift slider.

   Mask adjusts the non-masked area when the second Visibility button is selected. The amount of color adjustment will be based on the opacity of the mask.

   Image Luminance adjusts color based on the picture's light and dark values.

   Original Luminance adjusts color based on the source document's light and dark values.
4. Move the H (hue), S (saturation) or V (value) **Extents** sliders to widen or narrow the range of colors that are adjusted.

   Move the H (hue), S (saturation) or V (value) **Feather** sliders to adjust how much color adjustment is softened on the edges of color areas.
5. Move the **Hue Shift** slider to recolor the picture with different colors.

   Move the **Saturation** slider to increase or decrease color intensity.

   Move the **Value** slider to lighten or darken the picture.
6. *Optional:* Click Reset at any time to restore only the default Hue Shift, Saturation, and Value sliders settings.
7. Click OK or press Return.

To adjust brightness and contrast:

1. Choose Effects > Tonal Control > Brightness/Contrast.
2. Move the top slider (moon icon) to the right to increase contrast or to the left to decrease contrast.
   and/or
   Move the bottom slider (sun icon) to the right to increase brightness (lightness) or to the left to decrease brightness.

   Changes will preview in the image window immediately.
3. Click Apply.

Click Reset to restore the original Brightness/Contrast settings.

To lighten small areas manually, use the Dodge brush. To darken small areas manually, use the Burn brush. Use with a low opacity at first.

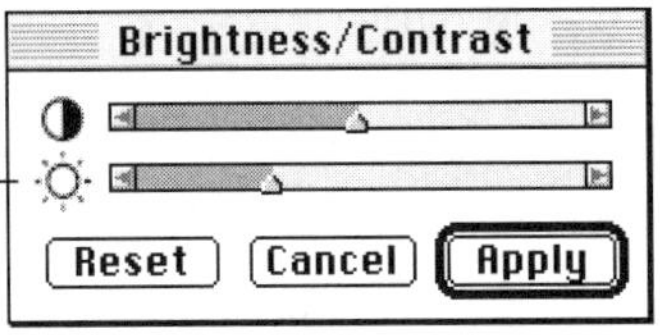

Brightness slider

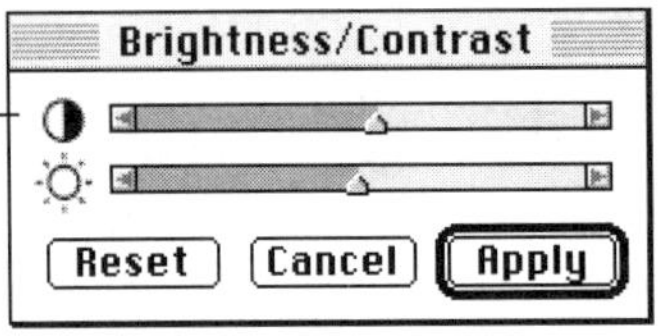

Contrast slider

*The original image: **18th Century Interior** by Ray Rue.*

*The **Brightness** lowered...*

*...and the **Contrast** increased slightly.*

The original image is at left, on the opposite page. The above image is after Equalize adjustments.

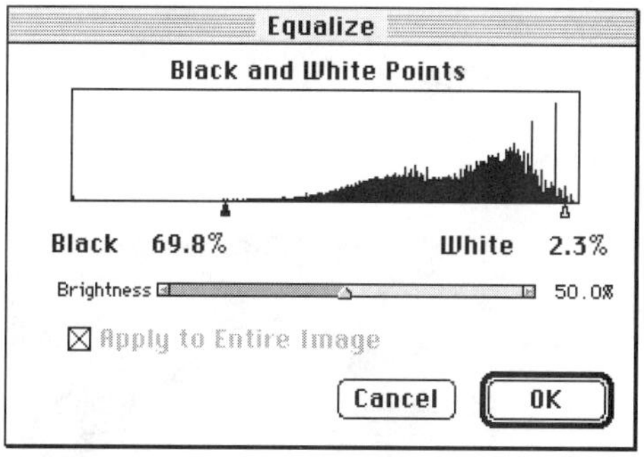

You can use the Equalize command to adjust the brightness and contrast of a picture's highlights, midtones, or shadows individually.

To equalize a picture:

1. Choose Effects > Tonal Control > Equalize (⌘-E). Automatic adjustments will be made, and will preview in the image window.
2. Do any of the following optional steps:

   Move the **White point** slider to the left to brighten the picture's highlights.

   Move the **Black point** slider to the right to darken the picture's shadows. The white and black points are the picture's darkest and lightest values.

   Move the **Brightness** slider to lighten or darken the picture's midtones (gamma).
3. Click OK or press Return.

To reduce previewing time, shrink the preview area by selecting an area on your picture. Then choose Effects > Tonal Control > Equalize and click the Apply to Entire Image box.

To create a negative of a picture:

Choose Effects > Tonal Control > Negative.

The original image.

After applying the Negative command.

Posterization reduces the number of color or shade levels in a picture. The fewer the Levels, the more dramatic the effect. Posterization can make a picture more adaptable to screen printing.

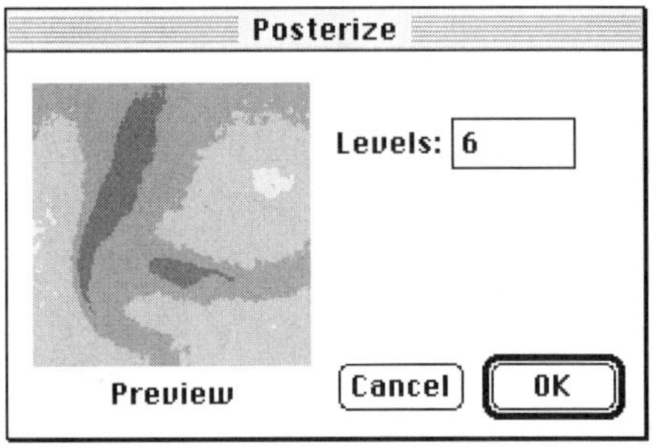

To posterize a picture:

1. Choose Effects > Tonal Control > Posterize.
2. Enter a number (2-128) in the Levels field.
3. Click OK or press Return.
4. *Optional:* Choose Effects > Toning Controls > Printable Colors to ensure the picture's colors are in the printable range.

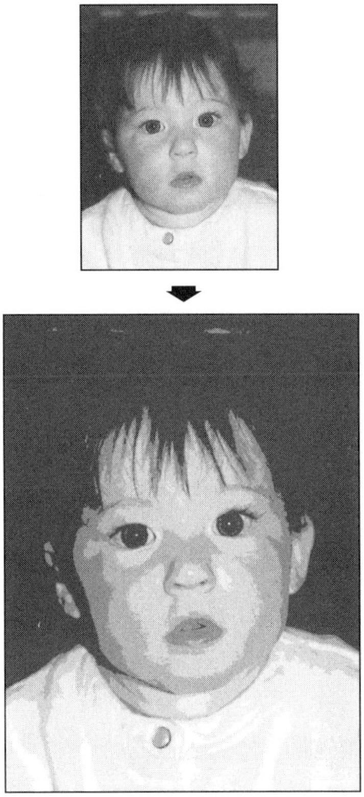

Six-level posterization.

Like the Posterize command, the Posterize Using Color Set command reduces the number of color or shade levels in a picture, but in this case, colors from a color set of your choice are substituted based on their closest brightness match to the picture's original brightness values. Apply this command to make a picture look more hand painted, to prepare a file for screen printing or a press that uses a limited number of inks, or to colorize a grayscale image. Spot color separations can't be produced from Painter.

Color Sets are discussed on page 23 and on pages 50-52. Use one of Painter's color sets, like Pastels, or use your own color set.

To posterize a picture using a color set:

1. Open or create the color set you want to become the picture's colors. If you create your own set, you can choose colors from any open picture using the Dropper tool (⌘). Try using a small set first (up to ten colors).
2. Choose Effects > Tonal Control > Posterize Using Color Set.

If the colors in the set have assigned names, you can use the Annotate feature to mark colors on the picture.

To apply a paper texture to your image

Choose Paper Grain from the Using pop-up menu when you apply any of these Effects menu commands: Adjust Colors, Adjust Selected Colors, Apply Screen, Apply Surface Texture, Color Overlay, Dye Concentration, Express Texture, or Glass Distortion.

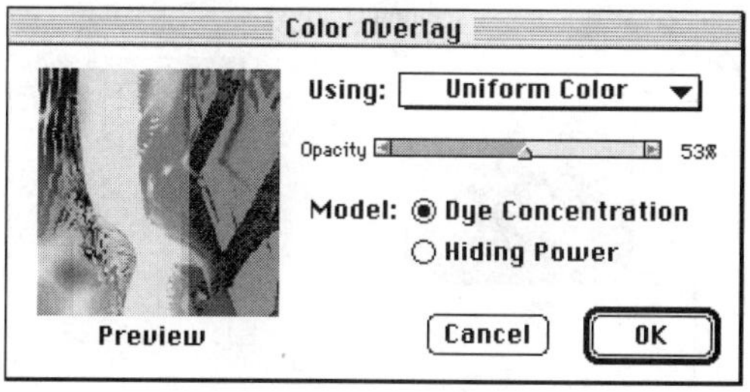

The Surface Control commands

Use the Color Overlay command to apply one overall color tint to a picture. You can also apply a paper texture at the same time.

To apply a tint:

1. Choose Effects > Surface Control > Color Overlay.
2. Choose a color from the Art Materials: Colors palette or from the Color Set palette.
3. Choose from the Using pop-up menu:

   Uniform Color applies a flat tint of the current Primary color. You can choose a different Primary color while the Color Overlay dialog box is open.

   Paper Grain applies the paper texture currently selected on the Art Materials: Paper palette. You can preview different textures while the Color Overlay dialog box is open.

   Mask colorizes the non-masked area when the second Visibility button is selected.

   Image Luminance colorizes the image based on the picture's light and dark values, which are preserved.

   Original Luminance colorizes a clone based on the source picture's light and dark values.
4. Click **Dye Concentration** to have the paper absorb the color.
   or
   Click **Hiding Power** to have the color cover underlying pixels more.
5. Move the Opacity slider to adjust the amount of color that is overlayed.
6. Click OK or press Return.

The Apply Lighting command casts one or more light beams on a picture. You can choose a preset lighting effect or you can create your own lighting effect by adjusting any number of variables, such as the light's color, shape, direction, or brightness. If you want the option to reuse a lighting effect that you've created, save it in the currently open Lighting library. To access the Lighting feature, use a Mac that has a Floating Point Unit (FPU), or use a Power Mac.

To apply lighting:

1. Choose Effects > Surface Control > Apply Lighting.
2. Click a preset lighting effect. Click the scroll arrows to display other choices.

   Click OK if you're happy with the preset lighting effect. If you want to customize the lighting effect, follow the remaining steps.
3. Do any of the following to customize the lighting effect:

   Move the **Brightness** slider to the right to make the light beam brighter or to the left to make it dimmer.

   Move the **Distance** slider to the right to increase the distance between the light source and where the light beam falls on the picture.

   Move the **Elevation** slider to the right to adjust the angle of the cast light. 90° shines directly down on the image, 10° shines at an acute angle.

   Move the **Spread** slider to the right to widen the light beam or to the left to make it narrower.

   Move the **Exposure** slider to the right to increase the exposure (brightness) of the whole image or to the left to lower the exposure.

   Move the **Ambient** slider to the right to raise the light level in the overall picture (except the light beam).

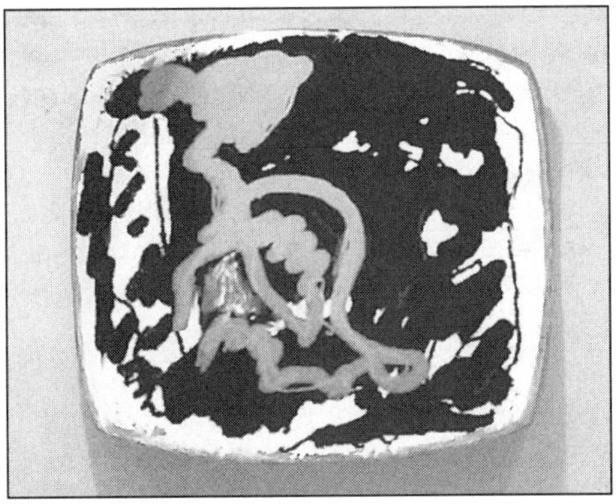

*Ron Gorchov, **Delihla.***

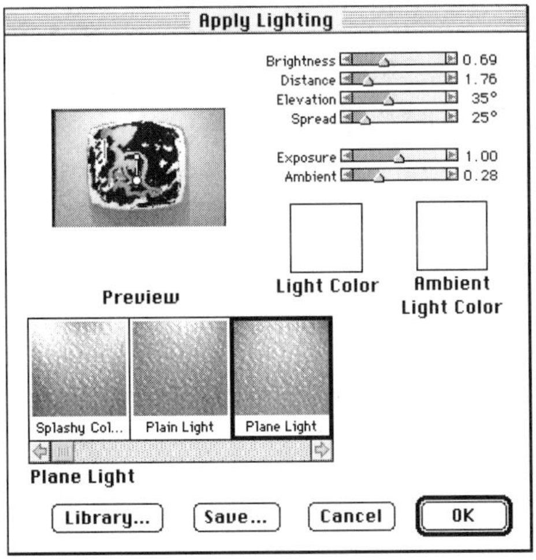

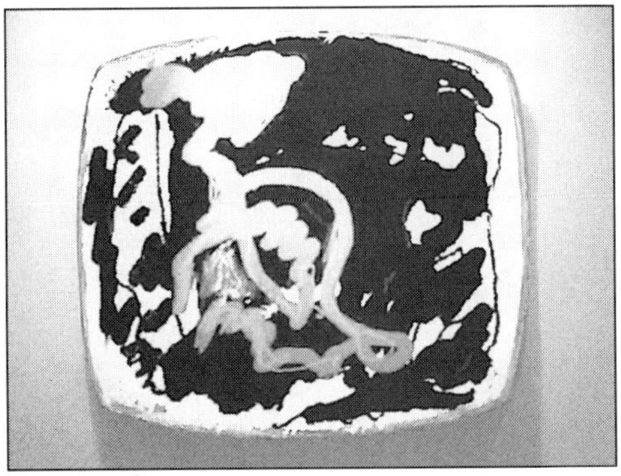

We applied the Readable lighting effect to Gorchov's painting. His version is better, of course.

Ron Gorchov

To produce his traditional media artworks, Ron Gorchov, a 1994 recipient of the Guggenheim Award, usually begins with an actual stretched, and specially curved, glue-sized linen canvas — convexly curved along the horizontal axis and concave on the vertical axis.

Gorchov uses the computer to develop a visual theme for his work on canvas. In Painter, he opens a CD-ROM photograph of a completed oil on canvas, and then "primes" his electronic canvas at 60% opacity over the existing image using a paint color that simulates traditional white lead. Over a faint ghost of the original image that remains, he paints directly, pastes and rearranges imagery from other electronic images, overpaints, and finally smudges the edges of any visible white lead ground. In addition to oil and chalk brushes, Gorchov also uses a variety of other Painter features: the Apply Lighting and Fade commands, the Outline Selection tool to cut out shapes, the Distort command to stretch them, and the Water brushes to create smudges and drips. In addition to Painter, he also uses NIH Image, a public domain program designed by Wayne Rasband of the National Institute of Health, which is normally used for medical imaging. It produces surprising color transformations that Gorchov likes.

Once he arrives at a promising theme on the computer, Gorchov turns his back to the computer and recreates the image on real-life canvas. Like a dancer or musician who rehearses a composition, the computer prepares him for his canvas "performance."

Ron Gorchov

To change the light source **direction**, rotate the square end of the light icon in the preview window. Click right on the icon, or else you will create another light source icon.

To **move** the whole light source, drag the round end of the light icon in the preview window.

To **add** another light source, click in the preview window. The new light will have the same color as the current light source.

To **remove** a light source, click on the light icon, then press Delete.

To change the color of a light, click on its icon in the preview window, click the **Light Color** square, choose a color from the Color Picker, then click OK.

To change the color of the area around the light beam, click the **Ambient Light Color** square, choose a color, then click OK.

4. *Optional:* To save the edited lighting effect in the currently open lighting library so you can choose it again from the Apply Lighting dialog box, click Save, enter a name, then click OK.
5. Click OK or press Return.

You can restore a lighting effect's default settings if you haven't saved it. Just click on a different effect.

To create or edit a lighting library, follow the instructions on pages 15-16.

Ray Rue uses lighting effects extensively in his work. Take a look at the opening page of this chapter and the same piece reproduced in the color section.

The Dye Concentration command is one of our favorites. It darkens (or lightens) colors without making them dull and makes them richer without noticeably changing their hue or making them gaudy. You can apply a paper texture as you adjust dye concentration.

To adjust color intensity:

1. Choose Effects > Surface Control > Dye Concentration.
2. Choose from the **Using** pop-up menu:

   Uniform Adjustment adjusts color without adding texture. Move the Maximum slider to adjust the intensity of the Dye Concentration effect.

   Paper Grain adjusts color and applies the paper texture currently selected on the Art Materials: Papers palette. You can choose a different paper texture while the Adjust Dye Concentration dialog box is open.

   To emphasize the paper texture more, move the Maximum or the Minimum slider to the right. The farther apart the sliders are, the more pronounced the paper texture.

   Mask adjusts outside mask using the Maximum slider or within the mask using the Minimum slider.

   Image Luminance adjusts color based on the picture's light and dark values.

   Original Luminance adjusts a clone based on the source picture's light and dark values.
3. Click OK or press Return.

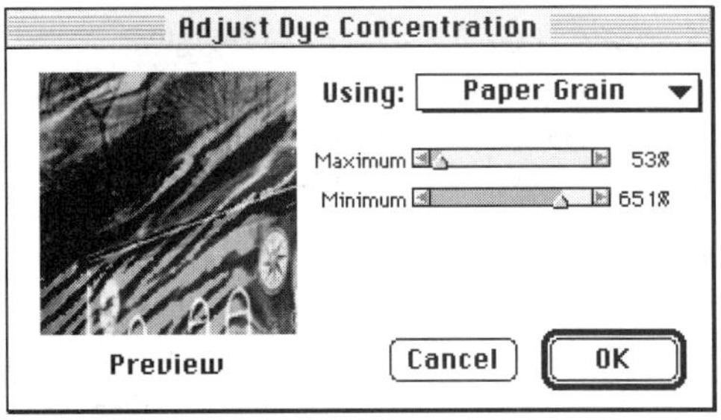

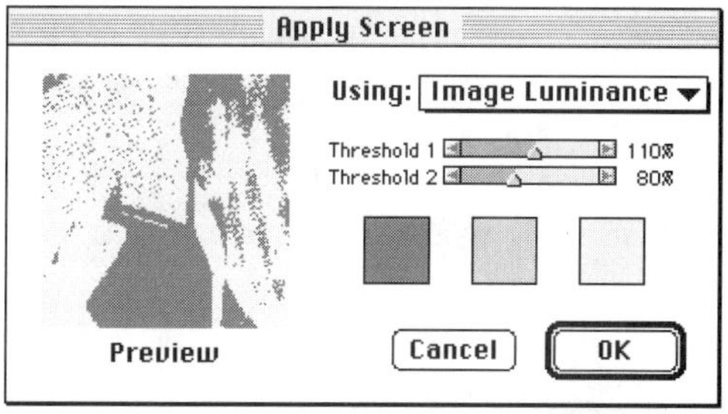

Lourekas

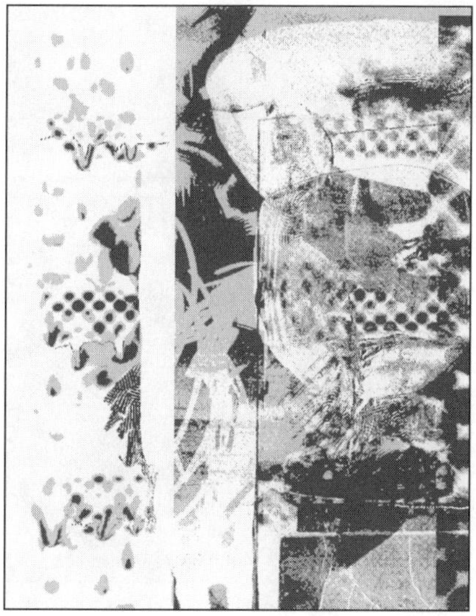

The Apply Screen command reduces a picture's colors to three colors that you specify. You can apply a paper texture at the same time. You can use Apply Screen to colorize a grayscale picture.

To apply a color screen:

1. Choose Effects > Surface Control > Apply Screen.
2. Click the first color square, choose a color (drag the vertical scroll box to change the brightness of the color wheel), then click OK. Repeat for the second and third color squares.
3. Choose from the **Using** pop-up menu:

   Paper Grain applies the paper texture currently selected on the Art Materials: Papers palette. You can preview different textures with the Apply Screen dialog box open.

   Mask. When the second Visibility button is selected, you can move the Threshold 2 slider to the left to apply the first color only to the masked area or to the right to apply the first color to the whole image.

   Image Luminance applies flat color to the image based on the picture's light and dark value distribution.

   Original Luminance applies flat color to a clone based on the source picture's light and dark values.
4. Move the Threshold 1 slider to the right to add more of the second color, or to the left to add more of the third color.
   and/or
   Move the Threshold 2 slider to the right to add more of the first color and reduce the second color, or to the left to reduce the first color and add more of the second color.
5. Click OK or press Return.

You can apply a surface texture to a completed painting or a selection using the Apply Surface Texture command. Where you draw subsequent brush strokes or use an Eraser brush, however, you'll **remove** the texture. Light Controls are included in Painter Version 3.1. To access the Apply Surface Texture command, use a Mac that has a Floating Point Unit (FPU), or use a Power Mac.

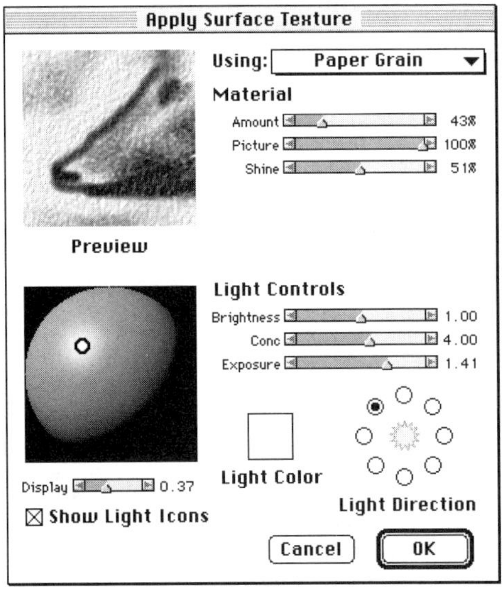

To apply a texture to a whole painting:

1. Choose Effects > Surface Control > Apply Surface Texture.
2. Choose **Paper Grain** from the Using pop-up menu to apply the paper texture currently selected on the Art Materials: Papers palette. You can choose a different paper texture with the dialog box open.

   Choose **3D Brush Strokes** to make strokes applied to a clone look more three-dimensional.

   Using **Mask** produces limited effects.

   Choose **Image Luminance** to create a raised surface effect.

   Choose **Original Luminance** to create a raised surface in a clone based on luminosity values in the source image.
3. Adjust any of the following Material controls:

   Move the **Amount** slider to the right to intensify the effect.

   Move the **Picture** slider to the right to reveal more of the original picture's color.

   Move the **Shiny** slider to the right to create a more reflective surface texture with stronger highlights.
4. Before you adjust any of the following Light Controls, check the **Show Light Icons** box, then **click on a light on the preview sphere to select it.**

   Drag the light icon to move the light source.

Jacquelyn Martino

Jacquelyn Martino

Two images from Martino's "Blue" series.

Jacquelyn Martino

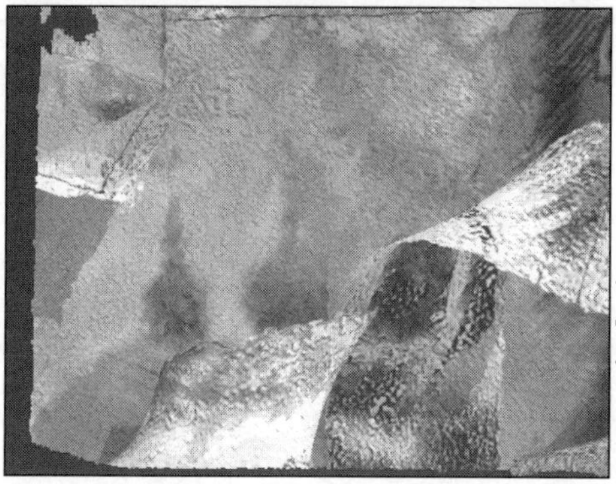
Jacquelyn Martino

Images from the "Tear" series

Jacquelyn Martino

To produce the pieces on these pages, which are part of an interactive multimedia piece exploring the city of Venice, Italy and issues of time, rejuvenation, and decay, Jacquelyn Martino started with her own Polaroid transfer prints of scenes in Venice. She developed the images further using various techniques, then photographed and scanned them. In Painter, Martino cloned the images using Water Color, Chalk, and Charcoal brush variants (the Use Clone Color box checked on the Colors palette) and using the Apply Surface Texture command (Original Luminance). She also used Bleach variants of the Eraser brush to lighten selective areas. The Tear Series images were used as color maps for 3D animations using SoftImage and then imported into Macromedia Director. The Blue Series still images were imported from Painter into Macromedia Director. To activate the multimedia piece, which includes a soundtrack, viewers turn pages of a real-life, handmade book in a candlelit room, which in turn "turn pages" on the computer.

Click a different **Direction** button to change the highlight-to-shadow direction.

Don't click a different Light Direction after adjusting other Light Controls — the single default light will be restored and all other lights will be deleted.

Move the **Brightness** slider to adjust the intensity of the light.

Move the **Conc** slider to adjust the width (spread) of the light.

Move the **Exposure** slider to adjust the overall brightness of the image.

Click the **Light Color** square, and choose a different color for the light.

Move the **Display** slider to lighten or darken the preview.

Drag a light source to **move** it.

To **add** a light source, click on the sphere. Each light source can have its own Light Controls settings, except for the Exposure setting.

To **delete** a light source, click on it, then press Delete.

5. Click OK or press Return.

To apply a tinted surface texture, choose Effects > Surface Control > Color Overlay, choose Paper Grain from the Using pop-up menu, and click the Hiding Power button.

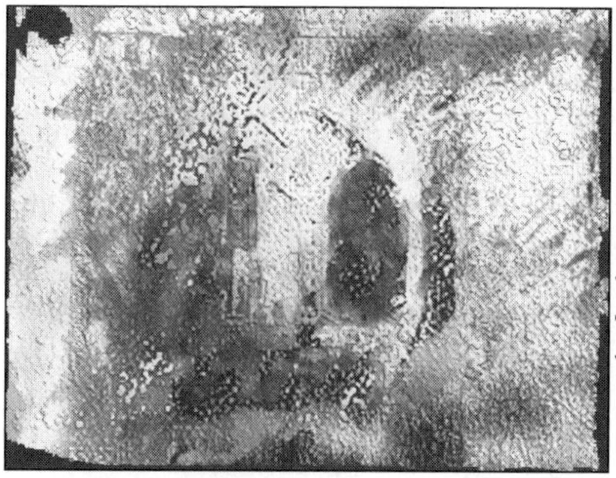
Jacquelyn Martino

To create a 3D textured shape:

Part I

1. Create text or a shape on a picture and turn it into a floater.
2. Choose Effects > Objects > Create Drop Shadow, check the Collapse to one Layer box, then click OK.
3. Drop the floater and its shadow.
4. Activate the path(s) on the Objects: P. List palette.
5. Choose a paper texture from the Art Materials: Papers palette.
6. Choose Effects > Surface Control > Apply Surface Texture.
7. Choose Using: Paper Grain.
8. *Optional:* Adjust the Light Controls sliders. Click the Light Color box to change the color of the cast light.
9. Click OK or press Return.

Part II

1. Select each path individually, and using the Path Adjuster tool, drag a corner handle inward to make the path shape slightly smaller. Repeat on the diagonally opposite corner.
2. Activate all the paths on the Objects: P. List palette.
3. Move the Controls: Path Adjuster palette Feather slider to around 13 for a 75 ppi document, around 35 for a 200 ppi document, or even higher for a higher res document.
4. Choose Choose Effects > Surface Control > Apply Surface Texture.
5. Choose Using: Mask.
6. Adjust the Amount, Picture and Shine sliders to produce the desired 3D effect. Amount controls texture build-up; Picture controls lightness/darkness; Shine controls the highlights.
7. Click OK or press Return.
8. Click the first Visibility icon on the extended Objects: P. List palette and deselect the paths.

Apply Surface Texture (Using: Paper Grain) command applied to text.

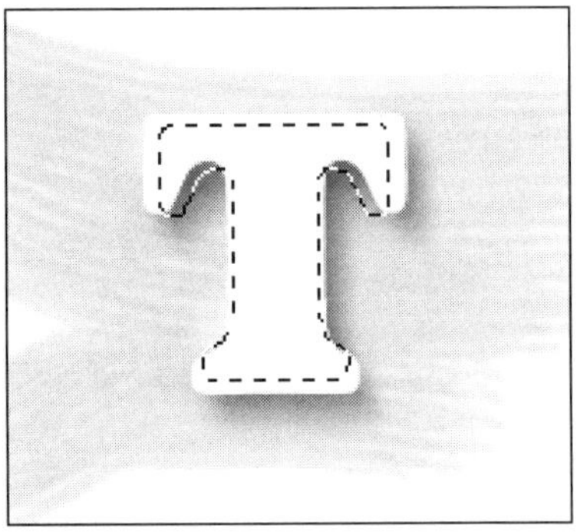

The path selection after scaling opposite corners using the Path Adjuster tool. We used a white fill in this illustration just for emphasis.

Apply Surface Texture (Using: Mask) applied for the second time now produces the 3D effect.

3D Shape

Texture combos produced using various methods

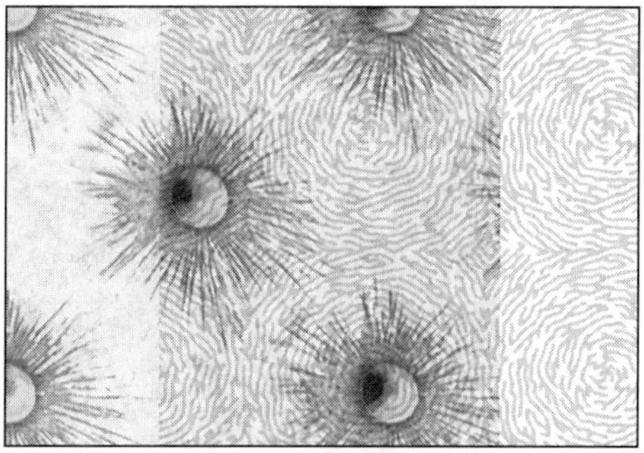

Circles (More Wild Textures file) Color Overlayed at 30% Opacity over Bolt Burst (Walls Library).

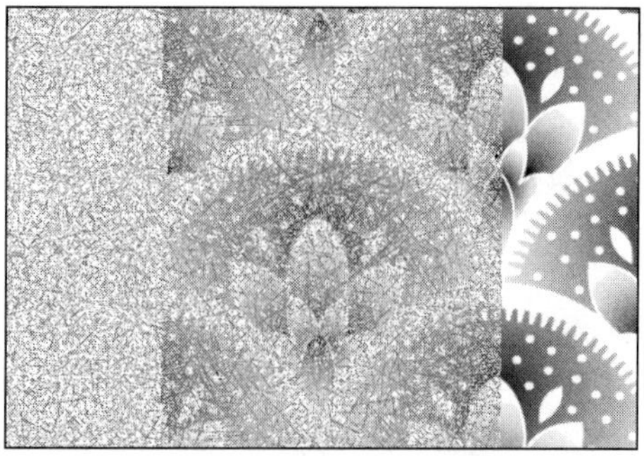

Fiber Fill (Weaves Library) floater (Dissolve Composite Method, 63% Opacity) over Deco Scallops (Walls Library) applied via the Color Overlay command.

Watercolor 2 (More Paper Textures file) at 43% opacity over Wood Squares (Walls Library) at 50% opacity, both floaters.

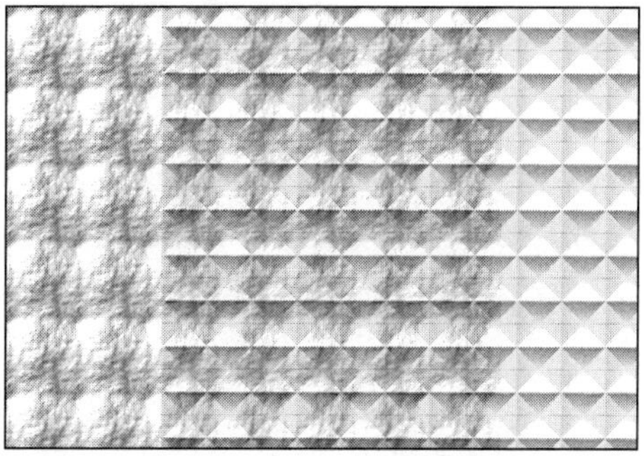

Texture on the left produced using Fractal Pattern, saved via Capture Texture, and applied to the picture via Apply Surface Texture (Paper Grain, Light Controls used to heighten contrast). Texture on the right produced via Make Paper Texture (Square pattern, Spacing 45), saved to the Papers palette, applied over first texture via Apply Surface Texture (Light Control options).

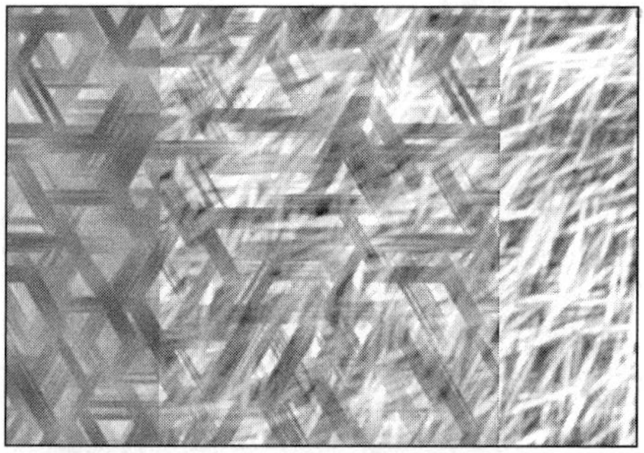

Basket 2 (Weaves Library) floater (Difference Composite Method, 100% Opacity) over Long Grain (Wild Textures) floater (Normal Composite Method, 87% Opacity).

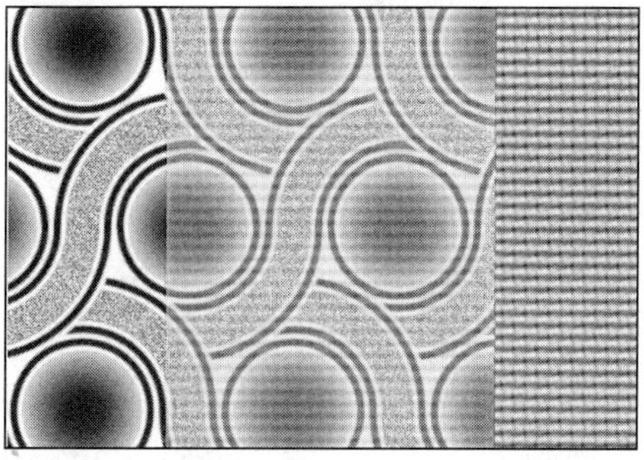

Raw Canvas (Grains) floater (Difference Composite Method, 27% Opacity) over Celtic Circles (Walls Library) floater (Normal Composite Method, 64% Opacity).

To translate a picture into grayscale values (Express Texture):

1. Choose Effects > Surface Control > Express Texture.
2. Choose from the Using pop-up menu:

   Choose **Paper Grain** to apply the current paper texture. You can choose from the Art Materials: Paper palette while the dialog box is open. Painter's Dottie and Circles textures are fun to experiment with. Or apply a texture that you've created.

   Choose **Mask** to restrict grayscale and contrast effects to inside the mask when the sliders are at their low settings. The paper texture isn't applied.

   Choose **Image Luminance** to apply grayscale values based on the pictures light and dark values.

   Choose **Original Luminance** to apply grayscale values to a clone based on the source picture's luminosity values.
3. Do any of the following:

   Move the **Gray Threshold** slider to control the balance between gray, black, and white. Move the slider to the right to add Black.

   If you chose Paper Grain from the Using pop-up menu, you can move the **Grain** slider to adjust the prominence of the paper texture. The higher the Grain setting, the more White in the picture.

   Move the **Contrast** slider to adjust the number of gray levels in the picture. Move to the right to heighten contrast.
4. Click OK or press Return.

If the original picture was in color, you can restore some color using the Edit > Fade command. Or apply the current Primary color to non-Black areas using the Effects > Surface Control > Color Overlay command.

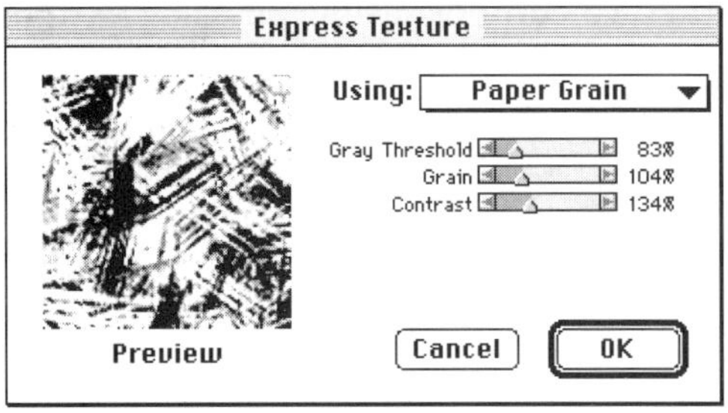

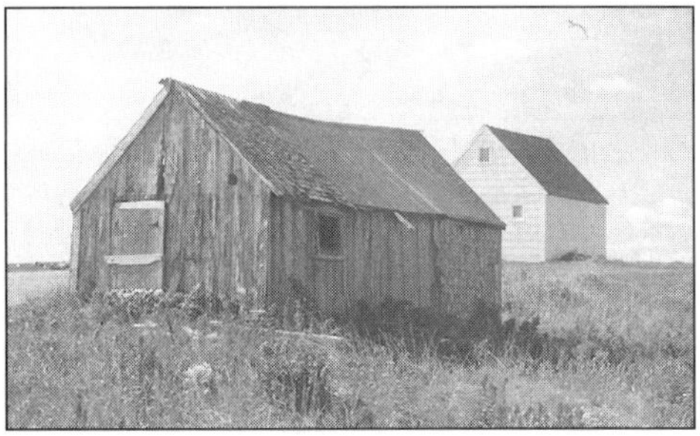

The original picture.

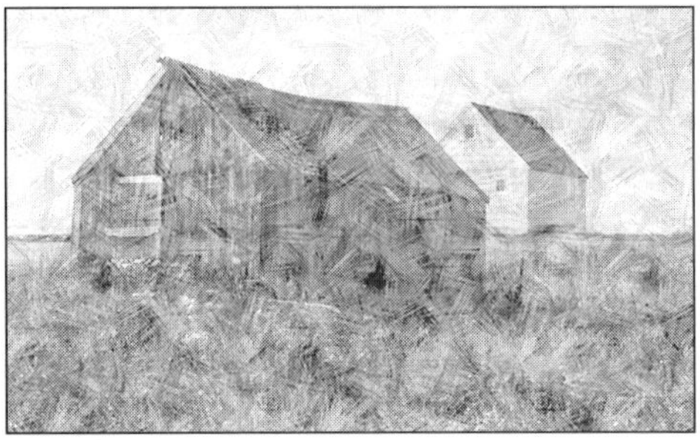

Express Texture (Using: Paper Grain) with Painter's Omniwicker texture (Invert box checked, Scale 133%), Gray Threshold 84%, Grain 72%, and Contrast 88%.

Painter's Omniwicker texture (Invert box checked, Scale 133%), Gray Threshold 83%, Grain 104%, and Contrast 134%.

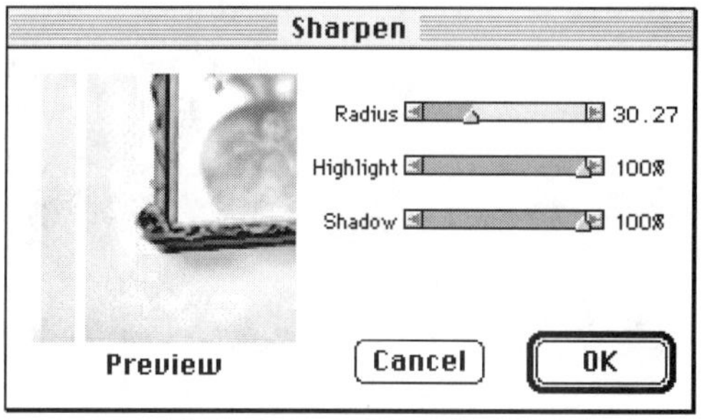

The Focus commands

The Sharpen command works by increasing the contrast between pixels.

To sharpen a picture:

1. Choose Effects > Focus > Sharpen.
2. Do any of the following:

   Move the **Radius** slider to the right to sharpen a wider area of each edge. Try a low Radius first to avoid oversharpening.

   Move the **Highlight** slider to the right to brighten the picture's highlights.

   Move the **Shadow** slider to the right to darken the shadows.

   Move the image in the preview window.
3. Click OK or press Return.

Ray Rue, 18th Century Interior

After sharpening (30).

To soften a picture:

1. Choose Effects > Focus > Soften.
2. Move the Radius slider to the right to increase blurring or to the left to decrease blurring. Try a low setting first.
3. Click OK or press Return.

Barbara S. Pollak

The Soften command applied to the background.

To motion blur an object or a picture:

1. Choose Effects > Focus > Motion Blur.
2. Do any of the following (try Radius and Thinness settings below 20 first):

   Move the **Radius** slider to the right to increase the motion effect (the distance pixels are moved).

   Move the **Angle** slider to change the direction of motion. 0° is horizontal, 90° is vertical.

   Move the **Thinness** slider to the right to blend and smooth edges at right angles to the Angle value and make the Angle less obvious. Too high a Thinness percentage will completely blur the image.
3. Click OK or press Return.

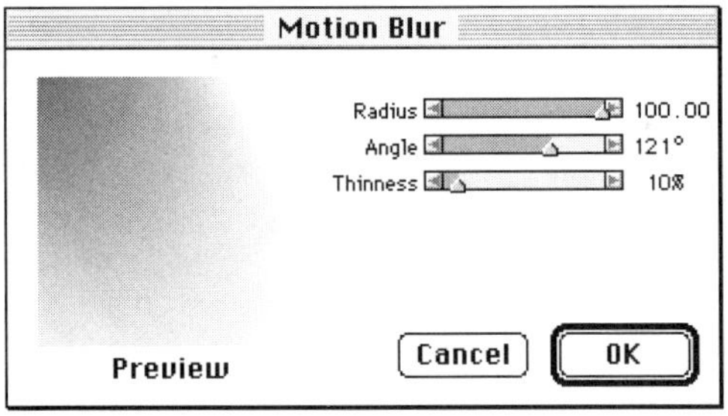

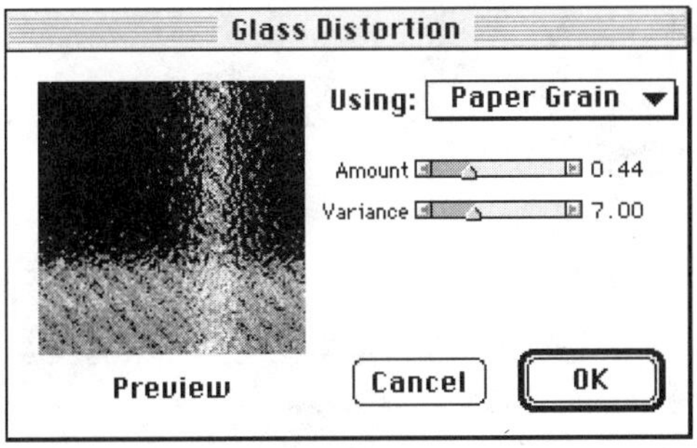

The original weave fill.

After applying the Glass Distortion command, Amount .44, Variance 6: a wool texture!

To apply the Glass Distortion command:

1. Choose Effects > Focus > Glass Distortion.
2. Do any of the following:

   Move the **Amount** slider to the right to intensify the effect.

   Move the **Variance** slider to the right to fracture shape edges more. Try using a low Amount setting and a high Variance setting.
3. Choose from the **Using** pop-up menu:

   Paper Grain to apply the paper texture currently selected on the Art Materials: Paper palette. You can choose a different texture while the Glass Distortion dialog box is open. Painter's Rougher, Basic Paper, Medium Fine, and Regular Fine textures produce believable glass effects.

   3D Brush Strokes distorts only areas in a clone to which brush strokes have been applied.

   Mask distorts the edge of a mask.

   Image Luminance displaces picture elements based on the picture's light and dark values.

   Original Luminance distorts a clone based on the source picture's light and dark values.
4. Click OK or press Return.

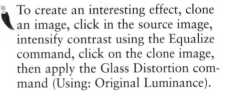

To create an interesting effect, clone an image, click in the source image, intensify contrast using the Equalize command, click on the clone image, then apply the Glass Distortion command (Using: Original Luminance).

Glass Distortion

The Esoterica commands

The commands grouped under the Esoterica submenu perform miscellaneous oddball distortions.

The blobs command dispenses shapes in liquid, like oil droplets in water. To access this command, use a computer that has an FPU (floating point unit), or use a PowerMac.

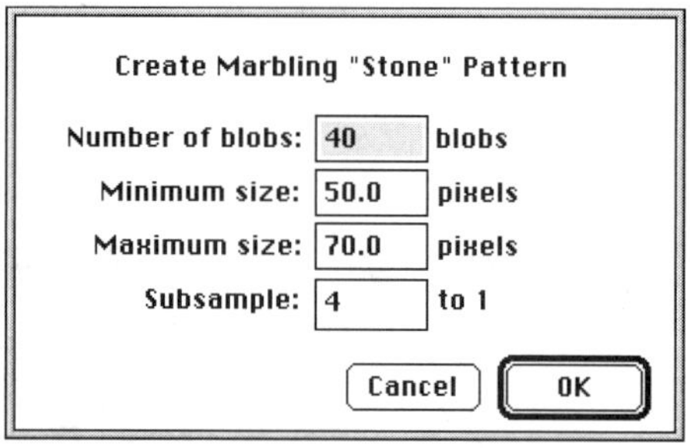

To create blobs:

1. To blob a picture element, select an area of any open picture or activate a floater, then choose Edit > Cut or Edit > Copy.

   If you don't put anything on the Clipboard, the command will blob the current Primary color. (To "clear" the Clipboard, fill a selection with a Primary color, then choose Edit > Cut or Edit > Copy.)
2. Open the picture you want to "blob."
   or
   To disperse the blobs on a blank background, create a new, blank document.
3. Choose Effects > Esoterica > Blobs.
4. Enter the Number of blobs, Minimum size, Maxmum size, and Subsample amount. Subsampling is anti-aliasing (smoothing).
5. Click OK or press Return.

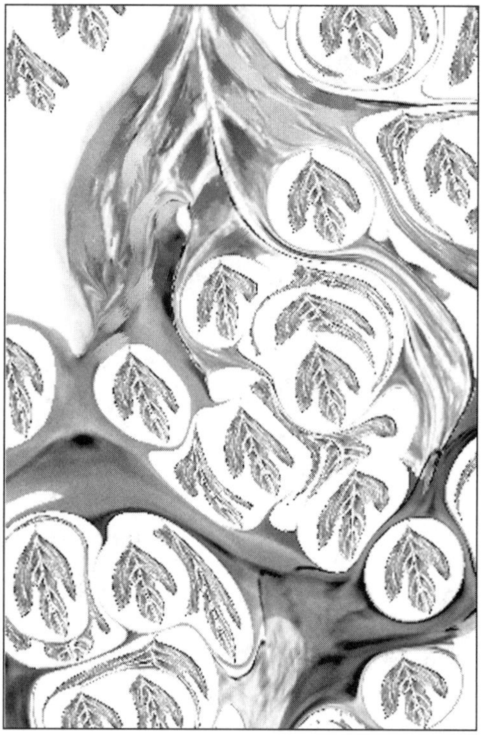

Blobbing an existing image with a picture element on the Clipboard produces the wildest results.

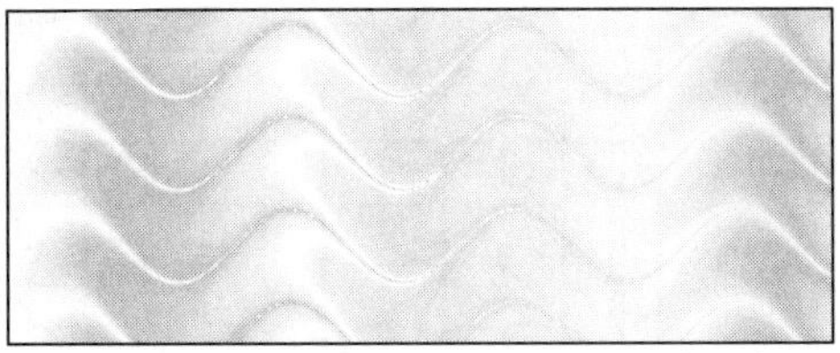
We used a gradient as a starting point for this image and for the images below.

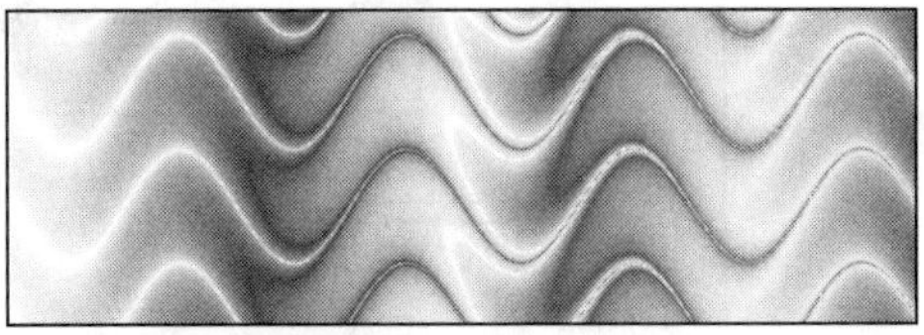
Default Marbling

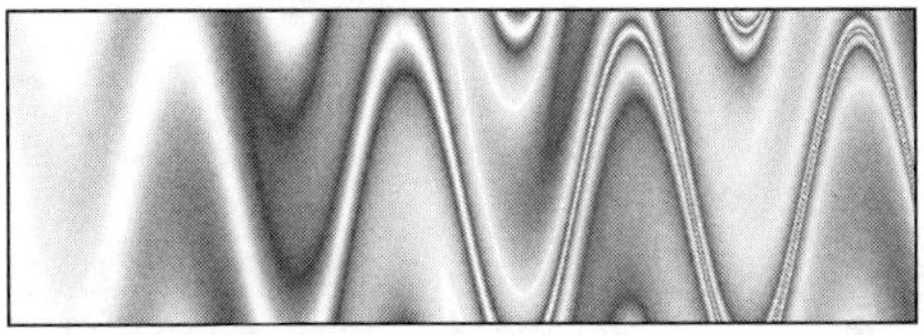
Spacing .51

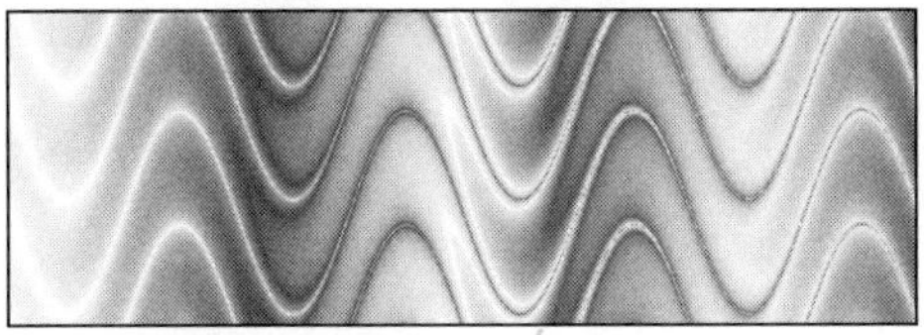
Waviness .89

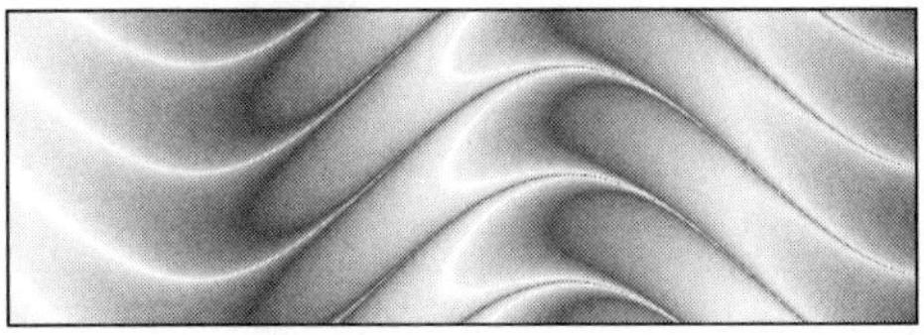
Wavelength .79

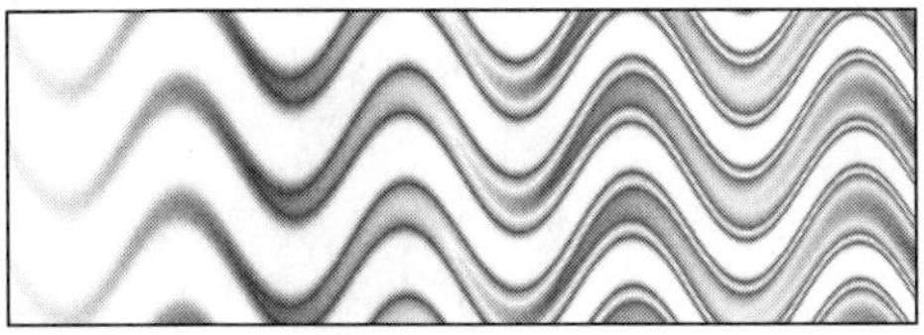
Pull 9

The Apply Marbling command mimics traditional marbling, a process by which a comb or rake is pulled through wet pigments to produce wave patterns. You can Apply Marbling after applying a gradient or the Blobs command. Don't apply it to a blank picture.

To apply marbling:

1. Choose Effects > Esoterica > Apply Marbling.
2. Adjust any of the following settings:

   Spacing: the distance between the rake teeth.

   Offset: the amount the rake shifts each time you reapply the command.

   Waviness: curve depth. Try a low Waviness setting first.

   Wavelength: the length (flatness) of the curves. A low Wavelength will produce gentle, flat curves.

   Phase: the position in the curve where the waves start.

   Pull: the amount of ink that is pulled. This option doesn't preview.

   Quality: anti-aliasing (smoothing). The higher the Quality, the longer Marbling takes to process.

   Direction: the direction the wave moves through the picture.
3. Click OK or press Return.

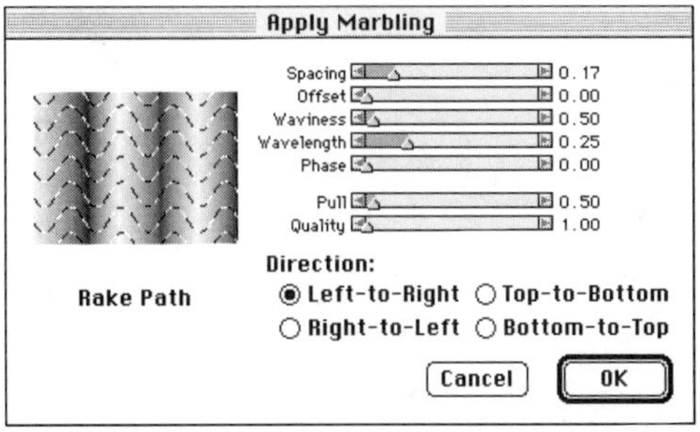

Unfortunately, there is no Reset button in the Apply Marbling dialog box. This screen grab shows the default settings.

Use the Image Warp command to distort all or part of an image around curvey, 3-D shapes. Unfortunately, once you drag in the preview window, you can't undo that preview and then preview different size and shape settings unless you Cancel out of the dialog box. Hopefully, this limitation will be corrected in a future version of Painter.

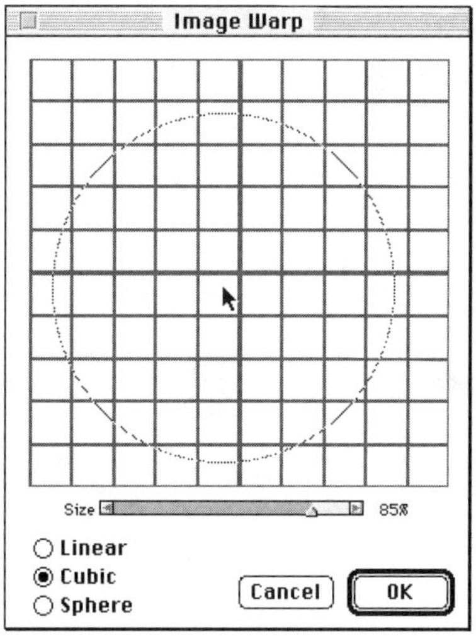

To warp a picture:

1. Choose Effects > Surface Control > Image Warp.
2. Click **Linear** to warp as if you were pulling straight up from the top of a cone, like a 3-D pyramid.
   or
   Click **Cubic** to pull straight up from the top of a cone, like the Linear method, but with soft curves toward the center of the warped area.
   or
   Click **Sphere** to warp pixels into a three-dimensional sphere.
3. Drag the Size slider to adjust the amount of the warp. Try a fairly high setting first (50% or higher).
4. Drag in the preview window to define the area to be warped.
5. Click OK or press Return.

(All 85% Size setting.)

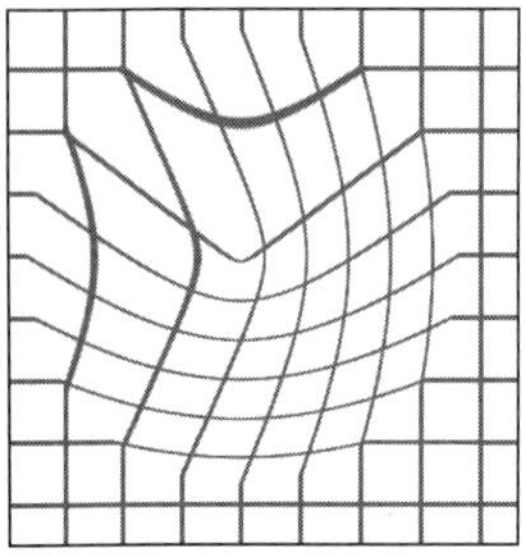

Linear Image Warp

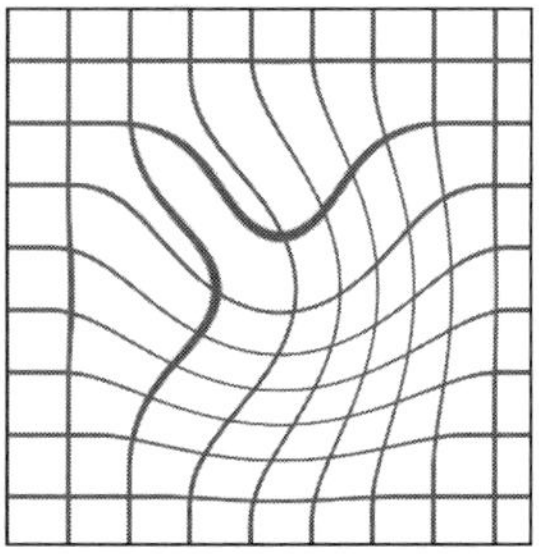

Cubic Image Warp

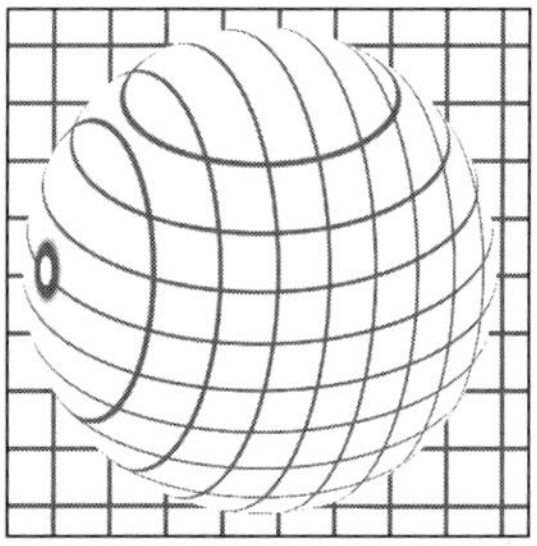

Spheric Image Warp

The original image.

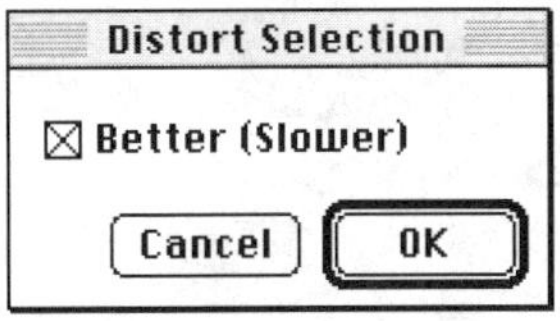

The Distort command isn't on the Esoterica submenu, but we're covering it in this section because it is interesting to compare its effects to the Image Warp command.

To distort a picture:

1. Choose Effects > Orientation > Distort.
2. Drag any corner handle.
3. *Optional:* Check the Better (Slower) box for cleaner rendering. Processing takes longer with this option checked.
4. Click OK or press Return. The image will automatically become a floater.

Barbara S. Pollak

After distorting the teacup.

The default Growth shape.

The Growth command produces organic forms — tree branches, flowers, parsley, Venetian glass, snowflakes — curved or axial shaped. Experiment with subtle slider adjustments to produce different kinds of shapes.

To use the Growth command:

1. Choose Effects > Esoterica > Growth.
2. Adjust any of the following settings.

   Flatness controls how far in toward the center of the shape the smaller

(Continued on the next page.)

branches meet the main trunks.

Thinout controls whether branches are thickest at the center of the overall shape or at the outer edges.

Random controls whether the branch pattern is symmetrical or asymmetrical.

Thickness controls the overall width of the branches.

Branch controls the number of main branches (1-20) from the center. The higher number, the more circular the shape.

Max Level controls the number of secondary forks off the main center branches. A high Max Level setting will produce a very complex shape and will preview slowly.

Fork controls how widely the forks spread. The Fractal box must be checked to use this option.

Fork Ratio controls the spread of the outer tips. The Fractal box must be checked to use this option.

Hard Edges: Uncheck to produce softer-edged lines.

Fractal: With the Fractal box checked, branches form cellular, honeycomb-like shapes, especially with a high Fork setting. Uncheck the Fractal box to make forks more symmetrical and the overall shape more circular.

3. Choose a Primary color.
4. Drag in the image window to preview the current shape on your picture. The further you drag, the larger the shape. Repeat steps 2-4 to add more shapes.
5. Click OK or press Return to accept the shapes that you previewed on the picture. Or click Cancel to remove **all** the shapes that you previewed on the picture and exit the Growth dialog box. **Growth shapes can't be removed individually, except with an Eraser brush variant.**

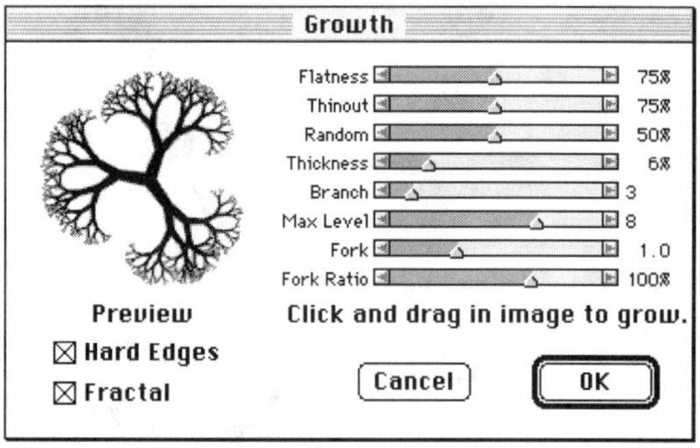

The default Growth command settings. ***To restore the default settings, you must relaunch Painter.***

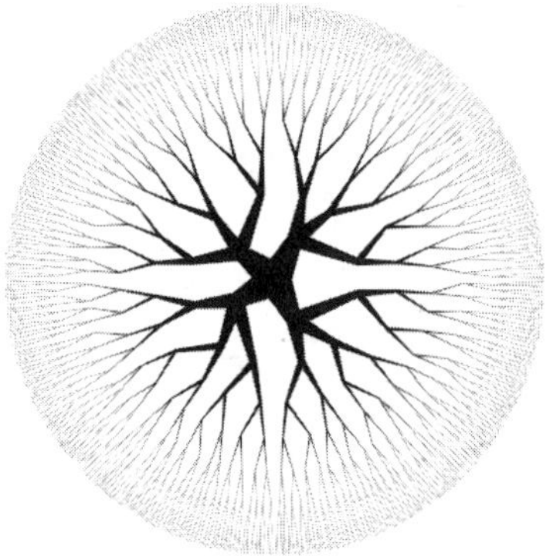

Flatness 92%, Thinout 48%, Random 50%, Thickness 6%, Branch 4, Max Level 8, Fork 1.0, Fork Ratio 100%, Hard Edges checked, Fractal unchecked.

Flatness 72%, Thinout 33%, Random 4%, Thickness 6%, Branch 12, Max Level 4, Fork 1.7, Fork Ratio 29%, Hard Edges and Fractal checked.

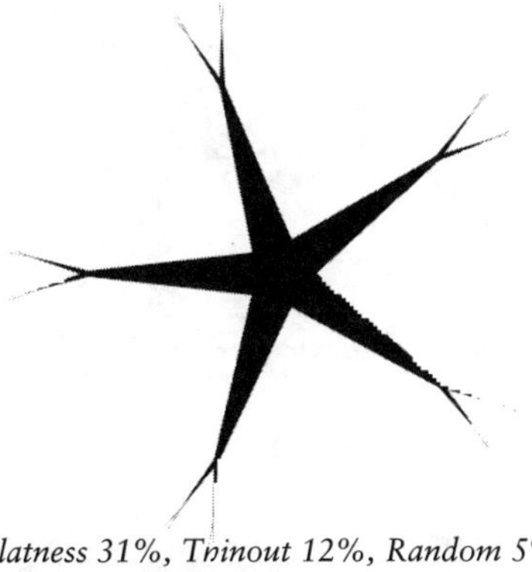

Flatness 31%, Thinout 12%, Random 5%, Thickness 9%, Branch 5, Max Level 4, Fork 0.6, Fork Ratio 29%, Hard Edges and Fractal checked.

Flatness 76%, Thinout 71%, Random 12%, Thickness 15%, Branch 11, Max Level 5, Fork 0.5, Fork Ratio 25%, Hard Edge unchecked, Fractal checked.

Flatness 87%, Thinout 27%, Random 4%, Thickness 10%, Branch 8, Max Level 2, Fork 1.7, Fork Ratio 25%, Hard Edges and Fractal checked.

Flatness 39%, Thinout 71%, Random 12%, Thickness 15%, Branch 6, Max Level 2, Fork 1.0, Fork Ratio 100%, Hard Edge and Fractal unchecked.

Flatness 17%, Thinout 33%, Random 4%, Thickness 6%, Branch 12, Max Level 4, Fork 1.0, Fork Ratio 100%, Hard Edge and Fractal unchecked.

Flatness 94%, Thinout 86, Random 50%, Thickness 6%, Branch 4, Max Level 8, Fork 1.0, Fork Ratio 100%, Hard Edges checked, Fractal unchecked. Lower the Random percentage to straighten the branches.

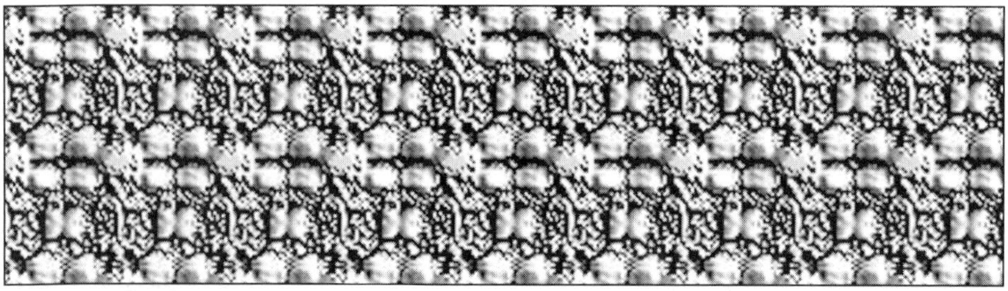

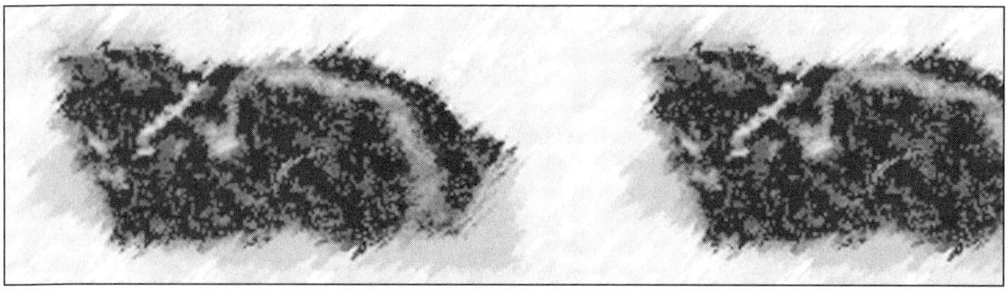

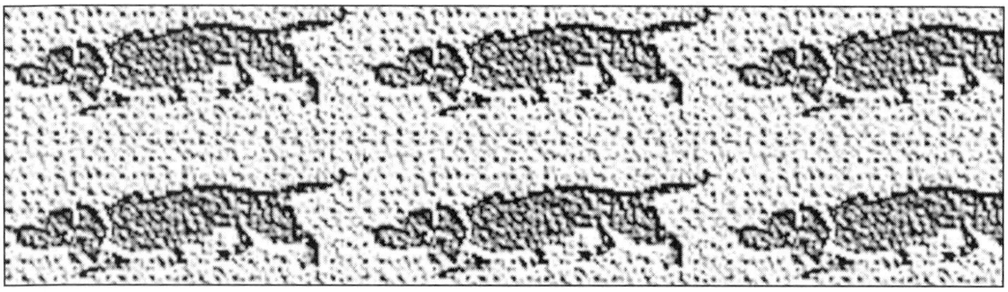

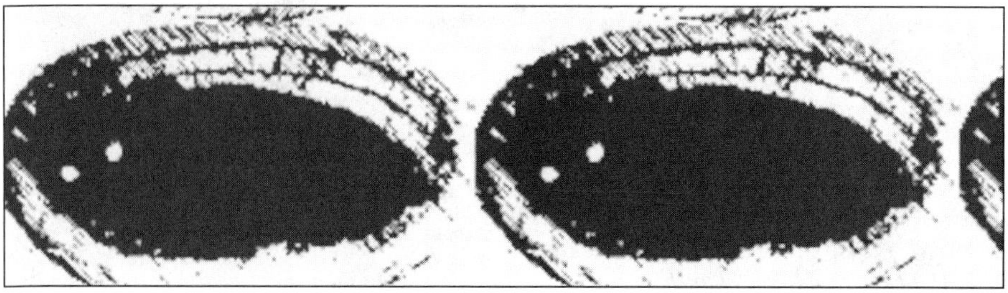

Sessions II

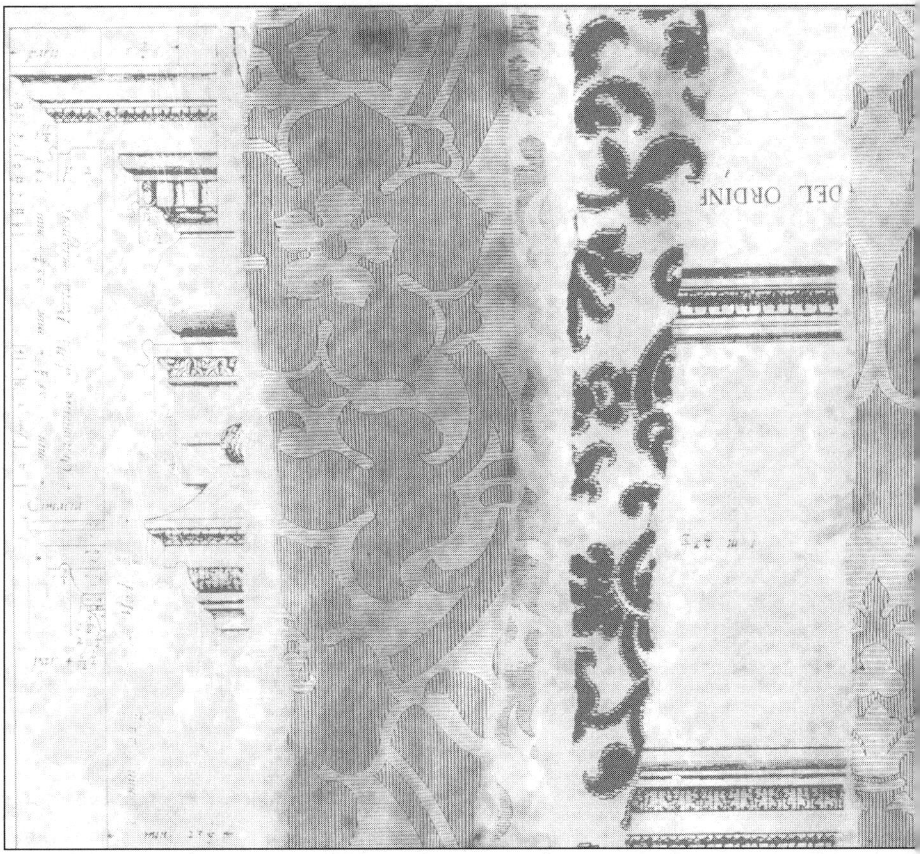

Fabric Effects, Inc.

Sessions

Sessions is Painter's instant replay feature. You can record and then replay any number of brush strokes, up to an entire work session. Use Sessions to demonstrate how you create your artwork, to replay one image on top of another, to create a movie, to recreate an image at a different resolution, or just to make a record for yourself of how you produce your artwork.

To record and replay one brush stroke instead of a whole work session, follow the instructions on page 162. To record a session as a movie, see page 161. To replay a session on a movie, see page 174.

This is what a session file icon looks like.

To record a session:

1. Choose Tools > Session Options.
2. Check the **Record Initial State** box if you're planning to replay your session using the same brushes and paper textures **2**.

   Uncheck **Record Initial State** if you want to replay your session using one brush and one paper texture that you will select at the time of replay. These Session options will remain in effect until you change them or quit Painter.
3. Click the Sessions icon on the Objects palette, and close the palette drawer.
4. Check the red record button on the Sessions palette **4** or choose Tools > Record Session.
5. Create your art work.
6. Check the square stop record button on the Sessions palette to stop recording **6** or choose Tools > Stop Recording Session.
7. Type a name for the session in the Save As field. To assign a keyboard shorcut to the session, enter "\" then a letter of your choice after the session name **7**.
8. Click OK or press Return. The session will be saved in the currently open Session library and an icon for the session will appear in the Objects: Sessions palette drawer.

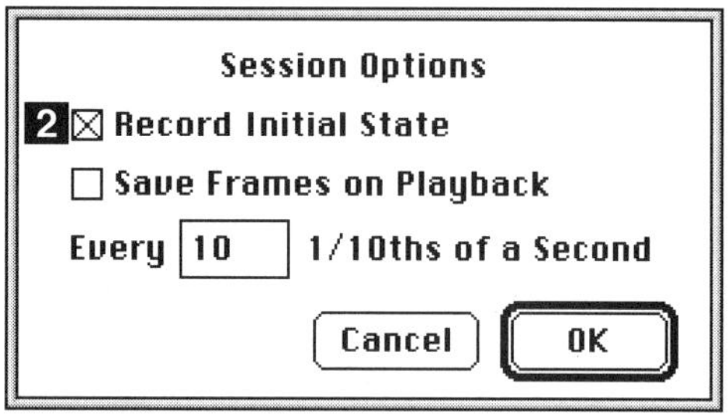

In case you're wondering...these buttons don't do anything yet. Hopefully, someday they'll become functional pause and fast forward buttons.

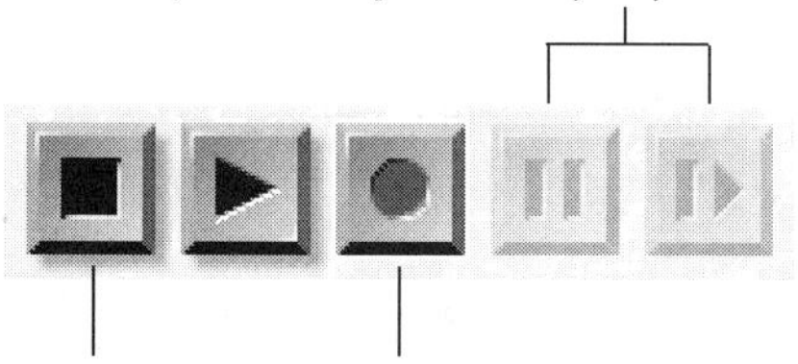

6 *Stop record button* **4** *Record button*

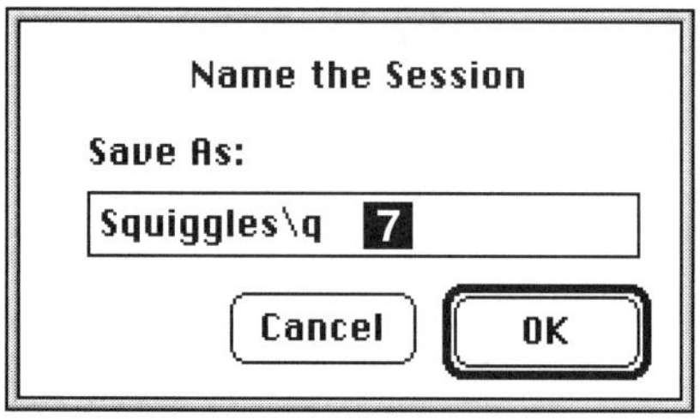

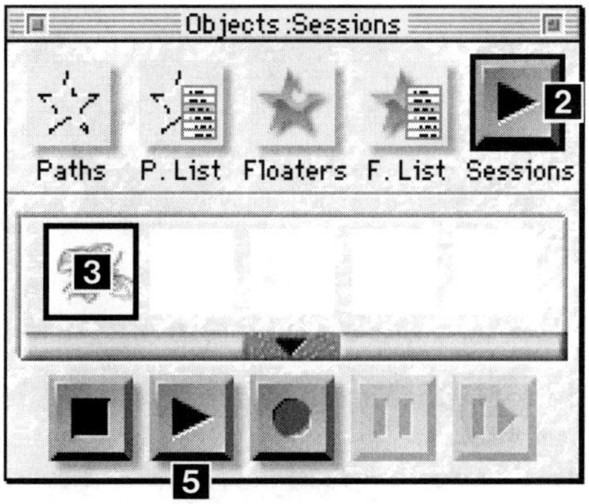

A session can be replayed by itself or right on top of another picture.

To replay a session:

1. Create a new document or open an existing document.
2. Click the Sessions icon on the Objects palette **2**.
3. Click the icon on the Objects: Sessions palette of the session you want to replay **3**. To access a session in a different library, click Library in the Sessions palette drawer, locate and highlight the library you want to open, then click Open.
4. Close the Sessions palette drawer.
5. *Optional:* If you unchecked the Record Initial State box before you recorded the session, you can choose one brush and one paper texture for the replay.
6. Click the play button **5**.

To end the replay before it's finished, hold down Command (⌘) and press ".".

To replay a session using a shortcut, hold down Command (⌘) and press "K", then press the letter you assigned to the session. You don't need to highlight the icon on the Sessions palette. *(See step 7 on the previous page.)*

To create or edit a Sessions library, see the instructions on pages 15-16.

If you're very ambitious, you can export a session as a text file, edit the actual steps in the session, and then convert the text file back into a functioning session. See the Session Script Tech Note in the TECHNOTE folder in the SUPPORT folder on the latest Painter Extras CD for more information about this procedure.

Replay a Session

High resolution files are slow to process and bulky to store. Though it's best to create a picture at its final output resolution, if you need to save storage space and speed up processing, you can record a session at a low resolution and then replay and save the picture later at a higher resolution. Replaying a session at a higher resolution is preferable to increasing a file's resolution via the Canvas > Resize command.

To record a session so it can be replayed at a different resolution:

1. Create a new document. Enter the appropriate starting Resolution.
2. Choose Edit > Select All (⌘-A).
3. Choose Tools > Session Options.
4. Check the **Record Initial State** box if you're planning to replay your session using the same brushes and paper textures.

   Uncheck **Record Initial State** if you want to replay your session using one brush and one paper texture that you will select at the time of replay. These Session options will remain in effect until you change them or quit Painter.
5. Click the Sessions icon on the Objects palette, and close the palette drawer.
6. Check the red record button on the Sessions palette.
7. Choose Edit > Deselect (⌘-D).
8. Paint your picture. *Note:* If you find that a very long or complex session causes playback problems, record your picture in more than one session.
9. Check the square stop button on the Sessions palette to stop recording.
10. Enter a name for the Session.
11. Click OK or press Return.

To replay a session at a different resolution:

1. Record your session following the steps at left.
2. Choose File > New.
3. Enter the desired Resolution. Don't choose a resolution that is more than approximately three times the resolution of the original file, or you may end up with color gaps. Also, Painter's brushes have a maximum size, so large brush strokes may not increase proportionally.
4. If you want this document to have a higher resolution but the same width-to-height ratio as the original document, increase the Width and Height by the same amount that you increased the resolution. If you change the width-to-height ratio, the image will become distorted.
5. Click OK.
6. *Optional:* If you unchecked the Record Initial State box before you recorded the session, you can choose one brush and one paper texture for the replay.
7. Choose Edit > Select All (⌘-A).
8. Follow steps 3-6 on the previous page to replay the session.

Tips

- To save the movie in a different format, choose File > Save As, then click "Save current frame as image" or "Save movie as QuickTime" or "Save movie as numbered files."
- If you replay a session recorded as a movie on another open picture, the movie will record over the picture, but it will be saved as a new movie file. Make sure no other movies are open when you replay the session and be sure to check the Save Frames on Playback box in the Session Options dialog box, otherwise the session will simply play back over the picture and will not become a frame stack movie.
- If you replay a session on a new document, the first few frames may be blank, but you can delete them later.
- After recording a session as a movie, choose Tools > Session Options and uncheck the Save Frames on Playback box so future sessions aren't recorded and replayed as movies.

If you save a session as a frame stack movie, you'll be able to edit the frames later in Painter. You can save the frame stack as a QuickTime movie later on.

To record a session as a frame stack movie:

1. Create a new document. Consider how the session will be played back when you choose dimensions (whether it will be applied to a movie or played over a picture).
2. Choose Tools > Session Options.
3. Check the Save Frames on Playback box.
   and
   Enter a number in the Every 1/10ths of a Second field. The more frames (the lower the number entered), the smoother the movie playback, but the larger the file size. 10 is the default.
   and
   Click OK or press Return.
4. Record the session (see page 158).
5. Choose Edit > Select All, then press Delete to remove the session brush strokes.
6. On the Objects: Sessions palette, click the icon of the new session.
   and
   Close the palette drawer, then click the play button (right pointing arrowhead).
7. Enter a name for the new movie.
   and
   Choose a location in which to save it.
   and
   Click Save or press Return.
8. Enter the number of Onion Skin layers you'll want to use.
   and
   Click a Storage Type for the movie (see page 166).
9. Click OK or press Return. The session will be recorded over several frames of the movie, depending on the length of the session.

Use the Record Stroke command to record any single stroke, including a stroke made with the Cloners brush. This command was used to create many of the brush stroke illustrations in this book. **You can save, close, then reopen a file in which you've recorded a stroke and still replay it, but the stroke will be lost if you quit Painter.**

A recorded stroke.

To record a brush stroke:

1. Choose Tools > Record Stroke.
2. Draw a brush stroke.

The stroke played back several times, the brush and color changed once. To produce this illustration, we enlarged our image window so we could click outside the "live" image area.

To replay a recorded brush stroke:

1. Choose Tools > Playback Stroke.
2. Choose the Brush tool.
3. *Optional:* Choose a different brush, variant, Primary color, or paper texture, or customize the brush.
4. Click in the image window. Keep clicking to replay additional strokes.
5. Choose Playback Stroke to turn the feature off.

If you record a new stroke and then want to replay it, you'll need to choose Playback Stroke again, even if the command has a check mark next to it on the Tools menu.

You can choose Playback Stroke again at any time to replay the same recorded stroke in any document until a different stroke is recorded or you quit Painter.

To replay a recorded brush stroke randomly:

1. *Optional:* Create a selection using the Outline Selection tool to confine the Auto Playback to that area.
2. Choose Tools > Auto Playback.
3. Click your mouse or press with your stylus to stop the playback. You can choose new art materials and then choose Auto Playback again.

Auto Playback.

Record and Replay a Brush Stroke

Movies 12

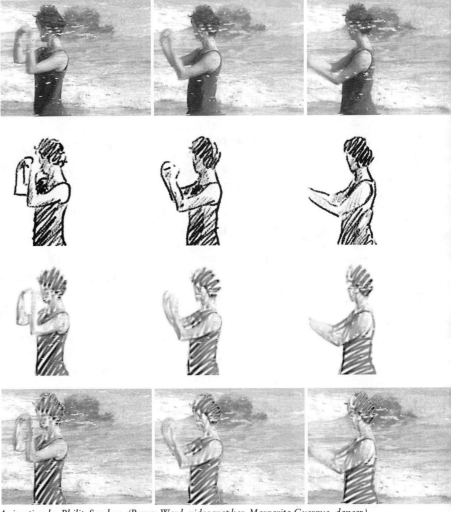

Animation by Philip Sanders. (Penny Ward, videographer. Margarita Guergue, dancer.)

Movies

Using Painter you can create a movie from scratch or you can edit individual frames of an existing movie using any Painter feature. Even if you've never made a movie before and you don't know anything about animation, try making a movie in Painter. You'll probably find making a simple movie to be relatively easy and fun. You can edit and save your movie in the QuickTime format or in Painter's own frame stack format.

QuickTime movies

QuickTime is a Macintosh system extension that enables applications to use data and resources needed for video. QuickTime runs on both the Macintosh and Windows operating systems, and you can use Painter to import from or export to either platform. A Painter movie saved in QuickTime format can be used in or further edited in a video editing application like Adobe Premiere, Adobe After Effects, or used in a multimedia application like Macromedia Director. (You can also import a series of numbered files from Painter into Director, where each file will become a separate cast member.)

If you have trouble importing a movie saved in Painter's QuickTime file format into a QuickTime compatible application, try importing the Painter movie into Adobe Premiere, resave the movie in Premiere's QuickTime format, and then import it again into the QuickTime compatible application.

Frame Stack movies

A frame stack is a sequence of movie frames that can only be edited in Painter. In the frame stacks format, you can use "digital onion skin paper," which, like traditional onion skin paper that animators use, will enable you to view previous frames behind the frame you're currently editing.

Digitizing video using hardware compression

You may encounter problems between hardware and software compressions if you digitize a video on one system and then move the digitized movie to another system. A digitized movie that uses custom hardware compression — like a video add-in board — won't play in software if the hardware isn't present in your system.

Surfer.QT2 — *A QuickTime movie file icon*

On the Beach — *A frame stack movie file icon*

Frame editing hints

- **You can use any Painter tool to modify an existing movie. You can even play back a recorded brush stroke or a session on a movie or apply a texture to a movie.**
- **When you move forward or backward to a different frame, Painter saves your changes, but you can't undo a change after you move to a previous or subsequent frame. You can choose File > Revert to undo multiple changes to a frame only before you move to another frame. To play it safe, work on a copy of a movie rather than the original (highlight the file name icon in the Finder, then choose File > Duplicate).**
- **To learn how to navigate through the frames of a movie, see the next page.**

The Frame Stacks palette

Frame Stacks palette buttons control the playback of movie frames. Up to five sequential movie frame thumbnails can be displayed at a time. The Frame Stacks palette opens automatically when you open a movie.

It's a flip book! ➔

Movie frame previews. The red arrowhead points to the frame that is currently displayed in the image window. Click a frame preview thumbnail to make that frame active in the image window, or control frame display using the buttons at the bottom of the palette. The number of previous frames that preview on the palette and in the image window behind the current frame depends on the number of onion skin layers you chose to use. Click the Tracing Paper icon in the upper right corner of the image window to display/hide onion skin layers.

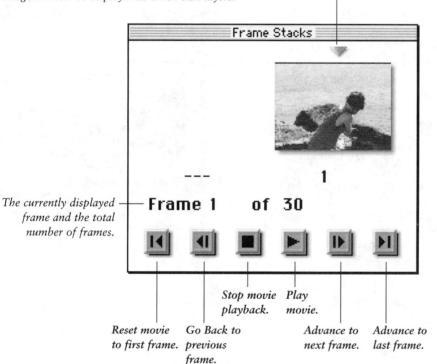

The currently displayed frame and the total number of frames.

Reset movie to first frame.

Go Back to previous frame.

Stop movie playback.

Play movie.

Advance to next frame.

Advance to last frame.

Frame Stacks Palette

MOVIE SHORTCUTS

First frame of stack	Home
Last frame of stack	End
Next frame	Page Up
Previous frame	Page Down
Stop at current frame	Option-Stop button
Stop and return to start	⌘-.

Follow these steps to create a new, blank movie (stack of frames), then follow the instructions on page 167, 169, or 175 to fill the frames with imagery.

To create a new, blank movie:

1. Choose File > New.
2. Enter Width and Height values and a Resolution of 72 dpi for the new movie.
3. In the Picture type area, click Movie, then enter the number of frames that you want the new movie to contain. You can add or delete frames later.
4. Click OK or press Return.
5. Enter a name for the new movie.
6. Choose a location in which to save the movie, then click Save.
7. Enter the number of Layers of Onion Skin you want to use. Onion skin layers are previous frames that are displayed semi-transparently behind the current frame.
8. Choose the Storage Type for the new movie: 8-bit gray (256 levels of gray), 8-bit color (256 levels of color with a Macintosh system palette), 15-bit color (32,768 colors) with an 1-bit mask (black and white mask only), or 24-bit color (16.7 million colors) with an 8-bit mask (grayscale). A 1-bit mask uses only black and white pixels, so shapes will have hard, aliased edges. An 8-bit mask uses many levels of gray, so mask shapes can have soft, gray edges.
9. Click OK or press Return. The first frame of the movie will appear in an image window and on the Frame Stacks palette. The movie will be saved as a frame stack when you close it (choose File > Close or click the movie window close box).

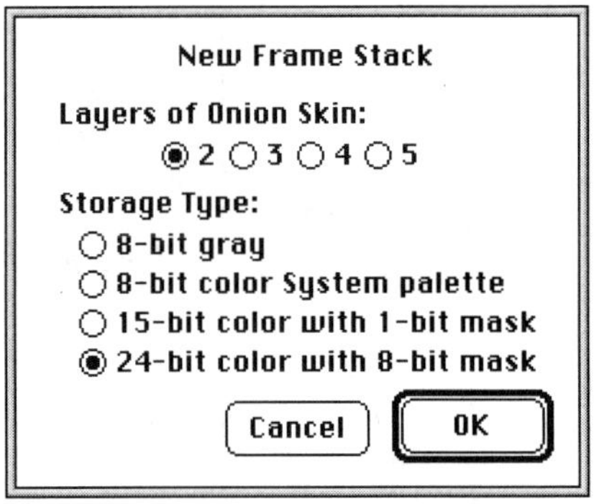

To save the movie in a different format, choose File > Save As, then click Save current frame as image, Save movie as QuickTime, or Save movie as numbered files.

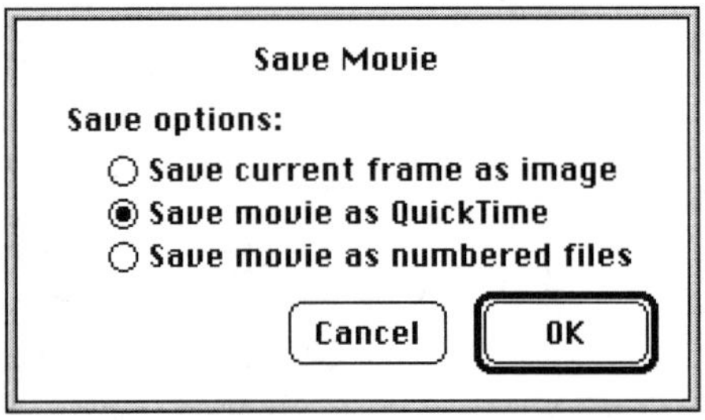

Use the following technique to add hand-drawn elements to a movie in increments. Each new frame will automatically fill with the contents of the previous frame, so you can build on previous frames without having to redraw them.

To use a floater to create repetitive frames:

1. Create a new one-frame movie (instructions on the previous page) that contains the desired background imagery.
2. Choose the Brush tool, a brush, and a variant, and paint on that frame.
3. Choose Edit > Select All.
4. Choose the Floating Selection tool (F).
5. Click on the frame to turn the whole frame into a floater.
6. Click the advance to next frame (fifth) button on the Frame Stacks palette. A new frame will be created and the floater will be copied onto it.
7. With the floater still active, click Drop on the Objects: F. List palette.
8. Select the Brush tool, a brush, and a variant, and paint on the image.
9. Repeat steps 3-8 to create more frames.

To open a frame stack or QuickTime movie:

1. Choose File > Open (⌘-O).
2. Highlight the name of the movie you want to open.
3. Leave the Open Numbered Files box unchecked, and click Open.
4. If it's a QuickTime movie, you'll need to save it as a frame stack movie. Enter a name, choose a location in which to save it, then click Save.
5. The first frame of the movie will be displayed in the image window and on the Frame Stacks palette.

Numbered files are a sequence of related files — one per movie frame — that is saved in a format that can be opened in Painter. For numbered files to be opened as a movie, all the names in the sequence must contain the same number of characters. For example, you could use the names "Movie.01," "Movie.02," etc. for a movie that contains 99 or fewer frames. Change the number of zeros for a movie that contains more than 99 frames.

To open a numbered files movie:

1. Choose File > Open.
2. Check the Open Numbered Files box.
3. Highlight the name of the first numbered file you want to open, then click Open.
4. Highlight the name of the last numbered file you want to open, then click Open.
5. Enter a name for the movie.
6. Click Save.
7. Enter the number of Layers of Onion Skin you want to use.
   and
   Choose a Storage Type (see page 166).
8. Click OK or press Return. The first frame of the movie will appear in the image window and on the Frame Stacks palette.

Artist Anna Kogan repainted the mouth on the clock face on this animation.

To paint on movie frames:

1. Follow the steps on the previous page to create a new movie, or open an existing movie.
2. Make sure the Frame Stacks palette is open and the first frame of the movie is displayed in the image window (click the leftmost button on the Frame Stacks palette, if necessary).
3. Choose the Brush tool, then paint on the first frame using any brush.
4. Click the Advance to Next Frame button (fifth button) on the Frame Stacks palette, and draw on the next frame. Repeat to edit other frames.
5. *Optional:* Click the Tracing icon on the vertical scroll bar to view previous frames (onion skin layers) under your current frame as you draw. Click the icon again to turn Tracing off.

   Your file will be saved automatically when you close it. See the "Frame editing hints" on page 164.

To edit a frame stack:
Choose any of the following from the Movie menu:

Add Frames. Enter the number of blank frames you want to add [1], then click the desired insertion point [2]: before or after a specified frame or at the start or end of the movie.

Delete Frames. Enter the range of consecutive frames to be deleted [3].

Erase Frames. Enter the range of consecutive frames to be erased [4] (the frame itself will become blank, but it won't be deleted).

Go To Frame: Enter the number of the frame you want to move to.

Clear New Frames: If you click the Advance to Next Frame (fifth) button on the Frame Stacks palette when the Clear New Frames option is checked and the last frame of the movie is currently displayed, a new, blank frame will be added to your movie. If Clear New Frames is unchecked and you click the Advance to Next Frame button, a duplicate will be made of the last frame of the movie.

Insert (a separate) **Movie:** Choose an insertion point [5] (before or after a certain frame or at the start or end of the movie). *Note:* The movie you insert must be saved in Painter's frame stack format and must have the same Width, Height, and Resolution as the movie into which it is inserted. In the Open dialog box, highlight the movie you want to insert, then click Open.

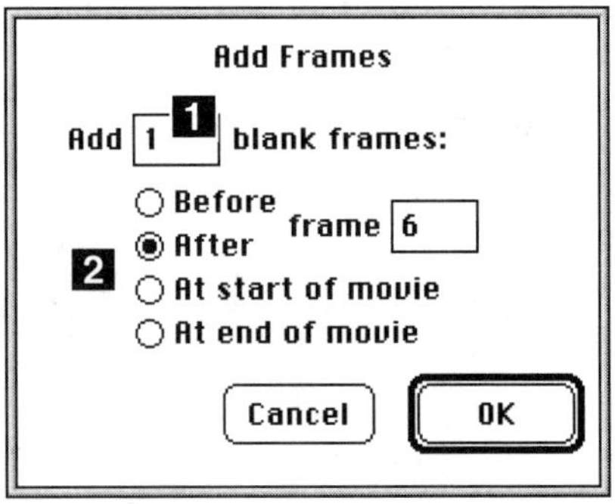

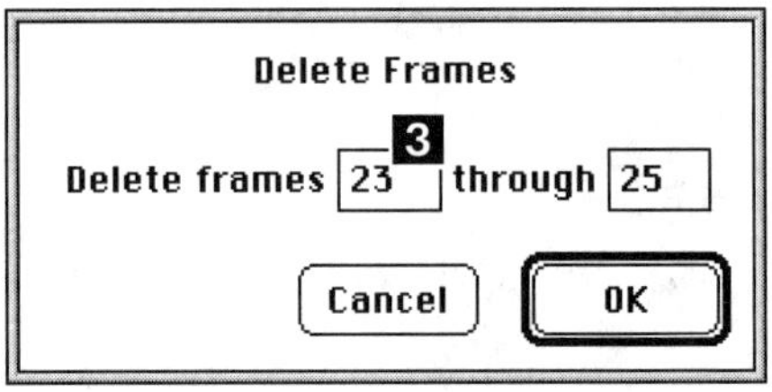

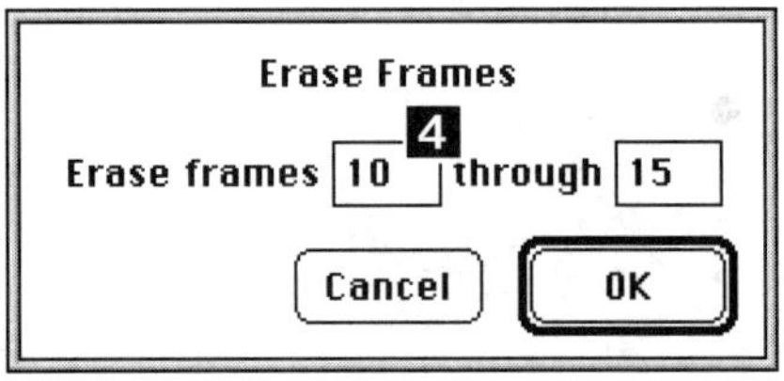

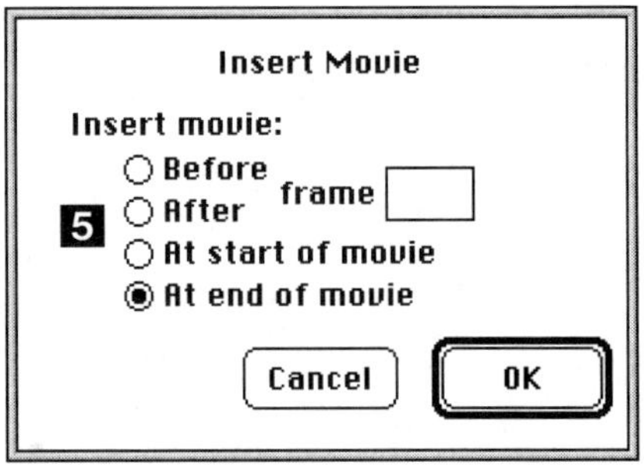

Penny Ward

Philip Sanders

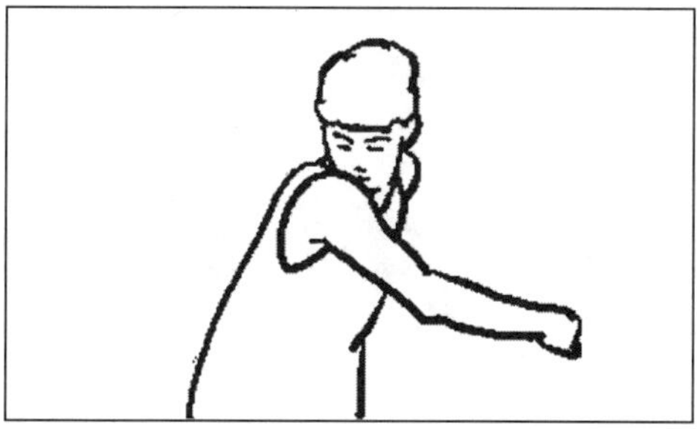

To trace a movie (rotoscope):

1. Open the movie to be the tracing source.
2. Create a new movie with the same dimensions and resolution and number of frames as the open movie. (Press the "i" icon in the lower left corner of the source movie window to display Height, Width, and Resolution info.)
3. Click in the source movie image window.
4. Choose Movie > Set Movie Clone Source.
5. Click in the new movie image window.
6. Click the Tracing icon on the vertical scroll bar to make the first frame of the source movie appear faintly behind the new movie frame.
7. Choose the Brush tool and a brush variant to trace with. Choose a hard-edged brush to draw solid line work.
8. Trace over the image in frame 1.
9. Click the Advance to Next Frame button (fifth button) on the Frame Stacks palette, then trace over the next frame. Repeat on other frames.

To darken the line work in the tracing to make filling with the Paint Bucket tool easier, choose Effects > Tonal Control > Equalize, then move the black point slider to the right. Also be sure to close all line shapes if you plan to use the Paint Bucket tool. See pages 120-122.

Trace a Movie

(Illustrations continue on the next page)

Penny Ward

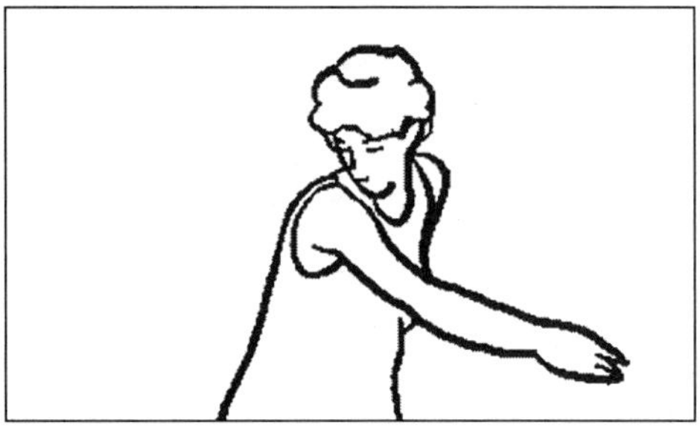

Philip Sanders

A drawback with the Apply Brush Stroke to Movie command is that it applies only a small section of the stroke to each frame. **If you use the Image Hose to produce the stroke, though, a complete nozzle file element will appear in each frame.**

To apply a recorded brush stroke to a movie:

1. Record a brush stroke using the Tools > Record Stroke command. If you record the stroke on the movie, choose Edit > Undo when you're finished.
2. With the movie image window active, choose Movie > Apply Brush Stroke to Movie. Pause while the brush stroke is applied to the movie.

If you use a mask when you apply a brush stroke, you'll have more control over the placement of the stroke.

To apply a continuous brush stroke to a movie using a mask:

1. Open the movie, and make sure Tracing Paper is off.
2. Choose a Masking brush variant.
3. Make sure the second Visibility (eye) button and the second Drawing button on the extended Objects: P. List palette are selected, and check the Transparent Mask box.
4. Choose Black as the Primary color.
5. Draw an entire, continuous masking stroke on any frame of the movie.
6. Click the third Visibility (eye) button on the Objects: P. List palette to turn the mask into a selection.
7. Choose a paintbrush and a Primary color. Make your brush tip size wider than the mask selection so you can easily cover the selection area.
8. Click the third Drawing button to paint inside the mask.
9. Draw a short stroke at the start of the active mask selection.
10. Click the Advance to Next Frame button on the Frame Stacks palette.
11. Press Return to activate the mask selection.
12. Draw a slightly longer stroke beginning again at the start of the active mask selection.
13. Repeat steps 10-12 until the entire mask selection is filled in.
14. Press Return when you're finished to deactivate the selection.
15. Click the first Visibility and Drawing buttons on the Objects: P. List palette so future edits won't be restricted to the mask selection. *Note:* If the brush stroke isn't confined to the active selection (isn't masked), choose Tools > Selections > Convert to Selection, then draw the brush stroke.

To apply a continuous brush stroke to a movie using tracing paper:

1. Turn on Tracing Paper: Click the Tracing Paper button at the top right corner of the image window (⌘-T).
2. Paint the stroke on the first frame in the series that you want to edit.
3. Click the Advance to Next Frame button to advance one frame.
4. When you start painting the next frame, paint over and then continue beyond the previous stroke. Repeat on consecutive frames.

You can record a session in which you apply Effects menu commands like Video Legal Colors or a series of brush strokes and then apply the whole session to every movie frame.

To apply a session to a movie:

1. Record a session (see page 158).
2. Open the movie you want to apply the session to.
3. Choose Movie > Apply Session to Movie.
4. Locate and highlight the session name.
5. Click Playback. The whole session will be applied to every frame.

Use the Command-**.** shortcut at any time to stop the application of the session to the movie.

Record a separate session for individual commands — like Brightness/ Contrast or Posterize — on the first movie frame, choose Edit > Undo, then follow steps 3-5 above to apply each session. Store the sessions in one folder so you can locate them easily and apply them as needed. Some commands may not work reliably if recorded in the same session with other commands.

To mask part of a frame

Use any Masking brush variant to mask areas on a frame. If you do this on each frame of a movie, you can then clone imagery frame-by-frame from another source within or around the masked area, depending which mask Drawing button you select on the Objects: P. List palette. Or, for a high contrast image, choose Edit > Mask > Auto Mask with its Using: Image Luminance option to mask dark shadow areas with a more opaque mask. Repeat this auto masking step on each frame of a movie to create masks for the whole movie.

You can also record a session using Auto Mask (Using: Image Luminance) and apply the session to the movie.

If all the frames in the movie contain an area of the same flat color, you can use the Dropper tool to pick up that flat color (it will now be the new Primary color) and use Auto Mask with the Current Color option.

To record and replay a session as a movie, see page 161.

Philip Sanders

Movie 1, a soft landscape background, to be cloned onto movie 2.

Philip Sanders

Movie 2, the dancer. The Magic Wand tool is dragged around the figure to create a mask so cloning can be limited, via the third Drawing button, to the mask (around the figure).

To clone between two movies:

1. Open two movies. Enter names for the new frame stack documents, if prompted to do so.
2. Click in the window of the movie you want to clone into, then choose the name of the document you want to be the clone source from the File > Clone Source submenu.
   or
   Click in the movie you will clone from, then choose Movie > Set Movie Clone Source.

3. *Optional:* Use the Magic Wand tool on each target movie frame to select a particular area of the frame to limit cloning to only that area.
   or
   Use the Dropper tool to pick up a flat color from a frame, and then use the Auto Mask command (Current Color option).
4. Choose a Cloners brush variant. The Straight Cloner or Soft Cloner variants will clone exactly.
5. Click, then press and drag on the clone (target) movie. Areas of the source movie frame will appear in the clone movie frame.
6. Click the Advance to Next Frame button (fifth button) on the Frame Stacks palette for the clone (target) movie. Do the same for the source movie, if you want to clone from a different frame. Drag again on the target movie frame.
7. Repeat steps 5-6 for each frame you want to clone into.

Record a stroke with a Cloners brush variant, then play it back on consecutive frames. Contents of the cloned areas will vary within the stroke.

Control-click in the source movie to define a new reference point to clone from. Otherwise the clone will start in the upper left corner of the source movie frame.

To apply a texture to a movie:

1. Record a session in which you use the Effects > Surface Control > Apply Surface Texture, Dye Concentration, or Color Overlay command to apply a texture (choose Paper Grain from the Using pop-up menu). If you want to make the grain move randomly (step 4), uncheck the Record Initital State box in the Session Options dialog box before you record the session.
2. Open the movie you want to apply the texture to.
3. Choose Movie > Set Grain Position.
4. Pick a Grain movement option: Grain Stays Still, Grain Moves Randomly, or Grain Moves Linearly.

   If you choose the Grain Moves Linearly option, enter pixel amounts in one or both Move fields at the bottom. Enter numbers in both Move fields to make the grain move diagonally. This will work well if the texture has a distinct pattern.
5. Click OK or press Return.
6. Choose Movie > Apply Session to Movie.
7. Highlight the session you want to apply to the movie.
8. Click Playback. Pause while the session is applied to the movie.

Use the Command-. shortcut at any time to stop the application of the session to the movie.

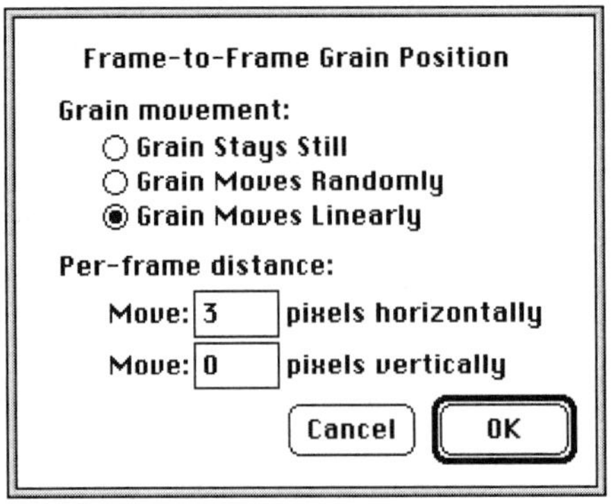

To produce this frame sequence, we chose the Grain movement moves Linearly option and entered values in both Move fields in the Frame-to-Frame Grain Position dialog box to move the grain diagonally downward and to the right.

Original animation by Philip Sanders

Preferences 13

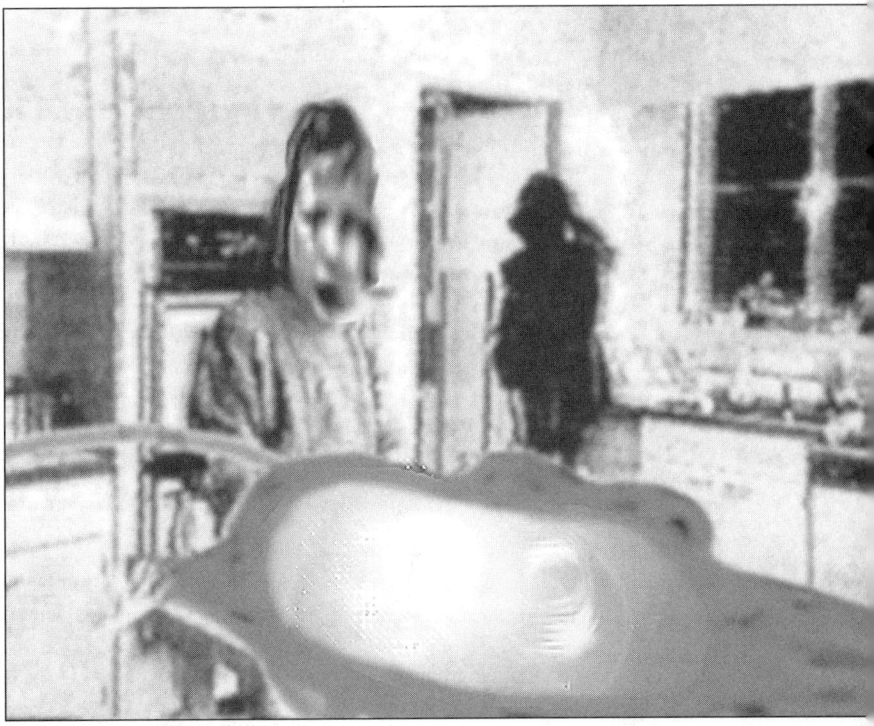

David Humphrey, ***Solarized Kitchen.***

General Preferences: (Choose Edit > Preferences > General)

(Preferences changes take effect when you click OK, except where otherwise noted.)

❶ Click **Triangle Drawing Cursor type** to see the cursor more easily on screen. Click **Single pixel** for more precise cursor placement.

Click a cursor **Orientation** button to tilt the triangle to suit your drawing style.

Click a cursor **Color.**

❷ Enter the maximum number of pixels in the **Floating selection pre-feather** field that a floating selection can be feathered using the Feather slider on the Objects: F. List palette. The maximum is 50. The larger the pre-feather amount, the larger the bounding box around the floater. Re-launch Painter to activate this default.

❸ Check **Indicate clone source with cross hairs while cloning** if you want to know which area of the source document is being cloned.

❹ Check **Disable automatic sync to disk** to speed up processing when Painter uses virtual memory.

❺ When **Draw zoomed-out views using area-averaging** is checked, screen rendering when the view size is less than 100% is faster, but less accurate. Uncheck for slower, more accurate rendering.

❻ With **Display warning when drawing outside selection** checked, a warning prompt will appear if you try to paint outside the boundary of a selection.

❼ Enter the name of the **Brushes, Paper Grains, Paths, Floaters,** and **Color Set libraries** that you want to appear in their respective palette drawers next time you launch Painter.

❽ Choose a **Temp File Volume** that Painter will use as a scratch disk for virtual memory when available RAM is insufficient for processing.

❾ Click a **Color Palette Type** for the Art Materials: Color Palette (illustrated on the next page).

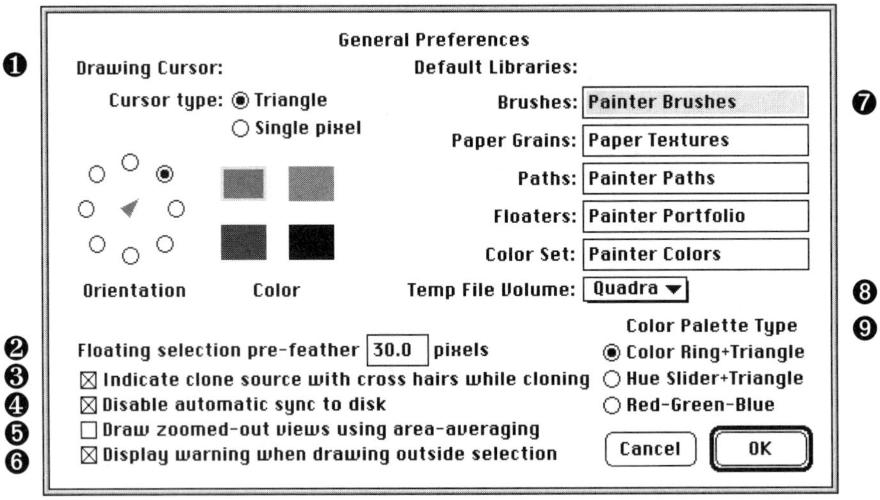

Undo Preferences are covered on page 13.

The three Color Palette Types (General Preferences)

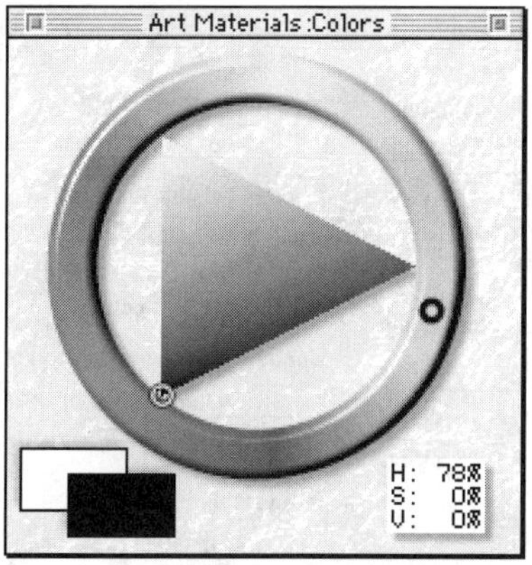

Color Ring +Triangle (Colors).

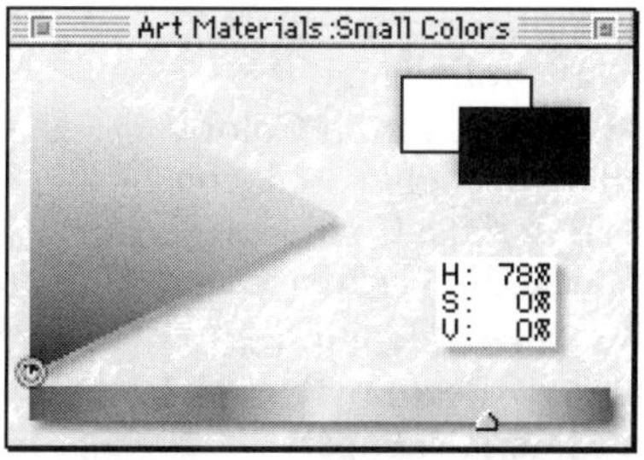

Hue Slider +Triangle (Small Colors). We like to use this configuration because it takes up the least amount of screen space.

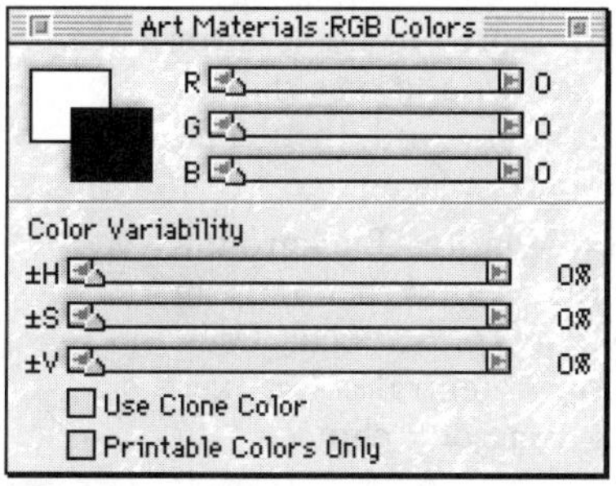

Red-Green-Blue *(RGB Colors). Use this palette type if you want to mix RGB colors by number.*

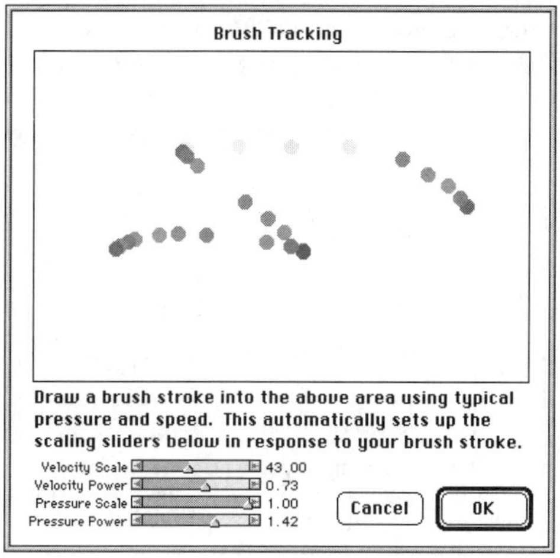

Painter's Brush Tracking dialog box defaults are restored each time the application is launched.

To customize stylus pressure and speed:

1. Choose Edit > Preferences > Brush Tracking.
2. Draw a stroke in the dialog box using your usual pressure and speed. If you're using a mouse, draw with your usual speed.
3. Click OK or press Return.

If you're in the mood to draw with an especially heavy or light touch, draw your Brush Tracking stroke that way.

To change the Painter interface:

1. Choose Edit > Preferences > Interface.

2. Watch any open Painter palettes as you do any of the following:

Choose a new **Icon Selection Color** (the frame color for highlighted icons) from the Art Materials: Colors palette, then click Use Current Color.

Choose a new **Palette Background Texture** or **Drawer Bottom Texture** from the Art Materials: Papers palette. To display the texture in grayscale, click "in grayscale," then click Use Current Texture. To display the texture in color, choose a color, click "in current colors," then click Use Current Texture. To use a pattern as a palette background, use the Define Pattern command, then click Use Current Pattern (see page 118).

Choose a new **Window Background Color** (the area around the image in the image window), then click Use Current Color. A neutral color like gray or black is a good choice.

3. Options you can't preview:

Enter **Rectangular Shadows** X-Offset and Y-Offset values for the shadows under palette icons. Enter a Softness amount for shadow feathering (1-10).

Enter **Rectangular Pillowing** X-Offset and Y-Offset values for all non-icon shadows on palettes. Enter a Softness amount for shadow feathering.

4. To save your custom interface preferences, click Save, enter a name, choose a location, then click Save.

5. Click OK.

Click Restore Factory Defaults to restore Painter's default Interface Preferences.

To load a saved interface, click Load, then double-click an interface. There are additional preset Painter interfaces in the INTRFCES folder inside the Goodies folder on the Painter 3 Extras CD.

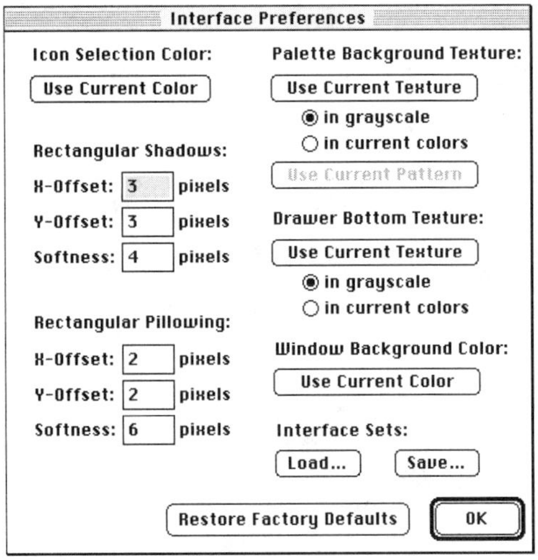

How to load plug-ins

PAINTER CAN ACCESS PLUG-INS FROM ONLY ONE FOLDER AT A TIME!

To load plug-ins, choose Edit > Preferences > Plug-ins, locate and highlight a plug-in you want to use, click Open, choose File > Quit, then relaunch Painter. Choose plug-ins in Painter from the Effects > Plugin Filter submenu. (We've loaded our plug-ins directly from our Adobe Photoshop application folder.)

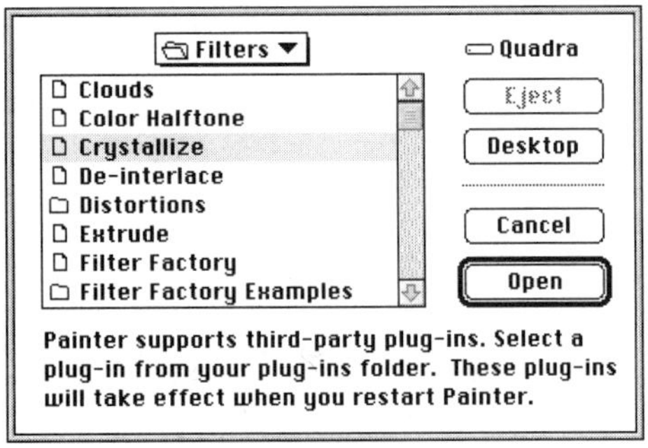

Output/Export 14

Diane Margolin.

Output devices

Standard size composite color printers

Composite color printers — like thermal wax, color laser copier, and dye sublimation — print the whole image on one sheet of paper. Composite color prints can be used as intermediary "comps," as final output, and even as proofs for press output if the printer is carefully calibrated to the film output device.

Thermal wax printers produce colors by printing Cyan, Magenta, Yellow and Black dots. Thermal wax printers usually have a resolution of around 300 dpi. Unfortunately, mixed color areas on thermal wax prints usually look very dithered, color accuracy is poor, and you must choose from a preset selection of paper stocks. To prepare your document for a thermal wax printer, save it at a maximum resolution of 150 ppi.

Fiery color laser copiers — like the Canon CLC — output computer files using a RIP (raster image processor). They produce continuous-tone color prints with no discernible dots. Colors are usually fairly accurate, though sometimes a little on the dark side, and you must choose from a preset selection of paper stocks. To prepare a file for a laser copier, save your file at a maximum resolution of 150 ppi in the Photoshop 3.0 format in Painter, and then save it again in the EPS format in Photoshop. (Double-check this with your service bureau.)

Scitex IRIS ink-jet printers produce very smooth continuous-tone color prints, and, if the IRIS is calibrated properly, fairly accurate color. Unlike many other printers, some IRIS models print on a variety of paper types — like cotton rag, glossy, and watercolor — and even onto fabric. The water soluble inks used to produce IRIS prints are environmentally sound, but, unfortunately, they also smear very easily with water. Your service bureau can laminate your IRIS print with a special coating that will provide some protection. Most IRIS inks are also fugitive, which means they will fade if they're exposed to light.

Output tips

- **If you're planning to color separate or color composite print your picture, you should choose paint colors with the Printable Colors Only box checked on the Art Materials: Colors palette. To make doubly sure your picture is printable, choose Effects > Tonal Control > Printable Colors to convert all colors to printable (CMYK) colors, or convert your file to CMYK Color mode in Photoshop.**
- **Ask your service bureau or print shop which file format to use for your target printer, and ask if they have any special instructions. If your service bureau doesn't output from Painter, save your file in the Photoshop 3.0 format.**
- **If your picture is in color and it contains photographic imagery, save your document at a resolution that is twice the printing press screen resolution using the Canvas > Resize command. If you created the image from scratch in Painter and it doesn't contain precise line work, one-and-a-half times the screen resolution will probably suffice.**
- **For slide output, no CMYK conversion is necessary, because a film recorder is an RGB device. Film recorders can output 2,000 or 4,000 pixels per line, depending on the desired quality and enlargement. Some service bureaus recommend using a Gamma of 2.2 when creating an image for slide output. Ask your service bureau what pixel dimensions and resolution to choose in Painter.**

The maximum IRIS printout size is approximately 36 by 50 inches. Save your document in Photoshop 3.0 format in Painter, and then save the file again in the EPS format in Photoshop at a resolution of 150 to 300 ppi, depending on how sharp you want the printout to be. But don't just take our word for it — verify this procedure with your service bureau.

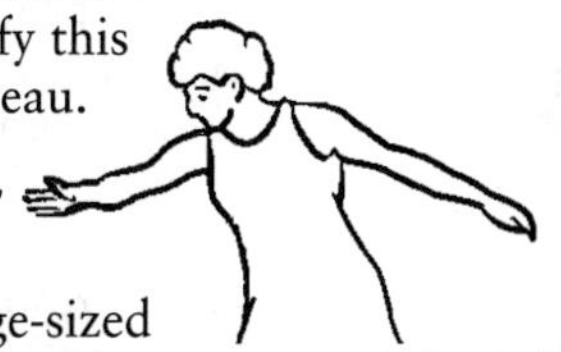

Large format composite color printers

The Vutek printer generates large-sized output (four feet wide by any length) on gessoed canvas. Vutek acrylic-based inks are permanent, and you can paint right on the canvas printout if you like. Save your file at a resolution of 18 ppi (yes, 18 ppi) in Painter in any file format that Photoshop reads, like Photoshop 3.0.

The Versatec printer outputs onto poster-size rolls of paper. The paper stocks that you can choose from may be limited (check with your service bureau). Save your file in Photoshop 2.5 or 3.0 format in Painter, and then save it in TIFF or EPS format in Photoshop.

Some output services, like Supersample Corporation, print water-based fabric dyes onto fabric using an ink-jet device. These dyes are more permanent, brighter, and produce a wider range of colors than standard printing inks. The printer resolution is 300 dpi and the maximum printout size is 36 inches wide by two to three yards long. To prepare a file for fabric output, save your file at a resolution between 100 and 150 ppi. A low resolution is appropriate for printing on fabric, which doesn't have a crisp surface like paper. Save your file in the TIFF format. Supersample Corporation recommends saving your file in Photoshop in Indexed Color mode. You can use the Posterize Using Custom Color Set command in Painter to reduce the number of colors in the image. Your output service may even recommend specific colors for you to use.

Color separations

For printed color work, you'll need to get high resolution film output (color separations), from which your print shop will produce plates for the final press. When a picture is color separated, one sheet of film is produced for each of the four process color inks — Cyan, Magenta, Yellow and Black — that are used for printing. For imagesetter output (1270-4000 dpi), save your file at twice the screen resolution of the final press, and save your file in the EPS format from Painter or from Photoshop.

Painter doesn't produce the best color separations because you can only work and save in RGB color mode — not CMYK color mode — and you can't tweak Painter's monitor, printing ink, or separation parameters. You can specify dot gain, monitor gamma, and halftone screen frequency and angle settings in Painter's Page Setup dialog box, but programs like ColorStudio and Photoshop offer greater control over these separation parameters and so are a better choice for producing separations.

If you decide to color separate from Painter, save your file in the EPS-DCS format, which produces a file for each color component (C, M, Y, and K), and a low resolution preview file. **You can't reopen an EPS-DCS file in Painter**, though, so be sure to save a copy of the file in a format that Painter opens.

Painter doesn't produce spot color separations. To reduce the number of colors in a document for screen printing, see the "To posterize using a color set" instructions on page 136 and "To annotate colors on a picture" on page 187.

Color proofing devices

There are several reasons to proof your computer artwork before it's printed. Firstly, the RGB colors that you see on your computer screen won't match the printed CMYK colors unless your monitor

If you decide to color separate your Painter file from Adobe Photoshop...

Ask your print shop these questions so you'll be able to choose the correct scan resolution (if you're using a photograph in your Painter picture) and the appropriate File > Preferences > Printer Inks Setup and File > Preferences > Separation Setup settings.

What lines per inch setting is going to be used on the press for my job? This will help you choose the appropriate scanning resolution if you use scanned imagery or choose the appropriate file resolution for a hand-painted image.

What is the dot gain for my paper stock choice on that press? Allowances for dot gain can be made using the Printer Inks Setup dialog box. Dot gain adjustments can be made in Painter, but it may be simpler to do all your adjustments in Adobe Photoshop.

Which printing method will be used on press — UCR or GCR? GCR produces better color printing and is the default choice in the Separations Setup box. (GCR stands for Gray Component Replacement. UCR stands for Undercolor Removal.)

What is the total ink limit and the Black ink limit for the press? These values can also be adjusted in the Separations Setup box.

Note: Change the dot gain, GCR or UCR method, and ink limits **before** you convert your picture from RGB Color mode to CMYK Color mode. If you modify any of these values after conversion, you'll have to convert the picture back to RGB Color mode, adjust the values, and then re-convert to CMYK Color mode.

Calibration tip

Order a laminated color proof (Chromalin or Matchprint) from color separations of a picture and then calibrate your monitor using Photoshop so it matches the proof as closely as possible. Better still, create a color set in Painter and a sheet of sample swatches, and then order a Matchprint for the swatches. Calibrate the monitor to the printout, and you'll have a reliable color set. For the color to be consistent, though, be sure to use the same prepress shop for your final output!

is professionally calibrated. Obtaining a proof will give you an opportunity to correct the color balance or brightness of a picture, or catch output problems like banding in gradations. And most print shops need a proof to refer to so they know what the printed piece should look like. Digital (direct-from-disk) color proofs — like IRIS or 3M prints — are the least expensive color proofs, though they're not perfectly reliable. An advantage of using an IRIS print, though, is that you can color correct your original electronic file and run another IRIS print before you order film. A more accurate but more expensive proof is a Chromalin or Matchprint, which is produced from film (color separations). Matchprint colors may be slightly more saturated than final print colors, though. The most reliable color proof, and by far the most expensive, is a press proof, which is produced in the print shop from your film negatives on the final paper stock.

Video and Multimedia

RGB is the native computer color model that is used to display images on screen. Choose Effects > Tonal Control > Video Legal Colors to convert your image into NTSC colors, which will reproduce reliably in video. For video, save your file in the PICT file format (the Macintosh native, on-screen image format), or the BMP file format (the Windows native, on-screen image format), depending on your target video platform, and save your file at 72 ppi — the monitor's resolution. You can save a Painter movie in QuickTime format or as numbered files (see Chapter 12, Movies). To output from a Macintosh to videotape (the 8500 Power Mac excepted), you will need a video board to convert the digital information to analog information. Images intended for video output should have a Monitor Gamma of 2.2 (Page Setup dialog box.)

To print a Painter file:

1. Choose File > Page Setup. (You can proceed directly to step 3 next time you print from Painter if the current Page Setup settings are correct.)

   If your picture is larger than the Paper size you have selected and you want Painter to shrink the image to fit on the paper, check the Size to Fit Page box.

   For PostScript color printing, let your print shop enter Printer/Press Dot Gain and Halftone Screens values.

   Change the Monitor Gamma only if you've calibrated your monitor with a calibration device that uses a different number. (The Gamma control panel supplied with Photoshop has a 1.8 setting.)
2. Click OK.
3. Choose File > Print (⌘-P).
4. Click Color Quickdraw only if your printer uses Quickdraw, and not PostScript.

   Click Color PostScript to output to a PostScript composite color printer.

   Your service bureau or print shop will click Separations if you request color separations.

   Click Black and White to output to a PostScript laser printer.
5. Click Print or press Return.

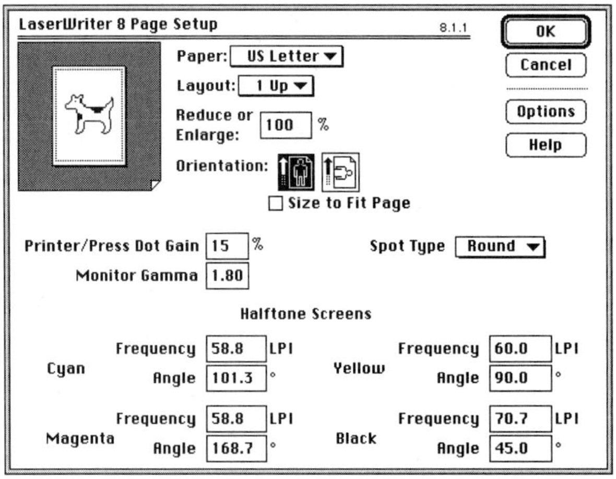

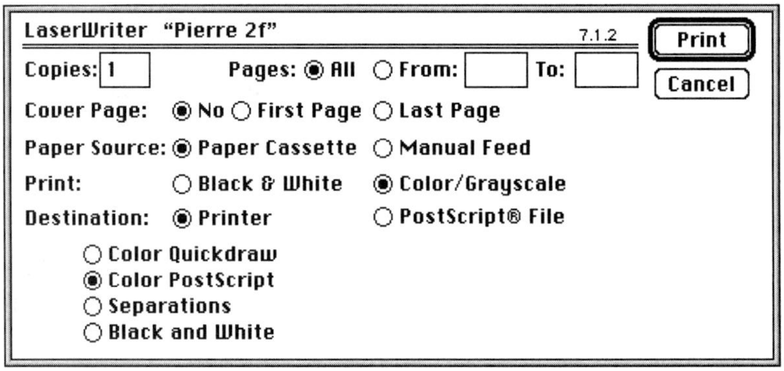

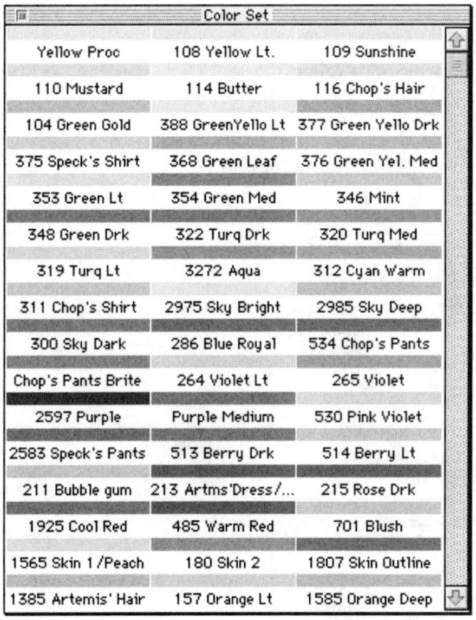

Rodney Alan Greenblat's custom process color set. To standardize his color output, Greenblat created and output a sample color chart using his custom colors, made sure they printed correctly, and now chooses from this color set when he paints.

Rodney Alan Greenblat's ***Springing****, with color annotations.*

To use the Annotate command, you must paint using colors from a color set, and the colors must have assigned names. To save a picture with annotations, it must be in the RIFF file format.

To annotate colors on a picture:

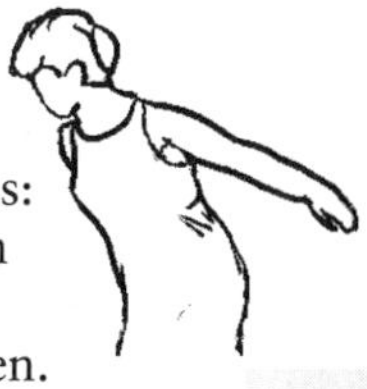

1. Make sure the color set you used to create the painting is the Current Color Set. If it's not, click Library on the Art Materials: Sets palette, then locate and open the picture's color set. The Color Set palette doesn't have to be open.
2. *Optional:* Use the Canvas > Canvas Size command to add more pixels around the picture to make more room for the color tags.
3. Choose Canvas > View Annotations. (The command should have a check mark.)
4. Choose Canvas > Annotate.
5. Press and drag a short distance on a color area you want to annotate. Repeat for other colors.
6. Click Done or press Return.

Choose Canvas > View Annotations to hide/display annotations.

To delete a color tag after you've clicked Done, turn on View Annotations, choose Canvas > Annotate again, click on the tag, then press Delete.

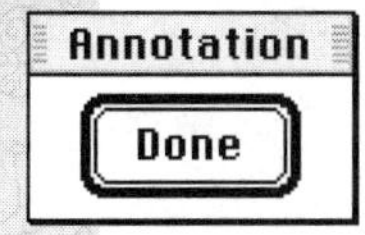

To prepare a Painter file for QuarkXPress:

Choose File > Save As, choose EPS from the Type pop-up menu, check the "Save PostScript data into preview file" box 1, and leave the Data options box unchecked to save it as a Binary file.

An EPS-DCS file consists of five files, one each for C, M, Y, and K, and a low resolution preview file. **You can't reopen an EPS file in Painter**, though, so be sure to save a version of it in another file format using the File > Save As command if you think you might want to work on it again in Painter.

If you don't want to create an EPS file and you have Photoshop 3.0, you can save your file in Photoshop 3.0 format in Painter (uncheck the Save Mask Layer box to not save any masks), open it in Photoshop, and save it as a TIFF. Remove the file's paths and extra channels in Photoshop. (If you have trouble reopening a TIFF in Painter, try resaving it in Photoshop 3.0 format first.)

To prepare a Painter file for PageMaker:

Choose File > Save As, choose EPS from the Type pop-up menu, check the "Save PostScript data into preview file" box, and check the "Data Options: Hex (ASCII) picture data" box. Remember, you can't reopen an EPS file in Painter.

To prepare a Painter file for Photoshop:

Choose File > Save As, then choose Photoshop 3.0 from the Type pop-up menu. An active mask group or path on the Objects: P. List palette will become a mask in Channel #4 in Photoshop if you also check the Save Mask Layer box, and any feathering on the mask will also be saved in the same Photoshop channel. Painter selection paths will appear on the Paths palette. If the Painter file contains floaters, each floater will be assigned its own layer in Photoshop.

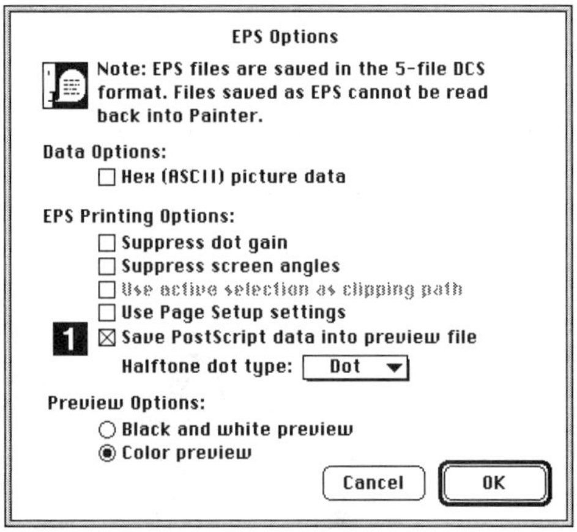

World Wide Web (Painter 3.1 only)

Choose the JPEG format to send a file via modem or to display it on the Internet's World Wide Web using more than 256 colors. When you save a file in the JPEG format, you will need to choose a compression option. Some image detail is lost with this format. The higher the quality, the less the distortion, but the less the file will be compressed and the longer it will take to transmit. Save your picture in the JPEG format after it's finished — not while you're working on it — so it won't be recompressed over and over.

You can also choose the GIF format to display your picture on the Internet's World Wide Web using only 256 colors and with a transparency option. For the GIF format, you will need to choose color options for the file, such as the Number of Colors and an Imaging Method. Choose the Quantize to Nearest Color Imaging Method to have Painter choose nearest colors or choose Dither Colors for smoother color transitions. If the file contains a mask, choose a transparency level for any masked areas using the Threshold slider. Click Preview Data to preview the GIF file. Transparent areas will preview as a lattice pattern.

To display a GIF file on the World Wide Web, click the Background is WWW Gray button. And check the Interlace GIF File box to make your picture render in successive low resolution passes until the higher resolution rendering is completed.

Image Transform

Image Transform produces output for fine artists using archival inks and papers at a variety of output sizes. For small to medium size outout, they can output on their customized IRIS printer using archival inks on 100% neutral ph rag paper. Save your Painter file in the EPS or TIFF format, 100-150 ppi resolution, and at the final printing dimensions. Before you output the file, Image Transform recommends that you do the following in Photoshop: Choose File > Preferences > Printer Inks Setup, and choose SWOP uncoated. Then choose File > Preferences > Separation Setup and set the Black Generation to Light. These Preferences settings will make your screen image closer to the IRIS printout. Finally, "proof" your image in Photoshop (choose Mode > CMYK Preview), and adjust the color, if necessary.

Image Transform uses the Translock print system for large output (up to 100 by 400 feet) on vinyl, canvas, or special adhesive-backed wallpaper. The file resolution should be 300 ppi, but the file does not have to be saved at the final output size. The printer uses ACO dyes that are guaranteed to be permanent.

For very large output — flags, banners or theater backdrops — Image Transform can print directly onto sailcloth (300 thread count). Save your file at 75-150 ppi.

(X+C) The Color Space

(X+C) The Color Space also does large format (35 by 50 inches) fine arts prints using their IRIS inkjet printer and special archival inks. They also use a patented coating on rag paper or fabric to control ink absorption. Save your file in the EPS or TIFF file format at 150 ppi for a very painterly image, or at 150-300 ppi for imagery that contains file lines or text.

(X+C) The Color Space also outputs on vinyl, canvas, theater scrims, mylar, or sail cloth using an inkjet Scitex Outboard billboard printer and MEK inks. They claim this method produces more accurate color ink delivery than other billboard type printers. Print sizes are 63 inches wide by any length. Save your file in the EPS or TIFF format, at 22 ppi.

Specialty output services

Cone Editions Press
Powder Spring Road
East Topsham, VT 05076
802-439-5751
Archival IRIS prints

Image Transform
106 Southwest 2nd Avenue
Des Moines, IA 50309
515-288-0000
Fax 515-288-6403
(See info at left)
Archival IRIS prints, canvas prints, billboard size output

Nash Editions
nashed@aol.com
310-545-4352
Fax 310-796-1418
Archival IRIS prints

Supersample Corporation
350 Great Neck Road,
Great Neck, NY 11021
516-482-4386
(See info on page 183)
Fabric prints

Vutek Company
Richard Noble, ordering agent
Noble & Company
899 Forest Lane
Alamo, CA 94507
510-838-5524
Canvas prints

(X+C) The Color Space
200 Varick Street
New York, NY 10014
212-366-6600
(See info at left)
Archival IRIS prints, canvas prints, billboard size output

This book weighs over 500MB,
and it contains over 800 pictures!

Appendix A
Painter Wizardry

Crackerjack Speed Tips

These suggestions won't make an artistic genie pop out of a bottle, but they may help to liberate you from technical constraints and from the frustration of waiting for effects to process, which in turn will clear the way for image-making to flow more freely. The less you get bogged down in technical snags, the more you can concentrate on painting.

- Use floaters so you can paint on image elements and move them around easily without affecting the background and conversely, so you can paint on the background without affecting the floaters.
- Use keyboard shortcuts. Start by memorizing just a few, and gradually add more to your repertoire. Some of the most useful shortcuts you can learn include the shortcuts for choosing individual tools.
- Work at the lowest resolution possible, bearing in mind the resolution required for your final output device. Unless you have a screamer of a Power Mac, high resolution files will test your patience.
- Create color sets for the colors you use most frequently so you can grab them quickly and so you don't have to re-mix them at each work session.
- Save your custom brushes in a brush looks library, or save them as new variants.
- If you copy or cut a large or high res image to the Clipboard, copy or cut a smaller-size image to the Clipboard when you're finished pasting the high res.
- Check the Disable automatic sync to disk box in the General Preferences dialog box to speed up processing when virtual (hard disk) memory is used.
- Allocate as much RAM as possible to Painter. If total available RAM is limited, consider allocating more RAM to Painter and working with fewer applications open at a time.

- Restore a brush's default settings quickly by Option-clicking its icon.
- Discover the power of cloning. Clone your document if for no other reason than so you'll have the option to restore areas from the source document.
- Screen your calls...order takeout.
- Save path shapes to a paths library so you can reuse them at any time on any image.
- Choose Drawing and Visibility options from the lower left corner of the image window so you don't have to hunt for the Objects: P. List palette or the Objects: F. List palette. (Doesn't the palette you're looking for always seems to be buried behind a zillion other palettes?)
- If you need to erase strokes, choose the Eraser variant for your current brush instead of switching to the Eraser brush. Ditto for masking. For erasing or masking, always remember to check the Controls: Brush palette Opacity slider setting.
- If you use a Water Color variant or any other brush with the Wet variant chosen, you'll be able to erase brush strokes on the Wet Paint layer without affecting linework or other kinds of brush strokes in the background, and you'll also be able to erase background strokes before you dry the wet strokes.
- Set your undo levels in the Undo Preferences to no more than seven or eight. Undo levels tie up memory.
- Make your image window larger than your image so you don't accidentally click or drag in the Finder.
- To mix a color similar to an existing color in an image, click on the existing color with the Dropper tool and then adjust its saturation or value using the Art Materials: Colors palette.
- Store all your libraries in the same location so you don't have to hunt for them when you need to open or edit them. Also store your movies in one place and your color sets in one place.
- Record and replay brush strokes or sessions to accomplish repetitive tasks.
- Use the Image Hose to quickly fill areas with interesting textures.
- Use the Fade command to partially undo a modification instead of undoing and redoing.
- Nag nag nag Fractal Design Corporation to create a brush variants palette for assembling and choosing frequently used or customized variants, the way the color set palette is used.

Keyboard Shortcuts

KEY: [click] *Click* [double-click] *Double-click* [press and drag] *Press and drag*

Palettes display/hide

Tools	⌘ 1
Brushes	⌘ 2
Art Materials	⌘ 3
Brush Controls	⌘ 4
Objects	⌘ 5
Controls	⌘ 6
Advanced Controls	⌘ 7
Color Set	⌘ 8
Display/hide all previously open palettes	⌘ H

File menu

New Picture	⌘ N
Open	⌘ O
Close	⌘ W
Save	⌘ S
File Information	⌘ I
Print	⌘ P
Quit	⌘ Q

Undo/Redo

Undo	⌘ Z
Redo	⌘ Y

Tools

Magnifier	M
Dropper	D
Oval Selection	O
Text	T
Rectangular Selection	R
Brush – Freehand	B
Brush – Straight Lines	V
Floating Selection	F
Paint Bucket	C
Path Adjuster	A
Outline Selection – Freehand path	H
Outline Selection – Straight lines path	L
Outline Selection – Bézier path	P

Document window

Zoom in	⌘ + *or* ⌘ Space bar [click]
Zoom out	⌘ – *or* ⌘ Option Space bar [click]
Screen Mode toggle	⌘ M
Use Grabber when another tool is selected	Space bar [press and drag]
Center image	Space bar [click]
Rotate image	Option Space bar [press and drag]
Un-rotate image	Option Space bar [click]
Constrain rotation to 90°	Shift Space bar [press and drag]

Clipboard

Undo	⌘ Z
Cut	⌘ X
Copy	⌘ C
Paste (Normal)	⌘ V

Paint

Load Image Hose nozzle	⌘ L

Brush Controls

Resize Brush	⌘ Option [press and drag]
Build Brush	⌘ B
Reset brush defaults	Option [click] brush icon
Constrain Straight Lines Draw Style to 45°	Shift [click]
Choose Opacity 1-0 keys (1 = 10%, 2= 20%, etc.)	

Wet Paint

Post-Diffuse strokes	Shift D

Cloning

Set clone source	Option Brush
Re-link clone source	Option–File > Clone Source
Tracing Paper toggle	⌘ T

Color Sets

Add current color to Set	Unlock Color Set, then ⌘ Shift K
Replace color in set	Option [click] swatch

Dropper

Dropper	⌘ with Oval Selection, Rectangular Selection, Brush, Floating Selection, or Paint Bucket tool selected

Gradations

Adjust spiral	⌘ ---↖ angle adjuster (red ball)

Canvas

Resize Image	⌘ Shift R
Grid on/off	⌘ G

Selections

Select All	⌘ A or ↖↖ Rectangular Selection tool
Deselect	⌘ D
Reselect	⌘ R

Rectangular Selection tool

Constrain to square	Control ---↖
Adjust current selection rectangle	Shift ---↖
Open Rectangle Selection dialog box after drawing rectangular selection	⌘ Shift E

Magic Wand

Add color to selection	Shift ↖

Paths

Outline Selection tool — Freehand

Edit path selection	Shift ---↖
Add to selection	⌘ ---↖
Subtract from selection	⌘ Option ---↖
Create a double-stroked path	Control ---↖

Outline Selection tool — Straight Lines

Constrain to 45°	Shift
Close path	Return or Enter

Outline Selection tool — Bézier

Corner/curve toggle	Control ---↖ handle
Equal length handles	Shift ---↖ handle
Make last created point corner	Option ---↖ handle
Delete last created point	Delete

Path Adjuster tool

Duplicate	Option ↖ or Option ---↖
Move path one pixel at a time	Arrow keys
Delete selected path(s)	Delete
Render/un-render selected path	Return or Enter
Resize/preserve aspect ratio	Shift ---↖ corner handle
Skew	⌘ ---↖ side handle
Rotate	⌘ ---↖ corner handle

Path List palette

Select/deselect multiple paths	Shift ↖ path names
Path Attributes	↖↖ path name

Floaters

Drop currently selected floater	⌘ Shift D
Change opacity	1-0 keys (1 = 10%, 2= 20%, etc.)

Floating Selection tool

Duplicate floater	Option ↖ or ---↖
Move floater one pixel at a time	Arrow keys
Hide/display marquee	⌘ Shift H
Floater Attributes for selected floater	Return
Delete selected floater	Delete

Floater List palette

Select/deselect multiple floaters	Shift ↖ floater names

Masks

Invert Mask	⌘ Shift I
Clear Mask	⌘ U
Measure mask density	Shift ↖ with Dropper tool

Effects

Last Effect	⌘ /
Second-to-last effect	⌘ ;
Fill	⌘ F
Equalize	⌘ E
Adjust Colors	⌘ Shift A

Sessions

Replay session	⌘ K, then user-assigned letter

Movies

First frame of stack	Home
Last frame of stack	End
Next frame	Page Up
Previous frame	Page Down
Stop at current frame	Option Stop button
Stop and return to start	x .

Appendix B
The Artists

We designed, wrote, tested, rewrote, partially illustrated, and, yes, argued passionately about this book, but it would be empty and spiritless without the contributions of artwork from the artists listed below. It was a pleasure and a privilege for us to meet with them, and we're enormously grateful for their generosity in sharing their work.

Phil Allen
424 East 83rd St., 5W
New York, NY 10028
212-873-3553
Omuck@aol.com
Painter
12, 120, 122, color plate

Arc Studios International, Inc.
137 East 25th Street, 3rd Fl.
New York, NY 10010
212-447-0001
Interactive multimedia. Arc images in this book are by Ray Rue, illustrator. (212-794-1210)
49, 56, 57, 91, 100, 112, 117, 131, 134, 147, color plates

Caty Bartholomew
198 Seventh Avenue, Apt. 4R
Brooklyn, NY 11215
718-965-0790
catyb@aol.com
Artist, educator
35

Jaime Davidovich
152 Wooster Street
New York, NY 10012
212-254-4978
jaimetango@aol.com
Mixed media artist
color plate

Fabric Effects, Inc.
RSL Digital Consultants
Richard Lerner, President
20 West 20th Street
New York, NY 10011
212-627-2070
rslerner@eworld.com
System design and hardware/software integration; fabric design, hand painting, dyeing, and silkscreening; computer assisted design and manufacture. Fabric Effects images in this book are by Mandy Leonard. (212-229-1401)
24, 42, 44, 101, 157, color plates

Johanna Gillman
GG Designs
65 West 90th Street
New York, NY 10024
212-580-1046
ggdesigns@aol.com
Painter, graphic designer
126

Ron Gorchov
Starin Place
RD1 Bx7C
Fultonville, NY 12072
212-334-0419
Painter
19, 45, 138, 139, color plates

Steven Gorney
280 Riverside Drive, Apt. 2E
New York, NY 10025
212-866-2373
Illustrator, designer, educator
35

(Continued on the next page)

Directory of Artists

Would you like to submit artwork for future editions of this book, or our Photoshop or Illustrator QuickStart Guides? Please mail your paper output to Peter Lourekas, c/o Communication Design Dept., Parsons School of Design, 66 Fifth Avenue, New York, NY 10011. We will review every submission very carefully and thoughtfully. **Paper output only, please!**

Rodney Alan Greenblat
Center for Advanced Whimsy
61 Crosby Street
New York, NY 10012
Fax 212-219-1758
rodney@voyagerco.com
Author, designer, and illustrator of children's books and interactive multimedia
1, 73, 75, 77, 82, 187, color plates

David Humphrey
439 Lafayette Street
New York, NY 10003
212-780-0512
Painter
5, 37, 47, 83, 177, color plates

Anna Kogan
KUB Inc.
30 West 21st Street
New York, NY 10010
W: 212-924-7700
H: 212-633-9240
Multimedia, 2D/3D animation, illustration
169

Diane Margolin
41 Perry Street
New York, NY 10014
212-691-9537
Illustrator, graphic designer, painter, educator, developer of a collection of over 1,000 original patterns and textures for computer artists.
30, 33, 43, 156, 181, color plates

Jacquelyn Martino
jam67@columbia.edu
Interactive multimedia artist
142, 143

Bernice Mast
mastmedia
201 East 30th Street
New York, NY 10016
212-683-1879
Home furnishings textile designer and producer of digital video
40, 64, 113

Barbara S. Pollak
1370 5th Avenue
San Francisco, CA 94122
415-731-0722
pyro406@aol.com
Painter, illustrator
148, 153

Philip Sanders
563 Van Duzer Street
Staten Island, NY 10304
718-720-0388
sanders@cgart.trenton.edu
or ps@acfcluster.nyu.edu
Artist, educator
163, 165, 171, 172, 175, 176

Nancy Stahl
470 West End Avenue, 8G
New York, NY 10024
Voice 212-362-8779
Fax 212-362-7511
NStahl@aol.com
Illustrator
31, color plates

Extra special thanks to the following individuals:
Cary Norsworthy, production manager at Peachpit Press, for her efforts to obtain the best quality print job for this book.

Mark Zimmer, John Derry, and Laurie Hemnes of Fractal Design Corporation, for patiently answering our technical questions, and to Daryl Wise for providing us with resources.

Philip Sanders, for his very substantial artistic and technical contributions to the Movies chapter.

And Ray Rue, for whipping up illustrations for us on short notice.

If you'd like to share any Painter, QuarkXPress, Photoshop, or Illustrator tips or tricks with us, or pat us on the back, or recommend future titles for us to write, or make suggestions or corrections for future editions of any of our books, E-Mail us at: Pixbill@aol.com.

Index

T

U

V

W

Z

Order Form

USA 800-283-9444 • 510-548-4393 • FAX 510-548-5991
CANADA 800-387-8028 • 416-447-1779 • FAX 800-456-0536 OR 416-443-0948

Qty	Title	Price	Total
	SUBTOTAL		
	ADD APPLICABLE SALES TAX*		
	SHIPPING		
	TOTAL		

Shipping is by UPS ground: $4 for first item, $1 each add'l.

*We are required to pay sales tax in all states with the exceptions of AK, DE, HI, MT, NH, NV, OK, OR, SC and WY. Please include appropriate sales tax if you live in any state not mentioned above.

Customer Information

NAME ____________________

COMPANY ____________________

STREET ADDRESS ____________________

CITY ____________ STATE ____________ ZIP ____________

PHONE (   ) ____________ FAX (   ) ____________
[REQUIRED FOR CREDIT CARD ORDERS]

Payment Method

❑ CHECK ENCLOSED ❑ VISA ❑ MASTERCARD ❑ AMEX

CREDIT CARD # ____________________ EXP. DATE ____________

COMPANY PURCHASE ORDER # ____________________

Tell Us What You Think

PLEASE TELL US WHAT YOU THOUGHT OF THIS BOOK: TITLE: ____________________

____

WHAT OTHER BOOKS WOULD YOU LIKE US TO PUBLISH?

____

MAC

PEACHPIT PRESS • 2414 Sixth Street • Berkeley, CA 94710